It
Could
Happen
to
Anyone

To battered and formerly battered women
and their children and to the advocates
who work so tirelessly on their behalf

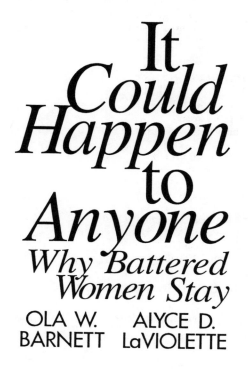

It Could Happen to Anyone

Why Battered Women Stay

OLA W. BARNETT   ALYCE D. LaVIOLETTE

Foreword by **LENORE E. A. WALKER**

SAGE Publications
International Educational and Professional Publisher
Newbury Park   London   New Delhi

For information address:

SAGE Publications, Inc.
2455 Teller Road
Newbury Park, California 91320

SAGE Publications Ltd.
6 Bonhill Street
London EC2A 4PU
United Kingdom

SAGE Publications India Pvt. Ltd.
M-32 Market
Greater Kailash I
New Delhi 110 048 India

Printed in the United States of America

Library of Congress Cataloging-in-Publication Data

Barnett, Ola W.
    It could happen to anyone : why battered women stay / Ola W.
Barnett, Alyce D. LaViolette.
        p. cm.
    Includes bibliographical references and index.
    ISBN 0-8039-5309-7. — ISBN 0-8039-5310-0 (pbk.)
    1. Abused women—United States—Case studies. 2. Abused wives—
United States—Case studies. I. LaViolette, Alyce D. II. Title.
HV6626.2.B27 1993
362.82′92′0973—dc20   93-12897
                                                                  CIP

94 95 96 97 10 9 8 7 6 5 4

Sage Production Editor: Tara S. Mead

● Contents

• Foreword

IN THE EARLY 1970S, when I first became aware of battered women, it was clear that the average person, even the average professional, believed it only happened to poor, passive women with lots of children and little education. Battered women, unlike battered children, were said to be masochists who somehow believed that they deserved the abuse they must have provoked by their behavior. "They must like it," I was told, "or else, they would leave." Even then, the psycSological effects of years of repeated abuse were noted, but not understood.

In less than 20 years, the dynamics of battering relationships and descriptions of the impact of abuse on battered women have become better understood because of new empirical research and clinical data. In *It Could Happen to Anyone: Why Battered Women Stay,* Barnett and LaViolette describe the psychosocial context that has been learned from this new knowledge. Battered women and their families break the silence and flock to whatever program is started for them; first the special sanctuaries or battered women shelters, then to the out-patient programs, legal advocates, and the specially trained mental health professionals' offices. Battered women and their children are everywhere because *It Could Happen to Anyone!*

This book describes the social psychological research that builds both socio-political context and learning theory to provide a comprehensive psychological understanding of domestic violence. Men beat women because no one stops them. There are few consequences for abusers while women and children are more likely to lose their lives, their sanity, and their developmental integrity. Living with fear takes an enormous emotional toll on victims—battered women often call it, "walking on eggshells." Barnett and LaViolette review the latest research and use case histories to document exactly how the batterer uses the woman's fear to gain control over her. Battering behavior is about the abuse of power and control. Most good treatment providers believe that men use the techniques of violence in a deliberate and conscious manner to gain power and control over women. The more frightened and humiliated the woman becomes, the easier it is to control her. Physical, sexual, and psychological violence lets him get his way with her.

New legislation has helped provide a better safety net for battered women and their children. The courts are more likely to take her words and bruises seriously, supporting the pro-arrest policies that insist on treating spouse abuse as the crime that it is. But what if the abuser is sent for inadequate treatment or worse yet, he gets a slap on the hand and is sent home to terrorize his family all over again. Little boys who watch their father abuse their mother are 700 times more likely to use violence in their own homes. If they are abused themselves, that risk factor raises to 1,000 times more. Girls who observe the abuse of their mothers often become victims of spousal abuse as adults. As we learn more about early abuse, however, it becomes clear that some women use the violence they have learned so well themselves. Those who never learned how to respect another person's boundaries are unable to do so even in therapy. Should their expectations not be met, they strike out just like the batterer taught them.

In an age when new health-care plans abound, it is gratifying to see the connection made between the impact of abuse and goals of treatment. Using a social-learning and cognitive-behavioral theoretical approach, the pages of this book explain how battered women lose the ability to predict that what they do will protect them. Learned helplessness can be turned into learned optimism or hopefulness to protect those still being battered, those who are struggling with a consistent optimistic outlook, and those who want to prevent the cycle of abuse from occurring in the next generation. It is time to start working on these ambitious plans now. Join Ola Barnett and Alyce LaViolette and become a catalyst for change.

Lenore E. A. Walker, Ed.D.

● Preface

SOME READERS MAY QUESTION the need for another book on battered women or on abusive relationships. This book is unique for several reasons. Learning theory, the cornerstone of this book, is extremely empirical and widely accepted in the field of psychology and related fields. Clear exposition of the research and its applications to learned helplessness, learned hopefulness, and other behaviors should help readers to recognize and better understand the causes of their own or their clients' behaviors. The case histories are racially and experientially diverse. They cover a range of abusive behaviors from moderate to the most severe. This book is organized around the common experiences of women's lives and their effects, cutting across racial, economic, educational, and religious dimensions and their influences. These commonalities explain the possibility of battering in any woman's life.

The following road map will help pinpoint those categories of information most valuable for shelter workers, social workers, therapists, police officers, researchers, students, nurses, judges, teachers, battered women, their families and friends, and others who will read this book.

Chapters 1 and 2 deal with the socialization of girls to women both within the family and within the larger culture. The common thread, despite cultural differences, is the learning of a belief system that devalues women, especially unmarried women, and creates a sense of female responsibility for the maintenance of an emotionally stable family. For individuals well read in feminist ideology, these chapters may seem commonplace or elementary. Nonetheless, much of the research is current and offers a few new twists on familiar arguments. The discussion of learned hopefulness is one such twist.

Chapters 3, 4, and 5 discuss the effects of victimization in general, the mechanisms underlying emotional learning, post-traumatic stress, and the appropriateness of extrapolating these concepts to battered women specifically. Data reported in the victimization chapter debunk the mythology surrounding the "type" of women who become battered. Information on victim-blaming, self-blame, conformity, the Stockholm Syndrome, and captivity help illustrate the universality of principles contributing to victimization, thus forming a common denominator linking "all people" to battered women.

These chapters also offer a thorough discussion of how battering evokes chronic fear. The relevance of learning theory is particularly striking as an explanation for the development and maintenance of fear in battered women and in persons who become involved in the battering relationship. These concepts appear along with homicide statistics and gender differences in motivations and outcomes of abuse, thereby providing support for the rationality of battered women's fear.

Chapter 5 describes the psychological impact of trauma on the victims of abuse. Once again, the parallels between battered women and other survivors of crises, such as Vietnam war veterans and victims of natural disasters, become apparent. A reexamination of learned helplessness theory in terms of its expanded parameters and an explanation of post-traumatic stress disorder as a predictable outcome of catastrophe help tie these components to the development of battered women's syndrome. Life in a battering relationship is analogous to life on a battlefield.

Because we did not want to present a problem without providing possible solutions, Chapter 6 presents a brief overview of prevention strategies and possible interventions at many levels: therapeutic, educational, legislative, and social. These catalysts should have an impact on the systems that have, whether by design or not, kept women trapped in abusive relationships. Although some of these exciting ideas have come to fruition in some settings, others are mere possibilities, worthy of future implementation.

The last chapter concludes with several personal revelations by women who not only survived but became empowered to effect change in their own lives. The case histories throughout the text represent heroic efforts by women. It seems fitting to give these survivors a chance to speak out and touch the lives of others.

Although it was impossible to address myriad other important issues, such as lesbian battering and cross-cultural differences related to battering, we have accomplished the book's principal goals. We believe that we have successfully explained how cultural mores, sexism, and other more specific learning pervade human experiences and reactions to those experiences. Finally, we believe that we have explained why "battered women stay" and how "it could happen to anyone."

Ola W. Barnett
Alyce D. LaViolette

● Acknowledgments

THE AUTHORS WISH TO EXPRESS their appreciation to Donald J. Barnett, Jean K. Fromm, and Carol V. Harnish for their careful reading of original manuscript drafts and for offering perceptive comments. We also thank the following reviewers for their comments and suggestions: Michèle Harway, Mildred Pagelow, and Lenore Walker.

Ola Barnett (OB) wishes to thank her parents, William L. King and Ruth Phillips King, for their years of support and encouragement, and her husband Don for being a devoted and enduring anchor.

Alyce LaViolette (AL) wishes to thank Jean, Jay, and Cori for their love, support, and everlasting patience, and her parents for teaching her to question the status quo and believe in herself.

OB wishes to thank AL for encouraging her to write a book and for composing the original case histories that have added so much emotional impact to the book's content.

AL wishes to thank OB for her tireless work, her ability to keep us focused, and for being a great writing partner.

● Introduction

Case History: Karen and Michael

On May 2, 1982, Michael Connell visited his estranged wife Karen and their son Ward. Karen and Michael had been separated for more than a year but were seeing each other again. A friend of Ward's was also visiting and the four of them were going on a picnic. They never made it.

At around noon, Karen staggered from the house, bleeding profusely from the neck. She collapsed into a neighbor's arms, gasping that her husband had stabbed her and was still in the house with their 5-year-old son and his friend.

The South Pasadena Police arrived on the scene to investigate. After several attempts to make contact with Michael or the children failed, they contacted the L.A. Sheriff's SWAT team. The SWAT team, using a bullhorn, requested that anyone inside the house come out.

Two boys walked out of the house with their hands up, pleading, "Don't shoot; we're the good guys." The SWAT team forced entry into the house at about 3:00. They found a man lying on the bathroom floor. He had massive slash wounds to his neck area and a stab wound to his chest. The wounds were self-inflicted. Michael Ward Connell was dead.

At the same time, Karen was undergoing an operation at Huntington Memorial Hospital. She had lost seven pints of blood, and her vocal cords had been severed. Her young son Ward had saved her life by jumping on his father's back and hitting him, screaming, "Don't hurt my Mom!"

The coroner's report stated, "Decedent apparently had marital problems with his wife for quite some time." Karen and Ward had been residents of Haven House, a refuge for battered women and their children. At the time of the attack, Karen had been a member of their outreach counseling group.

* * *

History of the Battered Women's Movement

Fortunately for battered women, batterers, and their families, the issue of domestic violence is coming out of the closet. In the early 1970s, the women's movement spawned the shelter movement along with advocacy for women's rights. When media attention focused on issues affecting women such as jobs, pay equity, and child care, the violence directed at women in their own homes came to public attention. *The New York Times* (cited in Tierney, 1982) indicated an increase in articles on wife abuse from zero in 1970 to 44 in 1977. By 1978, battered wives had become a separate topic, distinct from reports on assaults and murders.

Tierney (1982, p. 6) sums up the issue of public awareness as follows:

> Wife beating has become the object of media attention and government policy, not because of an increase in its frequency, or because the public has become more concerned, but because a social movement developed in the 1970s to help battered women. The growth of the battered women's movement illustrates both successful resource mobilization and the creation of a social problem.

Although the women's movement of the 1970s gave necessary impetus and attention to battered women through media focus and education, the first shelter for battered women and their children was started in 1964. Haven House, in Pasadena, California, was established through the efforts of Alanon members who saw the need to provide safety and shelter for the families of physically abusive alcoholics. These Alanon members held bake sales and small fund-raisers to pay rent on a house in Pasadena. From 1964 to 1972, there was no more than one paid staff person. All other staff were volunteers and the only program involved (until 1974) was Alanon.

Chiswick Women's Aid, established in London, England, in 1971 was the first widely publicized shelter for battered women. In 1972, Women's Advocates, Inc., established a crisis hot line in St. Paul, Minnesota. In 1975, NOW formed a national Task Force on Battered Women/Household Violence. Activists lobbied successfully for passage of broader protection laws for battered women in 1976. Rainbow Retreat opened in 1973 in Phoenix, Arizona.

Domestic Violence: The Facts

The drama and tragedy of woman abuse will touch most of us, at some time in our lives, in a very personal way. This could happen directly as a result of our own intimate relationships with lovers or through the experience of other family members and/or friends. Whether or not we have been raised in an abusive family environment, we are almost certainly going to have close contact with, and be affected by, someone who has. And that someone, unless he gets help, will carry the legacy of violence with him into his intimate relationships. Our understanding of battering becomes a significantly relevant issue when it is applied to our own personal experience.

> Violent crimes, particularly rape and violence against intimates, are vitally important to understand and to prevent. The debilitating effects of these crimes, most of which are against women, are dramatic and long-lasting for the victims and for society. Yet the very nature of these crimes and the consequences of them mean that victims are often unwilling or even unable to report them to the police or to a National Crime Survey (NCS) interviewer. (Harlow, 1991, p. iii)

Statistics on Violence Against Women

By the mid-1980s, domestic violence had reached such epidemic proportions (e.g., Finkelhor, 1984; Koss, Gidyez, & Wisniewski,

1987) that the U.S. Centers for Disease Control in Atlanta, Georgia, began to treat spouse abuse like any other epidemic by gathering statistics to include in its measurement section on the epidemiology of homicide and suicide ("Epidemiology of Domestic Violence," 1984). As much as 91% of spousal (or intimate) violence may never come to the attention of the police (Schulman, 1979; Teske & Parker, 1983). The majority of family crime committed by a relative is committed by a spouse or former spouse (58.6%). Of spousal violent crimes, 91% are attacks on women by their husbands or ex-husbands (Klaus & Rand, 1984). According to data (1979-1987) collected from Federal Bureau of Investigation *Uniform Crime Reports* (FBI, 1989), males perpetrated 5.6 million violent attacks on their female partners, an annual average of 626,000 (also see Flanagan & McGarrell, 1986). In a large sample of 3,002 currently or previously coupled women interviewed for the second National Family Violence Survey, 11.3% experienced minor violence in the previous year, while 5% experienced severe violence (Gelles & Harrop, 1989). Data on assault and injuries sustained during domestic disputes consistently reveal a greater amount of force used by males as compared with females (Straus, 1980).

A 1983 study (R. A. Berk, Berk, Loseke, & Rauma, 1983) examined police records in Santa Barbara, California, for information on domestic disturbances. Where injury was recorded, the woman was the sole victim in 86% of the cases; the male was victimized 6% of the time; and both parties received injuries 8% of the time. Saltzman et al. (1990) found that women were more than twice as likely as men to be victims of nonfatal intimate assaults.

The National Crime Survey (NCS), using interview data drawn from a large national sample of households, corroborates these findings. This survey also includes crimes that are not reported to the police. Schwartz (1987) analyzed NCS information from 1973 to 1982 and found that 94% of the victims of partner abuse were women. Of recorded injury cases sustained, 95% of the injured were females. The same statistic applied when the injured party sought medical treatment.

According to Campbell and Sheridan (1989), approximately 20%–50% of all female emergency patients (not just trauma victims) are battered women. Straus (1986) estimated that women make 1,453,437 medical visits per year for treatment of injuries resulting from an assault by a spouse. According to the Michigan Coalition Against Domestic Violence ("Did You Know That . . .," p. 9), "Women suffer 2,100,000 injuries annually as a result of domestic violence compared to 522,000 injuries from car accidents . . . [and] 131,120 injuries resulting from rape."

Mercy and Saltzman (1989) have determined that the leading cause of injuries to women is intimate violence. Toufexis (1987) spells out the statistical drama of spouse abuse in her article, "Home Is Where the Hurt Is": "An estimated two to four million women are beaten [annually] by their husbands or boyfriends, more than are hurt in auto accidents, rapes, or muggings" (p. 68).

In the early days of the shelter movement, Gelles and Straus (1979) coined the phrase "the marriage license as a hitting license." Researchers such as Roy (1977) and Straus, Gelles, and Steinmetz (1981) estimated that one in four wives were beaten during the course of their marriage.

As research has continued, investigators have found that violence also occurs in dating and cohabiting relationships (Rouse, 1988; Stets & Straus, 1989). Sugarman and Hotaling (1991) have estimated that a range of 9% to 60% of dating relationships include physically abusive encounters. Stets and Straus (1989) found that women who are cohabiting, but unmarried, were more often victimized than dating or married women. Along the same lines, Rouse, Breen, and Howell (1988) found that dating couples in a college sample were slightly more likely to use moderate force (shoving, slapping, or hitting with an object) to resolve conflict than a comparison sample of married couples.

In terms of intimate homicide, similar patterns have emerged. Over the 6-year period from 1983 to 1988, 64% of spousal homicide victims were female and 36% were male (FBI, 1989). In an examination of the data, Murphy and Meyer (1991) found that twice as many husbands killed wives as wives killed husbands. They found a comparable pattern for boyfriend-girlfriend homicide.

In addition, many women experience violence as they attempt to separate or become "unmarried." Lehnen and Skogan (1981), in analyzing data from the National Crime Survey, found that, contrary to popular beliefs, most victims were divorced or separated at the time the violence occurred. The U.S. Department of Justice (1983, p. 21) revealed that about three fourths of reported spousal assault victims were separated or divorced at the time of the incident. In Harlow's (1991) account, ex-husbands perpetrated 216,000 spousal assault incidents, more than in other categories (current boyfriend or spouse). Leaving, which was once thought of as the avenue to safety, is not as safe as once believed.

Some of the realities of domestic violence come from statistics. Most of the realities, however, come from the emotional, economic, familial, cultural, and legal burdens placed on battered women as they attempt to make decisions that will greatly affect their lives and the lives of their children.

Battered women face a number of difficult decisions as a result of living in a violent household. The most fundamental of these is the decision to stay or leave. If a woman remains with her abuser, she is criticized and quite often blamed for her own victimization. If she leaves, she is judged as demonstrating a lack of commitment and concern for the welfare of her children and her spouse.

It is not uncommon for theories in behavioral science to portray victims as provocateurs, people who incite the hapless culprit to violence, robbery, rape, or mayhem. We have held persons responsible for being burglarized because they did not have better locks or alarm systems. We wonder whether the victim of a drive-by shooting was actually an innocent victim or a gang member. It seems as if the mere act of victimization casts aspersions upon the character of the victim. This is a dilemma that few women can resolve.

As crimes become more "personal or intimate," we more closely question the culpability of the victim. We hold the rape victim accountable for her whereabouts after dark, and her dating practices, and wonder if her "turtleneck sweater" was cut too low! Defense attorneys have asked rape victims: "What did you do to indicate you did not wish to be raped?" By contrast, how frequently did they ask the victim of a burglary: "What did you do to indicate that you did not want to have your house burglarized?"

Similarly, there is a feeling on the part of some that battered women have "asked for it." Overall, there is little understanding of the reasons battered women would stay and little empathy for their plight. These problems are compounded by the ability of nuclear families to insulate and isolate themselves from neighbors, family members, and societal repercussion and also by the reluctance of the "system" to interfere in the private sphere of a sacrosanct institution. Nonetheless, spouse abuse parallels the existence of humankind. It has been an unwelcome, yet unchallenged stepchild residing in our families for generations.

Purpose of the Book

The following pages are an attempt to provide understanding and empathy regarding this complex issue and to present an integrated learning theory explanation of the conditioning that culminates in wife abuse, in the resulting state of the victim, and in the decision to stay with an abuser. We have asked battered women why they stayed in their abusive relationships, or why they left. We have asked about their survival both in and out of the relationship. This book represents, in part, their answers to these and other questions. Information has been gathered from both the scientific and the clinical sectors to formulate a comprehensive explanation that is also congruent with grass-roots experience. Our work is anchored in empirical data, especially data collected from the battered women themselves. We will include five original studies using battered women as subjects, and we will occasionally cite data gathered in several other original studies of batterers.

Last, actual case histories furnish graphic illustrations of the topics covered. Our case studies represent a range of battering situations. We have heard from a number of battered women who were unable to relate to the severity of abuse in many case histories. They may be in a state of denial, but battering relationships do vary in degree of injury, types of abuse involved, severity, and frequency. For these reasons, our case histories are diverse. Some may seem lacking in drama if you have seen *The Burning Bed,* but not to the women and children involved. *Fear, both emotional and physical, is present in every case.*

When we talk about battering in this book, we are not talking about an isolated instance of aggression. We are talking about an atmosphere that is created by many forms of abuse and a cycle that seems to increase over time in frequency and intensity (R. E. Dobash & R. P. Dobash, 1979; Pagelow, 1981b; Walker, 1979). One form of abuse does not occur in isolation from all others, and physical abuse does not have to occur frequently to create a climate of fear. Adams (1986) defines the battering control pattern as involving intimidation and pressure, withholding of financial or emotional support, issuance of ultimatums and accusations, and employment of children as confederates against the woman. We are using a definition of battering that includes four areas: physical (slapping, pushing, kicking, restraining, using a weapon), sexual (raping, beating genitalia, sodomizing, forcing unusual sex acts), destruction of pets and property (wall beating, breaking furniture, destroying valued possessions, misusing pets), and psychological (making threats, taking all the money, name-calling, ridiculing). *Violent relationships are characterized by fear, oppression, and control.*

Men who batter often find it difficult to recognize verbal and psychological abuse as *abuse.* They do not relate to the fear it can create and find it most difficult to change these kinds of behaviors. Much of the work that must be done in effective batterers' programs revolves around recognition of these forms of intimidation and halting nonphysical as well as physical abuse in the relationship.

We will attempt to address some of the "myths" surrounding domestic violence. There is an old saying: "If there are two stories, the truth is usually somewhere in the middle." Lenore Walker (personal communication, 1985) has created the new, improved version of this saying as it relates to spouse abuse: "If there are two stories, the truth is usually worse than either one of them."

We have also found that the truth is closer to her story than to his. Riggs, Murphy, and O'Leary (1989) found that perpetrators of abuse purposefully conceal undesirable interpartner aggression. That revision of reality makes sense. Emotional survival depends upon our ability to look at ourselves and to conclude: "I am a decent person." If our deeds are incongruous with that statement, it might be necessary to modify our perceptions and recollections of the deeds. For instance, it is more satisfying to our egos to say: "My partner and I mutually decided we were not compatible," rather than to say, "I got dumped."

When a man hits, belittles, or bullies someone he loves, he needs to create a framework by which to make that behavior seem reasonable. His emotional well-being depends upon it. Provocation is a great equalizer in this perceptual battle. Minimizing or forgetting details, or the degree of injury, is a tool that can be used to construct this framework. Jouriles and O'Leary (1985) found that the woman's perceptions of her partner's behavior and beliefs may be more accurate than her batterer's self-report.

A couple's report to a therapist:

His Story: I have not been really violent. I only hit my wife with a pillow.

Her Story: We had an argument. He took a small hard, couch pillow and hit me across the face 'til I almost lost consciousness.

He says: I wouldn't of hit her, but she attacked me with the phone.

She confronts him with a new, revised edition: I wouldn't have thrown the phone at you, but you were very angry and came across the room, ranting and waving your arms. You were on the attack and I was defending myself.

His rebuttal: Oh yes, that's right.

The cycle of violence. Lenore Walker's (1979) research and work with battered women enabled her to develop a theory of why women stay that is well accepted by other experts in the field of family violence. The "Cycle of Violence Theory" describes interpersonal aggression that intensifies in degree and frequency over time and holds the people involved in an established pattern of behavior.

The cycle of violence consists of three phases: (a) tension building—a phase in which minor incidents of violence may occur along with a buildup of anger. This phase may include verbal put-downs, jealousy, threats, breaking things and may last for an indefinite period of time. Eventually, this phase will escalate to the second phase: (b) acute battering—a phase in which the major violent outburst occurs. This violence, by contrast, can be seen as the major earthquake, and the episodes during tension building as the foreshocks. Following the second phase, the couple (or family if there are children) will enter the third phase: (c) the honeymoon or loving respite—a phase in which the batterer is remorseful and afraid of losing his partner. He may promise anything, beg forgiveness, buy gifts, be effusively communicative with a passion fueled by guilt, and basically be "the man she fell in love with." Over time, there is a change in this phase as the batterer externalizes the blame (blames others, primarily his wife) and she internalizes it (blames herself, not him). Over time, other researchers (e.g., Campbell, 1989a; Carlisle-Frank, 1991; Wauchope, 1988) and Walker (1979) herself modified this conceptual framework. Information from both women and men indicated that, in many cases, the alleged "honeymoon" was simply a cessation of violence and, for the abuser, repentance was short-lived.

Most of us say that we don't understand people who put up with abuse from a spouse or lover. Most of us say we would leave if that happened. To understand the battering relationship, it is necessary to understand that most relationships do not start out with one partner seriously injuring the other. Unless you are with someone who has battered several partners, the onset of battering is gradual and subtle. Our own theory is that you could live with Jack the Ripper or Ma Barker for at least a year and, if you were in love, you wouldn't figure it out. That would happen because most of us aren't looking, we're just feeling, and because Jack and Ma would be on their best behavior.

Let's make this a personal issue. We would ask the reader to think about a time when you were in an important relationship (lover, friend, job) and left that situation only to look back on it and wonder why you had stayed so long. Or did you find yourself asking how you had gotten there in the first place? How did you answer these questions? You might also ask yourself how you felt about your own anger and the ways you express it. What feelings do you usually have after you've gotten angry?

Put yourself in the beginning of your love relationship. Think about the intensity of your feelings and beliefs regarding your partner and the relationship itself. Most of us enter a marriage or important relationship feeling we will be nurtured, loved, and protected. Let's call our hypothetical couple Sam and Diane (for those of us who have watched *Cheers*).

Case History: Diane—The Story of a Typical Battered Woman

Sam and Diane have dated for more than a year and decide to get married. They know each other's friends and family. They have spent birthdays and holidays together and share many common interests, including religious beliefs. Diane's family and friends like Sam and vice versa, and everyone's excited about their marriage.

They are married and move into an apartment with their cat and two goldfish. They are setting up their home with many of the gifts they've received. Sam and Diane have had a few arguments while they've been together, but nothing serious.

After they have been married about 6 months, Sam comes home from work late again. He's been putting in lots of overtime. Diane's upset because dinner is cold, he hasn't called, and they haven't had time together. Sam is tired and grouchy and they begin to argue. Sam yells louder than he ever has, calls her a bitch, and throws his glass of water down, breaking a glass that was a wedding gift. How many of you think you would leave the relationship? Think about it.

Diane and Sam don't. Sam apologizes. They really talk to each other for the first time in a few weeks. He says he's tired and didn't mean to break anything. Diane feels his pain and remorse. He takes her out to dinner, and they feel close again. She understands and, when they get home, they make love. Diane may feel upset, but she puts it aside as she empathizes with Sam. After all, she thinks, people aren't perfect. It is important to be tolerant.

They go on a camping vacation that year to celebrate their first anniversary and share time with both families. Sam likes Diane's brother and they enjoy going to ball games together. Sam and Diane get rid of some hand-me-down furniture and buy a new couch and chair. They even own an electric toothbrush and a Seal-a-Meal. It is at the end of their second year of marriage that Diane announces she's pregnant, and it is shortly after that time that they have a major argument. They yell at each other, call each other names; then Sam hits the wall and slaps Diane once. How many of you would leave now? Why or why not?

After the birth of their first child, the families celebrate the baby's baptism at Sam and Diane's new home. There is reminiscing about the last 3 years and enthusiastic anticipation of the next holiday with the first grandchild. There have been several serious arguments during the first pregnancy, but only the one episode of hitting. Diane does find herself feeling apprehensive when Sam gets angry, but she reassures herself that it's only the financial pressure that set him off.

Sam begins to fear his anger and tries not to get mad but finds that, the harder he pushes anger away, the angrier he gets. He remembers his father's outburst, the terror on his mother's face, and his own fear. He knows he can control himself, except sometimes Diane just really pushes his buttons.

When the baby is 1 year old, Diane discovers she's pregnant again. Everyone's excited. Two days after her announcement, she and Sam argue over finances and her desire to return to work. Sam slaps her twice and pushes her. Then he leaves the house. Diane cries; she is almost hysterical. She is also afraid that Sam is gone. He calls several hours later, crying and begging for forgiveness. She is not ready to forgive, but she tells him to come home anyway. He returns, they reconcile, and neither of them tell anyone what has happened. Both Diane and Sam feel embarrassed about the aggression, and they don't want their friends or family to know about it. It has been 3½ years, one broken glass, two holes in the wall, two episodes of slapping, one push, 18 months of increasing fear, one house, many joyous holidays, 1½ children, shared memories, love, religious connections, economic security, and family bonds. How many of you would leave now?

*   *   *

As Diane and Sam develop their own cycle of violence, which includes tension over an indefinite period of time and outbursts and a honeymoon, they begin to close off emotionally from their friends and families.

The process is subtle. It begins with the first little lie. It continues when Diane and Sam don't go to friends' for dinner, because Diane "tripped" and hurt herself, or because she got the "flu," as opposed to that she was upset because she'd been slapped.

The lies chip away at their integrity and separate them from others. The lies also form a bond between the two people (or more if there are children) involved. Isolation develops slowly. Can you imagine telling your close friends that you have been slapped and pushed by your husband (whom they like and whom you still like)? Most of us want shared friends, want others to like our partners, and want others to think we have good taste.

Most of us establish "bottom lines" about relationships before we become involved. Bottom lines are the lower limits of our basic expectations of a relationship. "If she ever had an affair . . ."; "if he ever hit me . . ."; "if she doesn't have children . . ." are all examples of bottom lines. These basic expectations remain until they are confronted. Then, for most of us, it is easier to lower or alter them than it is to change our lives.

It is our purpose to demonstrate that battered women have *learned* to endure abuse and remain in their unhealthy relationships. Their learning occurs not only through common and "normal" socialization processes but also through exposure to the abuse itself. We hope to point out convincing analogies between learning in the laboratory using animal subjects and learning in the lives of battered women. That is, the principles of learning that control behavior discovered by such scientists as Pavlov, Skinner, and Seligman will ultimately be linked to the same principles of learning affecting the behavior of battered women.

Our theory of battering is eclectic. It includes the effects of male-female socialization, sex-role stereotyping, family history, and gender-related power differences. It also rests upon research conducted from behavioristic and cognitive learning perspectives as well as on social learning research and theory. In general, we assume, as does Kishur (1989), that family violence has multidimensional causes: intrapsychic dynamics (individual), intrafamilial dynamics (family), and environmental dynamics (cultural). The decision to leave an abusive relationship may be determined by a confluence of individual factors (Frisch & MacKenzie, 1991).

Experiences that cause stress-induced symptoms in other populations (e.g., Vietnam veterans) can be likened to the experiences of a battered woman. She is a human being responding to a crisis brought on by abuse, and her response is like the response of other human beings who experience similar intense and/or prolonged trauma.

A woman cannot know with complete certainty that the man she loves and plans to marry will not eventually abuse her (Avni, 1991a). A battered woman could be any woman or *every woman*. It is truly a case of "there but for the grace of God go I."

1

- ## Weaving the Fabric of Abuse: Learned Hopefulness and Learned Helplessness

Men are taught to apologize for their weaknesses, women for their strengths.

LOIS WYSE

Chapter Overview

THE ENIGMA OF BATTERING RELATIONSHIPS and why women remain in them begins with the long journey of learning to be female in this culture. To cover the topic of sex-role socialization, both in the family and in the world, is to explore the "Wonderful World of Women." The fundamental principle underlying female sex-role socialization is that female identity rests upon a woman's attachment and affiliation with a male partner, chiefly through marriage. The mores of the culture provide a psychosocial foundation for understanding the complexity of abusive relationships.

1

Case History: Lisa—For Better or Worse

I believe that you stay with your partner for better or for worse. I didn't know what "worse" was when I made that promise, but I promised. I believe my husband loves me, and I'm starting to believe he could kill me. I'm not sure how long I should stay and how "bad" is "too bad." I know I don't believe I should be hit. But I do believe if my relationship is a mess, I should stay to help make it better.

* * *

Affiliation and Socialization

Ferguson (1980) says that "women's identity is forthrightly and consistently defined in terms of the contexts of social relationships. . . . For most women, connection with others is a primary given of their lives, not a secondary option to be contracted at will" (pp. 159-160). "A woman's very sense of herself becomes organized around being able to make and then maintain affiliations and relationships" (J. B. Miller, 1976, p. 83). In Landenburger's (1989) judgment, a woman's conception of "self" acts like a filter through which she interprets the world.

According to Gilbert and Webster (1982), women first become trapped by daughterhood. Daughterhood is a common bond for all women and a beginning step for knowing and learning what it means to be feminine, to be a wife, and to be a mother. Girls learn to value themselves as they are desired by others. The only change in adulthood is that the most important source of esteem is no longer the parents, but the heterosexual partner.

Berger and Berger (1979) define *socialization* as the "process through which an individual learns to become a member of society" (p. 9). Learning applies not only to observable behaviors but also to cognitions (thoughts) and attitudes. Learning is strengthened through reward and punishment as well as through observation and modeling of others' behavior (Bandura, 1971). Ideally, an individual learns to discard nonproductive behavior and to retain healthy behaviors and beliefs through reward or reinforcement. (Turn to Appendix A for a description and explanation of technical learning terms such as *reinforcement*.)

Society exposes men and women, boys and girls, to differential expectations as part of learning their gender identity. Sex roles tend to magnify biological disparities. Carol Tavris (1992) believes that male and female behavior is not governed so much by genetic sex (chromosomal variation) as by the social context. In other words, if customs were reversed, men who had sole responsibility for the care of their children would learn to be child focused and nurturing, and women whose experiences centered on climbing the corporate ladder would learn to be businesslike. Opportunity to develop these aspects of personality plays an important role in their acquisition. "Practice makes perfect," and practice has been limited by gender.

The culture permits and encourages male aggression (Maccoby & Jacklin, 1974) but monitors its form. Female aggression, on the other hand, is tolerated primarily in defense of a loved one (particularly children; J. B. Miller, 1976). Marlo Thomas highlights this point with a bit of sarcasm: "A man has to be Joe McCarthy to be called ruthless. All a woman has to do is put you on hold."

In adulthood, masculinity is characterized by independence, while femininity is typified by dependence and passivity. Traditional success is also gender governed. While boys are afraid of failing, girls may be afraid of succeeding at traditional, male-oriented tasks. To avoid the conflict between achievement (male defined) and affiliation (marriage and motherhood) motives, most women learn to equate achievement with affiliation. Women may become anxious about success because they anticipate or expect negative consequences (Horner, 1972). Being smarter than all the boys is akin to being taller than all the boys.

Consequently, women have been inclined to shun public roles. Robin Morgan (1992) has phrased it well: "Women have lived out their days and nights in the private zone" (p. 1). When women have moved into public positions, they have tended to avoid activities and goals that threaten major affiliative relationships. Married women, for instance, frequently refuse job opportunities that separate them from their husbands. Female occupations are frequently atypical, safe, or low in status (Blau, 1984). Similarly, women may become professional volunteers or do club work, bringing qualities of aggression, competitiveness, and organizing skills to these "safer" activities.

Women learn that, to obtain the prized possession of a harmonious relationship, it is important to be "nice." Oprah Winfrey (1992) calls this the "disease to please." A glance at the titles of some current magazine articles gives an indication of the pressure placed upon women to find and maintain a relationship with a man.

"Beating the Man Shortage—Cosmo Finds the Best Places to Meet Them"
"Supporting a Husband Isn't the Worst Idea"
"Three Ways to Learn to Live with Your Husband's Infidelity"

Case History: Cindy

Cindy was abandoned by her parents at an early age and raised by strict, moralistic relatives. She and her sister were taught to be "nice" girls with traditional values. Disagreement was not tolerated, nor was "unladylike" behavior. Verbal abuse in the form of put-downs or threats was part of "normal" life. Mild slapping and pushing were common forms of discipline for unacceptable behavior.

Cindy decided early in life that the price of breaking family rules was too high. She had very few friends, did not stay out late, got good grades, and did not date often. She married young and quickly learned that her husband's "rules" were much like her aunt and uncle's. Cindy believed that she had no power to change the situation. Mild abuse was chronic, a familiar pain, endurable. She believed that maintaining her marital relationship was the most important achievement in her life. To fail was to fall short of being a woman.

* * *

Landenburger (1989) maintains that the complexity of abusive relationships requires a multifaceted explanation anchored in the psychosocial framework provided by the culture. Barnett and Lopez-Real (1985) quantified several reasons that battered women stay in abusive relationships that fall under the rubric of attachment: (a) "You loved your partner"; (b) "you thought you would feel lonely without your partner"; and (c) "you were afraid to live without a man" (see also Frisch & MacKenzie, 1991). These rationales are not exclusive to women living in a battering relationship. Unhappily married, nonbattered women in Procci's (1990) study gave the same explanations for staying.

Affiliation pressures on battered women, however, are even more intense than those put on women in general. Gilligan (1982) adds that women perceive marital aggression as a "fracture of the human condition." A woman may think that the violence represents a failure in her relationship rather than an impulsive act by the perpetrator to control her. Threat of a rupture in her relationship, or isolation from or rejection by her male partner, may cause even more apprehension than her fear of sporadic physical aggression (see Frisch & MacKenzie, 1991).

As part and parcel of fulfilling attachment mandates, women have learned how to emotionally support men. A description of today's woman includes adjectives that have described virtuous women over the centuries: *patient, self-sacrificing,* and *long-suffering.* Self-sacrifice for women has a long and noble history. As Anna Quindlen (1992, p. 10), a writer for *The New York Times,* wrote in her column:

> The fact is that there's still a tacit agreement in American society, despite decades of change, that women support. Like a French word that always takes "la," self-sacrifice remains a feminine noun. It is a deal that works beautifully for men, which is why you hear so much about how natural it is, even that it was God's idea; that there is a theological basis for women's inevitable compromises.[1]

Roiphe (1986, p. 308), writing about women and self-sacrifice, quotes Pat Nixon as saying: "I gave up everything I considered precious in this world to advance my husband's political career." Women pay a heavy price for their selflessness. Self-sacrificing women show up in doctors' offices on a regular basis suffering from chronic headaches, backaches, stomach and digestive disorders, eczema, and physical problems directly associated with repression of feelings (Millon, Green, & Meagher, 1982).

Women who display these attributes, but are not physically battered, are considered good women; those who are battered are not. Ascribing traits such as martyrdom or masochism to battered women not only fails to take female socialization into account but also fails to acknowledge research evidence refuting this myth (Caplan, 1984; Kuhl, 1985; Symonds, 1979).

Sexism and Power

Sexism is a system of combined male controls: physical control, psychological control, derogatory beliefs about women, and institutional policies and regulations that discriminate against women (Adams, 1984). Perhaps it is fair to say that part of the "job description" for being male is the ability to control women, or as West and Zimmerman (1987) have put it: "In doing gender, men are also doing dominance and women are doing deference" (p. 130).

Sexism occurs in the family, in psychiatric medicine, in language and the media, in organized religion, in government, and in the legal system. Acceptance of sexist stereotypes have been used to justify unequal treatment of women. "If you are a female, that's one strike against you; if you are either a poor female or a nonwhite female, that's two strikes against you; if you are a poor, nonwhite female, you have struck out" (Julian & Kornblum, 1983, p. 337).

Webster's (1947, p. 152) definition of *power* (cited in Murphy & Meyer, 1991) is as follows: "Power is the probability that one actor within a social relationship will be in a position to carry out his own will despite resistance." Other related concepts are decision making and dominance. Of interest, the definition fails to incorporate personal power and the ability to accomplish goals in a participatory fashion. Gilbert and Webster (1982) contend that power is the reward for doing masculinity well; powerlessness is the reward for doing femininity well. A girl who becomes the woman she is meant to be receives love, but never power.

Coleman and Straus (1986) examined the relationships between marital power, marital power consensus, conflict, and violence in 2,143 representative American couples. Contrary to the view that the customary model of male head-of-household best preserves the family unit, the research found that an egalitarian, shared-power, marital relationship exhibits the lowest level of conflict and aggression. This finding was true even when both partners agreed that the husband's role should be dominant. In fact, consensus about marital power reduces the level of marital strife. When discord does arise, it is associated with much higher levels of violence in nonegalitarian marriages (Coleman & Straus, 1986).

Power and battering. Physical, economic, and social power differentials are significant contributors in the battering of women (e.g., Dutton & Browning, 1987; Yllo & Bogard, 1988). From a feminist perspective, Adams and Penn (1981) and Breines and Gordon (1983) hold that battering occurs within a wider context of society's permission for men to be violent toward women and children. In the view of DeKeseredy (1990), battering is at the extreme end of the continuum of controls meant to reinforce male dominance of women. Murphy and Meyer (1991) state that "there are striking parallels between the use of violence as a means of control in marriage and in the larger culture outside of the family" (p. 97). In sum, a battering relationship is both cause and effect of stereotyped roles and the unequal power relationship between men and women (S. Smith, 1984).

Gondolf and Russell (1986) allege that battering is a consequence of a socially imposed need to control women rather than an anger-derived, psychological manifestation. Ptacek (1988) adds another dimension by describing violence as a deliberate, chosen behavior that batterers believe is warranted, given the situation. In contrast, Breines and Gordon (1983) argue against using sexism as the sole explanation for wife abuse. "One difficulty with this perspective is that it does not seem to explain why wife beating is not universal in our society, but is only practiced in some relationships" (Maertz, 1990, pp. 48-49).

Cultural Support for Male-to-Female Violence

Although only a small number of men repeatedly and severely commit violent acts toward women, it benefits men in general (Brownmiller, 1976). Fear of violence tends to keep a woman in her place. Consequently, violence becomes a solution to problems for men rather than a problem itself.

Straus (1976) identified a number of cherished cultural standards that not only permit but also encourage husband-to-wife violence: (a) greater authority of men in our culture; (b) male aggressiveness (compulsive masculinity), that is, the notion that aggression positively correlates to maleness and that aggression is not only an acceptable tool for a man but also a way to demonstrate male identity; (c) wife/mother role as the preferred status for women; and (d) male domination and orientation of the criminal justice system, which provides little legal relief for battered women.

DeKeseredy (1990), in a review article, identified a number of behaviors classified as male peer support for abusing women: (a) information and advice (e.g., get an attorney so she can't ruin your career); (b) silence (seeming agreement with abuse by failing to support the victim's position); (c) pressure to use sex as a demonstration of male prowess, even at a woman's expense; and (d) esteem support (approval for his "keeping the upper hand"; see also M. D. Smith, 1990).

M. D. Smith (1990) has provided additional empirical evidence (as in Ellis, 1989) that patriarchal norms contribute to wife beating (see Deschner, 1984b). The beliefs identified by Smith's (1990) study include the following: (a) The man has the right to determine if his wife may work; (b) the man has the right to decide if his wife may leave the home at night; (c) it is important to show the wife that he is the head of the household; and (d) a man is entitled to have sex with his wife even if she does not want to (the "woman as chattel" theme; see also S. F. Berk & Loseke, 1981).

Case History: Trisha

Trisha called the hot line for information. She wanted to find out whether her marriage was "typical" in terms of highs and lows. She said that she didn't get black eyes; she was just pushed and shoved. Verbal outbursts and threats were just a fact of life. She said, "The kids and I just try not to make Daddy mad." Her husband's male psychiatrist had told her that she needed to "take the good with the bad." Her male minister told her to "turn the other cheek and be more loving."

Trisha's husband, the psychiatrist, and the minister are symbols of power. Male authority figures in the community tell women that they must keep their families intact at all costs. The culture encourages women to become chameleons, to adapt to their environments, to camouflage themselves and their feelings.

*   *   *

Battering happens because society somehow has given its consent. R. Stark and J. McEvoy (1970) found that many people condoned behaviors such as slapping a spouse under certain circumstances. Ellis (1989) found that married men approved of slapping women for some of the following reasons: (a) she insults him privately, (b) she insults him publicly, (c) she comes home drunk, (d) she hits him first, (e) she has an affair, and (f) she does not do what he tells her to do. In a national survey of family violence, Dibble and Straus (1980) documented that 27.6% of respondents thought that slapping a spouse could be necessary, normal, or good. One third of this group had actually slapped a spouse. More recently, Briere (1987) demonstrated that 79% of a sample of college males rated themselves as having some hypothetical likelihood of hitting a woman in a variety of situations. The likelihood of battering was associated with violent attitudes toward women.

In contrast, other studies have revealed that strong norms exist against male-to-female violence. The characteristics of the perpetrators (e.g., age, gender) and their relationship (e.g., married), however, affect one's evaluations of violence (Harris, 1991; Koski & Mangold, 1988). Overall, the more intimate the violence, the more the victim is assigned responsibility for its occurrence (Kalmuss, 1979).

Although society pays lip service to the belief that male-to-female violence is unacceptable or at least less acceptable than the reverse, reality provides a conflicting norm. There may be a dichotomy between what people say and what they actually believe, and culturally, there may be a state of cognitive dissonance residing in our collective psyche.

Sexism and Therapy

Many agents of social change reflect that state of cognitive dissonance, not the least of which are psychotherapists. In a revealing study, Swenson (1984) investigated the judgments of experienced psychotherapists concerning the relationship between sex roles and mental health. Results indicated that the psychotherapists rated a "healthy" person (sex unspecified) as having *masculine* traits, not as possessing both favorable masculine and favorable feminine characteristics. These findings coincide with those of early researchers showing that subjects valued masculinity more highly than femininity (Broverman, Vogel, Broverman, Clarkson, & Rosenkrantz, 1972).

Gender bias can also affect a therapist's ability to recognize intimate violence. During a counseling session, a therapist is reacting to what he or she believes about the power dynamics in relationships. Hansen, Harway, and Cervantes (1991, p. 2) used two hypothetical cases to study the abilities of family therapists to recognize marital violence and recommend appropriate protection strategies. In one of the two "test" stories, Carol told her therapist privately that she had sought an order of protection because James "grabbed her and threw her on the floor in a violent manner and then struck her." In the other vignette, Beth claimed that Tony "punched her in the back and stomach and caused her to miscarry." Tony asserted that Beth tried to hit him and punched herself in the back.

Of the 362 therapists, 22% correctly identified the problem as violence/battering and 17% as an abusive relationship. Others classified the problem as conflict (8%), anger (5%), a power struggle (4%), lack of control (1%), or other (4%). The remaining participants did not categorize the problem as any type of conflict. Only 45% of the therapists advised crisis intervention; 48% called for further assessment; 60% suggested work on a nonviolent marital problem; and 28% recommended couples counseling. Only 10% addressed the need for protection.

In another study, Hall-Apicella (1983) assessed the attitudes of three types of mental health professionals toward battered women. The 232 volunteer counselors came from graduate training programs, battered women's shelter programs, and community mental health centers. They completed a number of tests such as the Attitude Toward Women Scale (Spence, Helmreich, & Stapp, 1973) and the Davis-Carlson Scale (Davis & Carlson, 1981) of liability for the abuse. On the basis of her findings, Hall-Apicella (1983, p. 6) speculated that battered women would receive the least appropriate help from "a male psychiatrist, who worked at a community mental health agency, and was over 60 years old." They would be best served by selecting a "female who worked at a battered women's facility, had a master's degree, a high amount of experience with battered women, and was between 20-29 years old."

Case History: Bernice—A Tall Woman

We are both therapists. Trying to find someone to counsel us, and not feel completely exposed, was difficult, and I was desperately seeking help. I was afraid and feeling trapped at this point. We finally found a marriage counselor who was well known; he had written books and articles on relationships.

During the second session, I mentioned the battering. I began to get angry and agitated when the marriage counselor did not address the violence directed at me. Instead, he talked about *my* height and *my* anger. He said I was very tall for a woman, something I was always self-conscious about. He asked my partner if my size, my anger, and my verbal ability (otherwise known as nagging) were intimidating to *him*.

* * *

Families

One is never finished with the family. It's like the smallpox—it catches you in childhood and marks you for life.

Sartre

TV families. Television families, such as the Cleavers, defined "normal" for a generation of Americans. Fathers held down good jobs and "headed" the families. Mothers provided support and nurturing, remained at home, and wore dresses, high heels, and smiles while vacuuming. Parents were always fair and reasonable (often beyond reason). There were no signs of corporal punishment or verbal outbursts; if conflict did occur, it was handled with consistency, diplomacy, and goodwill.

Until the last few years, TV portrayed "healthy" families as white, middle or upper-middle class, together at mealtime, and having an at-home mother. Even when TV became more racially and socially integrated (e.g., *The Cosby Show* and *Kate and Allie*), the quality of the families remained the same. Problems became more contemporary, but problem solving was still handled with consistency, diplomacy, and goodwill.

Can you imagine the Beaver walking into his attractive, split-level home only to find his mother, June, drunk and passed out on the couch? Gelles and Cornell (1990) claim that showing family violence on TV is a taboo. Even with the advent of docudramas such as *The Burning Bed* and an occasional episode on *L.A. Law*, depiction of family violence does not appear at a level anywhere close to its actual rate of occurrence.

Real families. In real families, mothers and fathers struggle with the obligations and restrictions of their sex roles. Although both parents may share the breadwinner role to some degree, they do not equally share the nurturing and domestic duties (Hartmann, 1981). Conflict arises not only from daily hassles and work loads but also from power struggles and the challenge of changing sex-role expectations (Eisler, Skidmore, & Ward, 1988). Although times have changed, old stereotypes have remained intact (Snodgrass, 1990). Marital harmony is difficult when one lives in a democratic country *and* in an autocratic home.

Learning within families. Because families vary and have diverse coping styles, the definition of "normal" differs from family to family. In fact, an unhealthy family is quite likely to define "unhealthy" behaviors as normal. The family creed takes the form of rules used to survive within the family of origin. Children accept the family standards and quite often go on to practice them, regardless of their later usefulness. Children may develop interpersonal "survival" skills and beliefs perceived to be normal, only to find subsequently that they stand in the way of building healthy relationships. These skills become internalized responses, and their expression is almost reflexive. When an adult feels pushed against the wall, the old behavior patterns (survival skills) rear up. People do what they have *learned* to do, and they do it with the rapidity of a knee jerk.

From this viewpoint, family members might learn to suppress anger and other emotions or to use drugs, alcohol, and aggression as coping mechanisms. Maladaptive behaviors do not simply reflect a lack of learning; rather, they also represent the outcome of inadequate family and cultural teachings. Kahn (1980), a professor from the University of Arizona who studied aboriginal islanders, offers a final word on this topic. He commented about the custom of wife beating: "Severe injury or damage . . . cannot be condoned, but to totally condemn the practice [of wife beating] may be to negate an important aspect of island culture" (p. 731). (By the way, we were unable to reach these women for comment!)

Dysfunctional families. John Bradshaw (1988), a practitioner whose expertise stems from his work with recovering addicts, describes dysfunctional families in his widely read book *Bradshaw: On the Family.* These families are shame-based, unable to solve problems, bound by fixed and frozen roles, unable to set appropriate boundaries, enmeshed, conflicted, and unable to recognize or communicate feelings. One of the Bradshawisms quoted with some degree of regularity is that 96% of all families are to some degree emotionally impaired: "The range of compulsive, addictive behavior in modern society is awesome. Three-fourths of the population is seriously affected" (p. 21).

According to Bradshaw's calculations, the possibility of meeting someone who is emotionally healthy is almost nil. To extrapolate, *dysfunctional* could be synonymous with *normal,* and *normal* could be equated with *unhealthy.* This premise refutes the commonly held myth that battered women are seeking out men who will eventually batter them or that something is inherently wrong with them. In fact, research documents that 12% to 40% of all men can be classified as physically abusive (e.g., Browne, 1983; Deschner, 1984a; Hotaling & Straus, 1990). It is not simply a case of sick people gravitating toward each other.

Hotaling and Sugarman (1986) pointed out that the greatest predictor of becoming battered is simply being female. Certainly not all battered women are from dysfunctional families. In fact, many women come from loving families. The family history of battered women is much less uniform than the histories of men who batter (Hotaling & Sugarman, 1990). The common denominator for women is that they were all raised in a culture where females are one-down in terms of actual power and where the incentive to hope, to believe in change, and to "Stand by Your Man" is paramount. Because beliefs about marriage and commitment, about being men and women, husbands and wives, and fathers and mothers guide relationship choices, a woman coming from a healthy family has no guarantee that she will live with a healthy partner (Avni, 1991a).

Lenore Walker (1985b) cites several modern myths about battering relationships. One myth is that it is impossible to love someone who hits you. Love and physical force often occur together. The commonly heard phrase, "If he ever lays a hand on me, I'll leave," does not mirror reality. As Lloyd (1988) noted, physical aggression does not "herald the demise" of a marriage. Indeed, most adults have grown up in homes where loving parents spanked them as a form of physical discipline, "for the child's own good." Adults have come to believe that in families a certain amount of physical force is not a denial of love but can even be tangible proof of it. (See Appendix B, section 1, for a review of the Ayllon & Azrin, 1966, study.)

When you're in love, you put up with things that, when you're out of love you cite.

Judith Martin

Case History: Bianca and Damian

Bianca had lost her husband after an 11-year marriage. She had two children and a supportive family, but she was depressed and vulnerable. After 18 months, she met a man at work who was understanding, seemed to love children, and was divorced. He had two children of his own. She began to date him.

After Bianca and Damian moved in together, the emotional and verbal abuse began. He became angry when she spent too much time with her family, calling her "mama's girl." He was jealous of her friends and wondered why he wasn't enough for her. He got upset when their plans changed because her children were ill. His kids were older and out of the house most of the time. He wanted quiet, romantic dinners alone, sans children, on a routine basis. She gave up what was important to her a little at a time.

Bianca came from a family that was close and enjoyed time together. She had no context for understanding abusive behavior. When she confronted Damian, he told her that she was too sensitive. By the time that Damian began to hit her, she was confused about her own perceptions.

* * *

Human beings tend to adapt to their situations regardless of the quality of their environment, a sort of *chameleon effect*. In the isolation of a battering relationship, the batterer's reality becomes the family's reality. In the words of Claudia Black (personal communication, April 1981), who works with adult children of alcoholics, "When you invite a healthy person into a sick family, you give him or her the opportunity to become sick."

The Role of Learning and the Cycle of Violence

A scientific analysis of such processes as socialization and emotional dependency leads one inevitably to an inquiry of the common, underlying mechanism—learning. That is, women learn to be feminine, to rely on a husband, and to follow prescribed religious concepts. The following illustration demonstrates the basic role that learning plays in behavior. (Appendix A presents a brief review of operant conditioning.)

Case History: Heather and Ron

Heather had learned to iron her husband Ron's shirts just the way he wanted them. She had mastered nearly all of his favorite recipes, and she had worked very hard to teach the children to be quiet and pleasant when Ron was at home. She graduated in the top 10% of her "Fascinating Womanhood" (Andelin, 1963) course.

If Heather performed well (e.g., ironed, cooked, and got the children to bed quietly—"operants"), she and Ron often had an enjoyable evening watching TV and just "hanging out" together (reinforcement). At such times, they shared happy, intimate moments and often ended the evening by making love. She had learned that having a pleasant evening with Ron depended upon her ability to please him. (Heather had been operantly conditioned.)

*   *   *

Walker's (1979) "Cycle of Violence" theory refers to a three-stage sequence of events repeatedly occurring in violent relationships and helps to explain the staying/leaving dilemma experienced by battered women. During the first phase of the cycle, tension builds as a result of verbal outbursts, muttering, confrontation, minor acts of violence, emotional threats, or controlling behavior. Tension escalates until a violent incident erupts (second phase), and then a respite occurs. That respite can include loving, contrition, apologies, gifts, or simply a cessation of violence. During the third phase, the battered woman experiences what she sees as the "real" man whom she fell in love with initially.

Here she receives discernible reinforcement of her identity as the good wife and her importance to her partner. Here she recovers from her battle scars. Here she remembers that abuse is not the only significant aspect of her relationship. She recognizes that she loves him too. She cares about how he feels, his health, his survival if she leaves, his reputation, and so forth. She seems concerned about his relationship with the children and with friends and family. In fact, if she has left him, she may return because of love (Barnett & Lopez-Real, 1985; I. M. Johnson, 1988).

Wetzel and Ross (1983) describe the abusive male partner's loving behavior as a form of intermittent reinforcement. (See Appendix A, section 1B.7, for information on intermittent reinforcement and other variables controlling reinforcement.) Intermittently reinforced behaviors resist change. About 85% of battering men cycle through this last phase of remorse, promises of reform, and appeals for reconciliation (Browne, 1984; Walker, 1984). About 50% of batterers skip the last phase when battering becomes habitual (Browne, 1984; Stacey & Shupe, 1983). For some battered women, the absence of violence may become the respite (Walker, 1984).

Learned Hopefulness

The honeymoon phase and hope. For many women, the third stage of the cycle of violence provides reason to hope. Muldary (1983) called this outcome *learned hopefulness*. Learned hopefulness is a battered woman's ongoing belief that her partner will change his abusive behavior or that he will change his personality.

Pagelow (1981b) indicated that 73% of one shelter sample returned home because the batterer repented and they believed he would change (also see Frieze, 1979; Frisch & MacKenzie, 1991; I. M. Johnson, 1988; Pfouts, 1978). Mars (1990) emphasized the same result with an added twist: "It's not that I really believe the relationship will change, but that I want to believe that it will be different." What an individual believes about his or her own reality is more important than an outside observer's perception (Swann & Read, 1981).

Muldary's (1983) study of shelter residents identified the following list of reasons for staying or returning to a battering relationship: "I wanted to save the relationship"; "I thought we could solve our problems"; and "I loved my partner." Barnett and Lopez-Real (1985) found "hoped partner would change" to be the *number one* reason women said they remained with their abusive partners ("feared revenge" was number two). Some women in their study made the following comments:

> "That he would change was still a thought in the back of my head."
>
> "I was always hoping since he had gone to A.A."
>
> "I kept making excuses for him."
>
> "After living together for so long without the abuse, I was hoping he would go back to his old self. I don't understand the change in him."
>
> "He's got a lot of pluses. Hopefully he will help himself, and become a better person overall."

Relationship hope seems to be an internalized and reinforced notion characteristic of women in general. Families, friends, song lyrics, literature, religion, and the media all encourage women to hope and believe that they can change their male partners and that they should persevere to see the results of their labor of love—the reward will be great. Isn't it true that behind every good man is a woman (who changed him)?

Other factors can create sufficient hope for a battered woman to return. For example, Thompson (1989) found that a few counseling sessions and promises from her husband that the violence would stop engendered battered women's hope. Indeed, Okun (1983) reported that battered women returned home as soon as their violent husbands enrolled in therapy, even *before* any changes in behavior had occurred.

Gondolf (1988b) also asserted that the batterer's psychotherapy was a key factor in a battered woman's return. Indeed, batterers frequently resort to counseling as a means of manipulating their female partners and not as a means of changing their own behavior. One of the authors (AL), who works with batterers, contends that "men do not come into therapy because they think personal growth is 'far out,' and they can't wait to change. They come in either because their partner left, or they really believe that she will leave, or because God speaks to them through the SWAT team."

Hope also springs from the fact that an abusive male is not unidimensional. Women report that their partners can show kindness, romance, and intensity (Dr. Jekyll) and then flip to the other side (Mr. Hyde). Research has validated this two-sided profile of some batterers. Hastings and Hamberger (1988, p. 43) describe this group of men as follows: "In superficial interactions, for example, batterers may appear entirely 'normal,' appropriate, and even charming. A casual observer might conclude that these are 'typical males.' Such behaviors usually serve to ingratiate the batterer with others and help him control and manipulate the relationship to meet his needs." The batterer's negative behaviors (intimidation and violence) only emerge when his sense of control is threatened. Conflict arises for some battered women from the ongoing hope that Dr. Jekyll will return.

Case History: Sylvia and Dan

Even after Sylvia left Dan, she was torn by mixed feelings. Dan would call and offer support. He sometimes picked up the children and would spend a little time with them. He sounded interested in her and what she was doing for the first time in years. After they talked, he would ask her to consider reconciliation.

Between the "bouts of reason," he would call her, screaming and condemning her as a wife and mother. He harassed her at work. He had his mother call Sylvia to implore her to "think of the children." As the holidays approached, they talked less, and Sylvia felt relief. He began to pay the back child support he owed her and saw the children more regularly.

And then one day, she met Dan in the park. He came to pick up the kids. Instead, he attacked her. He choked and hit her. The children were terrified and crying. A passerby pulled Dan away so that Sylvia and the children could escape. Dan threw himself in front of her car screaming to his daughters: "Mommy is trying to kill me." He has called her since the incident, alternately asking for forgiveness and blaming her for his rage. He threatens to kill her.

This pattern of hope and caring followed by brutality and fear kept her confused and immobilized for years. His vacillation continues to keep her off balance even 8 months after their separation.

*   *   *

Other Reasons for Staying

Strube and Barbour (1983, 1984) discovered that psychological commitment was significantly related to the decision to stay or leave. Keeping the relationship together "no matter what" significantly differentiated women who left an abusive relationship and those who did not (Frisch & MacKenzie, 1991).

According to Rusbult's (1980) model of commitment, individuals committed to an unsatisfactory marriage remain if their investments (i.e., time, emotional energy) are high and their alternatives are few. In applying the model to spouse abuse, Bauserman and Arias (1990) demonstrated that substantial investment was associated with higher commitment.

Commitment to a relationship is usually seen as a positive attribute. It seems, however, that such characteristics in battered women are yet another sign of "sickness." To leave is to abandon her commitments; to stay is to be beaten. To define seemingly healthy traits as sick because of their context is to "pathologize" human behavior. To define battered women as mentally ill, codependent, or unhealthy because these very traits have entrapped them is to negate their socialization.

Ferraro (1981) noted that "even women who are able to overcome the financial obstacles to independence return to violent husbands. Perhaps a major reason for doing so is loneliness" (pp. 436-437). The psychodynamics specific to a battering relationship may intensify a battered woman's fear of loneliness. Turner and Shapiro (1986) verified this hypothesis. Of the women who left their abusive partners, 70% returned because of feelings of loneliness and loss generated by the separation. Like widows, battered women mourn the loss of their relationships.

Varvaro (1991) listed 12 losses encountered by battered women: safety, everyday routine, living in a home, personal possessions, self-esteem, a father figure for the children, love and caring from a spouse, success in marriage, hopes and dreams, trust in mate, view of the world as a safe place, and status and support system. These losses were associated with their loneliness. They had varying levels of attachment and investment in their relationships, even if their relationships had been short-lived.

Procci (1990) noted that the failure of a marriage to meet one's expectations causes bitter disappointment. Both abusive and non-abusive couples devise plausible reasons for hanging on to unhappy relationships (Vaughn, 1987): (a) belief in commitment, (b) legal binding together, (c) desire not to hurt the partner, (d) fear about not finding a better person who is available, (e) belief in ability to make the relationship better, (f) avoidance of being a quitter, (g) the need to protect children and parents, and (h) religious convictions. In general, couples hide their troubled relationships from others. They develop rationalizations, such as "all relationships have trouble" or "after a while, all couples lose interest in sex."

Ellard, Herbert, and Thompson (1991) compared battered women still involved in abusive relationships with those who were not. Similarities existed in regard to psychosocial attributes such as mutual trust, love and respect, satisfaction with sex, and sharing of household chores. The key difference was that enmeshed women tended to see other women as having comparable problems. They cited many positive aspects of their relationships and did not perceive a diminution of love as connected to the battering. They developed methods for processing the meaning of their situations positively, thereby providing themselves with concrete reasons for staying (see also Campbell, 1989a).

Women who were raised in nonviolent families may not recognize abusive behavior in its early stages because they have no frame of reference. According to McLeer (cited in "The Battered Woman,"

1989, p. 108), "Early on, she may be trying to figure out how to decrease the violence but keep her relationship intact. It can take a long time for her to recognize that she can't do anything about his violence—he's a violent man—all she can do is get out."

Conflict

Animal research. Early psychologists attempted to understand human conflict through animal studies. Using rats, N. E. Miller (1959) demonstrated all of the following kinds of conflicts (translated below into human examples): approach-approach, avoidance-avoidance, and approach-avoidance. (See Appendix B, section 2, for a description of this study.)

When an individual has a choice between two desirable options (e.g., going on a vacation to Hawaii or going to Alaska), an approach-approach conflict arises. That is, the person would like to go to both Hawaii and Alaska. At other times, a choice occurs between two undesirable alternatives (e.g., cleaning the oven or cleaning the garage: "caught between a rock and a hard place"). This circumstance also gives rise to ambivalence (avoidance-avoidance conflict). When one choice includes both desirable and undesirable features (the house you want to buy is inexpensive but 60 miles from your job), one may enter an approach-avoidance conflict. When two choices contain both positive and negative elements, the person finds herself in a multiple approach-avoidance conflict. People caught in such conflicts vacillate, first going toward one goal, then retreating, and then going back to the first goal.

Conflict in battered women. Approach-avoidance behavior seems relevant to reasons that battered women remain. The combination of benefits (learned hopefulness) and costs (fear) inherent in most battering relationships leads to ambivalence, conflict, and frustration. A battered woman becomes trapped in a double approach-avoidance conflict. On the one hand, her relationship meets many of her emotional and economic needs, but it is degrading and dangerous. She wants to approach the hope that is positive and run from the fear that is negative. She wants to move toward safety but avoid losing her relationship. For a while, the conflict is reflected by her ambivalence about staying or leaving.

Summary

This chapter has attempted to explain the role cultural mores and sex-role socialization play in a woman's decision to remain with her abuser. A woman *learns* gender identity in her family. She learns that affiliation with a man gives her status and worth. Battered women form attachments and become emotionally dependent upon their male partners in the same way that other women do, following the same path as their nonbattered sisters.

Society's acceptance of male dominance and aggression, along with its disavowal of male-to-female violence, creates a societal dissonance. Battered women also experience this conflict as they recognize the abuse in their own relationships. They may erroneously assume that their relationship struggles correspond to those faced by other women in their marriages.

A woman also learns about hope and commitment in her family, qualities continually nourished by cultural messages. Her primary reason for remaining in or returning to a battering relationship is her hope and need to believe that her abuser will stop the violence, a need called "learned hopefulness." Some of the traits most valued in women, such as commitment and tolerance, may be used to "pathologize" her behavior and to blame her for staying. Cultural mores coupled with the likelihood of meeting a dysfunctional mate support the contention that becoming a battered woman could happen to anyone.

Note

1. Copyright © 1992 by The New York Times Company. Reprinted by permission.

2

● Institutional Battering:
The Power of the Patriarchy

The thing women have got to learn is that nobody gives you power. You just take it.

ROSEANNE ARNOLD

IN ANCIENT TIMES, virgins were sacrificed to appease vengeful gods. A virgin was not a high price to pay for rain or bounteous crops. It was an honor for the parents and the hapless virgin herself to be offered up in this way. As civilization has advanced, the powers that were, and are, no longer sacrifice maidens. They ask only that the maiden agree to sacrifice herself (Roiphe, 1986).

Chapter Overview

This chapter explores some of the practical issues faced by battered women trying to leave their abusive partners. Among these issues are economic dependency; patriarchal, social, and religious

23

practices; and the failure of the medical and criminal justice systems to adequately address the question. A battered woman finds little institutional support for leaving an abusive relationship.

Below the Poverty Line and Below the Belt

Women represent two thirds of all economically poor adults, according to the U.S. Bureau of the Census. Duncan (1987) calls single women and children the "new poor" in this country, and Burkhauser and Duncan (1989) have shown that women are at much greater risk for an economic loss over the course of their lives than men.

Generally, women contribute 22% of the family's total income (Arendell, 1987). Full-time female workers earn about 60% as much as full-time male workers (Blau, 1984). "More than 80% of women who work full-time earn less than $20,000 a year" (cited in Faludi, 1991, p. xiii). The average female college graduate today earns less than a man with a high school diploma, just as she did in the 1950s. "Though business leaders say they are aware of and deplore sex discrimination, corporate America has yet to make an honest effort toward eradicating it" (Faludi, 1991, p. xiii). Despite the rumor that women have made it to the executive washroom in large numbers, economic realities paint a not-so-vibrant watercolor.

Women have much to fear from poverty. For example, poor women are disproportionately exposed to crime and violence (Belle, Longfellow, Makosky, Saunders, & Zelkowitz, 1981, pp. 28-37), to illness and death of children (Children's Defense Fund, 1979), to the imprisonment of husbands and inadequate housing (G. Brown, Bhrolchain, & Harris, 1975). "These conditions, which enforce the economic dependence of women, have been viewed as a means of maintaining power and control over women in our society" (Shepard & Pence, 1988, p. 55). Battering exacerbates the plight of poor women. Battered women who go to shelters are often representative of women with the least money.

Ferraro (1981) highlighted the obstacles that battered women living in a shelter faced in their attempts to achieve economic independence. Most of them were young, high school graduates with relatively few job skills and with one or more small children.

For the most part, the battered women in her study (a) had no cars and lived in cities with no public transportation, (b) were waiting up to 2 years for a vacancy in the small number of subsidized housing units, and (c) could not find affordable child care. For a moment, stop and imagine yourself in this situation. How would you cope?

Case History: Liz

Liz arrived at the shelter following a 2-week stay in the hospital for a fractured ankle that required surgery. Over the course of her 8-year marriage, she had developed a first-name relationship with several nurses. Staff had stopped believing that she was accident prone, and on this occasion medical staff persuaded Liz to call the local shelter.

Liz was an at-home mother with two young sons, 3-year-old Ben and 6-year-old Patrick. She was taking medication to control the occasional seizures she suffered because of head injuries inflicted by her husband. Over the course of the relationship, she had received numerous injuries such as broken bones, concussions, facial stitches, and torn ligaments, not to mention myriad cuts and bruises.

Her case was a complicated one. She was virtually unemployable because of her injuries, and she had an inconsistent job history prior to her stay in the shelter. She was financially dependent upon her husband, and although he made a decent living and they owned a home, she had no independent funds. After she entered the shelter, her husband took all of the money from their joint savings account, leaving Liz with no money.

Within a week of entering the shelter, her sons, Ben and Patrick, tried to stab another child with a dinner knife. Liz had a difficult time keeping up with the boys, as she was on crutches and discipline was not her strong suit.

Filing for divorce was the only avenue she saw to having access to any money so that she could leave the shelter. She appeared at the initial hearing to obtain a restraining order, which included a kick-out order (her husband would have to leave the home), temporary custody, and child support. Although the judge ordered her husband to pay temporary child support, he determined that *she* should be restrained from staying in the house, as her husband would know where to find her and she wouldn't be safe.

Liz's husband remained in the house but selectively forgot to pay child support. He filed a counterpetition demanding visitation with his children. That order was granted by the court. Liz had been in the shelter for 5 weeks, still had no money, was dependent upon emergency food, and was unable to return to her home. She was also now in contempt of court for failure to allow visitation while living in the shelter. (As a safety precaution, staff may not allow visitation during a shelter stay.) Her husband's refusal to pay child support left her and the children penniless and unable to leave the shelter.

Liz felt discouraged as she watched other women and their children come and go. At the end of 8 weeks, Liz received her first disability payment, which she needed to save for rent on her own apartment. She had just begun to look for a job, but, with her injuries and few marketable skills, she was financially better off with disability. Another month passed before she received her second disability payment and her first child support check. Liz and her husband finally put their house up for sale. Liz looked for an apartment and was able to find an affordable one-bedroom in a poor section of town. With the assistance of shelter staff, she and the boys moved in. The boys had calmed down after they had some consistency and nonviolence in the shelter. Altogether, it took almost 4 months before Liz was able to leave the shelter and another year before she was able to find a job. Ten years after her stay in the shelter, Liz called to serve as a volunteer.

* * *

Much like Liz's husband, other men have penalized their wives and children economically. Inspection of court-ordered support data revealed that 62% of fathers failed to abide by the decree fully the first year, and 42% never made any payment. By the tenth year, 79% were in total noncompliance (Weitzman, 1974; see also U.S. Bureau of the Census, 1989). After a divorce, men's standard of living usually rises, while women's and children's decreases (Corcoran, Duncan, & Hill, 1984).

From the perspective of battering relationships, women are in an economic "no-win" position. Hornung, McCullough, and Sugimoto (1981) provided evidence linking educational and occupational differences in couples with an increased risk of psychological abuse, physical aggression, and life-threatening violence. In another investigation of status inequality, C. Smith (1988) also confirmed a virtual "no-win" status conflict for women:

In the case of lower status husbands, resource theory explains how traditional values of male dominance can lead to violence against higher status wives. Conversely in the case of higher status husbands, the distributive justice hypothesis explains how more contemporary values of status advancement may lead to violence against lower status wives. (p. 15)

Economic Dependence and Remaining With an Abuser

Pence and Paymar's (1986) model of battering proposes that abusive behaviors, including economic abuse (threats or prevention of economic security), help men maintain power and control over women. Batterers may use physical force or threats to control the woman's ability to participate in the workplace. While physical abuse allows an abuser to maintain control, economic abuse further restricts a woman's ability to escape.

Shepard and Pence (1988) found that battering resulted in absenteeism from work in 55% of battered women, lateness or leaving early in 62%, job loss in 24%, and batterer harassment at work in 56%. In addition, 33% of the battered women in this sample reported being prohibited from working, 59% were discouraged from working, 24% were not allowed to attend school, 50% were discouraged from attending school, and the abuse prevented 21% from finding work. Ending the abuse enabled 48% to change their employment or school status (see also Frisch & MacKenzie, 1991).

Many researchers have observed the economic dependency/ failure to leave connection (e.g., Barnett, Haney-Martindale, Modzelewski, & Sheltra, 1991; Kalmuss & Straus, 1982; Pagelow, 1981b; Strube & Barbour, 1983). In a study of 426 shelter residents (e.g., I. M. Johnson, 1988) and in another of more than 1,000 women (Aguirre, 1985), the probability of staying in the violent relationship was highest for women whose husbands were the sole breadwinners.

Barnett and Lopez-Real (1985) reported a constellation of reasons for staying given by the battered women in their sample that can be labeled as resource and economic dependence. These were some of the comments:

"I still feel scared of supporting the kids and bringing home enough money because I can't depend on him."

"I'm facing eviction now. I'm scared."

"I've never worked and have no high school education."

"I am disabled because of his battering."

"I feel one of the keys to this whole thing is for women to be economically independent, so as soon as they find themselves in a destructive relationship, they have the means to get out."

"I only left once, but I came back because I didn't have any money, but money isn't everything."

"I know I'll eventually get out of this situation, that is, finding a place to live, getting a job, and supporting my children."

For battered women, economic realities reinforce economic fears. Using resource theory, Pagelow (1981b) disclosed that women with the fewest resources (e.g., job, money, a car) are the most likely to remain with an abuser. To manage economically, many women who are leaving the shelter join together to form an "extended" family. Two families may move into a one- or two-bedroom apartment and share rent, household expenses, and child care. Between the two of them, they maintain a home until they can find a better job or receive family assistance. For many women, coming to the shelter constitutes their first experience of being on any kind of public assistance (e.g., unemployment, welfare, disability) and being part of the "system."

In coping with the ambivalence about whether to remain, many battered women use a cost-benefit analysis (Frisch & MacKenzie, 1991; Pfouts, 1978). Fleming (1979) describes this conflict as economic support versus economic deprivation. In accord with exchange theory (Thibaut & Kelley, 1958), I. M. Johnson (1988) suggests that the survivor who decides to return to her abusive relationship perceives her alternatives within the marriage as more rewarding and less costly than her alternatives outside the marriage. For example, a woman with little or no income and insufficient work skills is likely to perceive her alternatives outside the marriage as costly while perceiving those within the marriage (e.g., a home, love, security) as more rewarding.

Perception of one's situation plays a crucial role in the decision to leave. Kalmuss and Straus (1982) analyzed data from Straus's 1979 national sample of 2,143 individuals (960 men and 1,183 women). They concluded that women remained in abusive relationships because of *perceived* dependency. Those who misjudged themselves to be dependent experienced minor aggression, but those who really were dependent experienced more severe violence at the hands of their abusers. Similarly, Frisch and MacKenzie (1991) noted that battered women who did not escape, compared with those who did, were significantly more likely to feel unable to make it in the work world because of poor job skills.

A well-known psychological theory describing human behavior and growth seems to apply to a battered woman's decision making. Maslow's "Hierarchy of Needs" describes the path to self-actualization, or becoming a whole human being (Maslow, 1970). The basic tenet of this theory is that movement up the ladder is contingent upon meeting lower-level needs. The scale ascends from basic needs, such as air to breathe, food and water, shelter, and safety, on to affiliation, esteem, cognitive or intellectual needs, aesthetic needs, and the need for self-fulfillment. It is obvious that a battered woman whose needs for food, shelter, and safety are not met will have little physical or emotional energy to invest in achieving higher-level needs. Social expectations imposed on battered women to move up the ladder usually fail to address survival needs. For many battered women, it may feel like "two steps forward, one step back."

Seeking Shelter

Finding a safe place for a woman alone or a woman with children is a critical early step up Maslow's hierarchy. Many women are unaware of the existence of emergency shelters. Even those who know about them might encounter difficulty finding available space (Frisch & MacKenzie, 1991). Because of lack of space, shelters in Southern California turn away about 15 to 20 appropriate referrals for every battered woman they accept. In fact, a 1988 study funded by Victim Services identified 21% of the homeless as battered women (cited in Friedman, 1991). In spite of these circumstances, Gordon Humphrey, a conservative Republican senator from New Hampshire, expressed his distress over shelter activities:

"The federal government should not fund missionaries who would war on the traditional family or on local values" (quoted in "Domestic Violence Conference Bill," 1980, p. 1).

On the positive side, hot line counselors and shelter staff are generally very creative and aware of community resources. Shelter workers explore options with a battered woman to help her devise a safety/housing plan. Referrals may include a funded, after-hours hotel, other emergency shelter (mission or church), a 24-hour coffee shop, or a friend or relative's home. Usually, within a week, space will become available in a battered women's program. For safe space outside of the area, a battered woman sometimes can obtain a small financial grant through such agencies as Traveler's Aid, Catholic Charities, Lutheran Social Services, or the YWCA.

Many women do eventually leave but return more than once to their abusive partners. Many factors affect a woman's return home. Fear, financial needs, and love are but a few. When women reenter a shelter, their reasons for returning resemble those for entering in the first place (M. N. Wilson, Baglioni, & Downing, 1989): (a) The most important factor influencing a woman's decision to seek shelter again was the average age of her children. Those with mobile children (not toddlers and infants) were more likely to seek readmission to the shelter. (b) The second most influential variable was the source (not amount) of the woman's income. Women who worked outside the home were far more likely to leave it when violence occurred.

Case History: Glenda

Glenda attended a woman's group run by the YWCA in her hometown. The group's theme was "Women and Self-Esteem." She had been in the group for several months before she hinted at "not having her needs met" in her marriage. A few weeks later, she came to group with bruises on her face and an Ace bandage on her wrist. After she told the group that her husband had hurt her, the other women comforted her and wanted to help.

The group leader had heard about a shelter for abused women somewhere in California. None of the other women knew of any safe place for Glenda to go. After a 2-day search, the group facilitator obtained information about the shelter. With the help of other group members and the counselor, Glenda packed up her children and her household belongings and boarded a bus to California to become one of the first women to enter one of the first shelters in California.

*   *   *

Religion

It's hard to fight an enemy who has outposts in your head.
Sally Kempton

The Judeo-Christian ethic has greatly affected American culture. God and religion are mentioned in the Declaration of Independence, the U.S. Constitution, the Gettysburg Address, and in other important documents. The Judeo-Christian heritage exerts an influence on anyone who lives in this country, whether he or she is denying it, condemning it, actively participating in ascribed religious practices, or somewhere in between.

Marie Fortune (1987), an ordained Christian minister and author of *Keeping the Faith*, made the following claim:

> The majority of women in the United States were raised in Christian homes or as adults have affiliated themselves with a Christian Church. This is a sociological reality. Therefore, when a woman is battered by a member of her family, she will likely bring to her experience her background and values as a Christian woman. Also likely, is that her experience of violence in her family will not only be a physical and emotional crisis, but also a spiritual crisis. (p. 2)

This crisis of faith is not limited to Christian women. Most women of faith struggle with their spiritual principles when confronted with personal violence inflicted by the person that they have loved and trusted. It is essential to acknowledge the dilemma of those who feel bound to their relationships by the very tenets of their religious beliefs.

A woman with deep convictions looks to her minister, rabbi, or priest to interpret God's word and to ensure her eternal consequences. She turns to her spiritual adviser and to other members of her religious community for support. For a battered woman in particular, the quality of the assistance she receives can have life-and-death results. At the very least, the advice she is given can alter her life, her children's lives, and perhaps have a significant effect on her batterer.

Clarke (1986), in her book *Pastoral Care of Battered Women*, states:

> Theological beliefs become an integral part of one's being and these beliefs are very powerful for a religious woman in a battering relationship. If a battered woman's religious convictions lead her to believe that a wife is subordinate to the husband, that marriage is an unalterable life-time commitment, or that suffering is the lot of the faithful, then those convictions have the sanction of God. (p. 61)

Case History: Claudette—A Christian Woman

Hitting had gone on for a few years before we went for help. We were members of a strict Protestant denomination. They had a counseling center and we wanted Christian counseling. We talked to the counselor about our marriage, our children, about everything, except the violence. Finally, I told him I was afraid of my husband. The counselor told me in front of my husband to be a better wife and mother, to pray harder, to be more submissive. He told my husband he shouldn't hit me. When we got home, my husband only remembered the part about how I should be more submissive.

* * *

Religion and patriarchy. Nineteenth-century suffragette Mathilda Gage (Stanton, Anthony, & Gage, 1881/1889, p. 763) asserted that "the church, which should have been the great conservator of morals, dragged women to the lowest depths." Gage went on to explain that "the most grievous wound ever inflicted upon women has been in the teaching that she was not created equal with man, and the consequent denial of her rightful place and position in Church and State" (p. 754).

Many of the writers who assert that a sexist society is the fertile soil that allows for woman abuse also contend that traditional theologies have contributed to the victimization of wives by supplying biblical evidence that God ordains patriarchy (R. E. Dobash & R. P. Dobash, 1979; D. Martin, 1978; Pagelow, 1981b; Star, 1980; Walker, 1979). Stacey and Shupe (1983, p. 97) conclude that "the overwhelming role played by religion in the lives of the violent couples . . . was a regressive, and unwholesome one."

Clergy and battered women. Alsdurf (1985) believes his research data show that clergy's beliefs mirror society's acceptance of patriarchal practices. He mailed a two-page questionnaire to 5,700 ministers in Protestant churches in the United States and Canada. Responses indicated that 26% of the surveyed pastors agreed that a wife should submit to her husband and trust that God would honor her action by either stopping the abuse or giving her the strength to endure it. About 50% of the pastors expressed concern that the husband's aggression not be overemphasized and used as a justification to break up the marriage.

Results also revealed that 33% of the ministers felt that abuse would have to be severe to justify a Christian wife's leaving her husband. According to 21% of these clergy, no amount of abuse would justify a separation. Only 17% believed that seldom-expressed physical violence was compelling enough to allow a woman to separate from her husband.

Case History: June

June was married for 22 years to a helping professional who battered her and terrified the children. They were both faithful church members, and she prayed daily. Her faith was the fundamental factor in her decision making. She was a devout and very intelligent woman, yet she felt confused and guilty in regard to her own angry feelings, which had recently surfaced.

June's husband broke things around the house, screamed and hollered, threatened, and beat her and the children. When he attacked their older son, she tried to stop it, but he hit her and threw her out of the way. Chaos was a way of life in their family. The mood of the family changed when her husband came home from work. June and the kids ate dinner silently. They responded to any quick movement from the head of the household and were ready to duck or run to defend themselves.

When she spoke of her fear and some of the problems at home to her friends in the church women's group, she was advised to submit to her husband and not to even think of leaving him, as leaving would damn her children's souls. Her husband was, after all, a deacon and very well respected. After that first attempt to gain support, June didn't risk approaching anyone at her church for a while. Her next attempt was with an assistant minister, who advised her to pray and to endure, that her husband would eventually change.

Several years later, after a particularly violent argument, June went to the minister in charge. This time she had evidence. She pulled up her sleeves to show the bruises on her arms and pulled down her turtle neck collar revealing the finger marks on her throat. She explained calmly about hearing her children's screams as she lost consciousness. At that point, the minister decided the situation was very serious and wanted a conference with June and her husband. After the conference, June's pastor advised her to take the kids and run. And so she did.

* * *

A clergyman's specific beliefs profoundly influence his approach to helping a battered woman. Although a survey by Pagelow (1981b) revealed that the church was the institutional resource most frequently contacted by battered women, a study by Roy (1977) maintained that, compared with friends, lawyers, relatives, police, women's groups, and psychologists, clergy had the highest negative influence in counseling battered women.

Bowker (1982) surveyed 146 battered women, 59 of whom reported consulting clergy in connection with the abuse. Of the clergy (rabbis, priests, ministers, and pastors), 93% did attempt some form of assistance. The women's written responses disclosed that the helping behaviors included everything from passive listening to physical confrontations with the batterer. Advice was commonly given, both somewhat helpful and outright bad.

Bowker and Mauer (1986) reported that, after the first battering incident, wives were more likely to contact the clergy than any other helping group except the police (also see Pagelow, 1981b). As battering incidents continued, however, battered women contacted clergy less often. When the 59 women who sought clergy counseling later identified the system most effective in helping them stop the abuse, 33 specified women's groups and 18 cited social service agencies. None of the women mentioned the clergy.

Actual responses of the clergy to victims were most frequently multiple, but limited. They furnished information about treatment programs, provided extended counseling, or suggested that the victim obtain professional therapy. Much less frequently, they advised the women to call the police, obtain a civil protection order, or separate from the abuser. They rarely assisted women to leave, although more than half relayed information about shelters (S. E. Martin, 1989).

Some clergy alleged that they do not help because they are seldom asked. Other considerations were the clergy's lack of information about treatment programs or state laws, lack of time to meet the congregation's needs, and lack of training in counseling. Although J. M. Johnson and D. M. Bondurant (1992) documented an increase in ministerial training (from 30% to over 50%) about domestic violence from 1982 to 1988, they found that clerics remained ambivalent. Even when mandated by law to report certain types of child maltreatment, they reported only 3.2% of the actual cases recounted to them. Their "institutional nonresponse" most likely reflects their dispute over the authority of the state to intervene in family matters. Thompson (1989) contends that battered women and sexual assault victims become isolated further when ministers and churches deny their needs.

> *Guilt is the gift that keeps on giving.*
> Erma Bombeck

Moral dilemmas. Barnett and Lopez-Real (1985) reported that battered women also identified other reasons of principle or morality for staying with their abusive spouses: (a) "Children need both a mother and father" was the most significant of these ethical reasons; (b) "you thought it would be distressing to leave your children"; and (c) "you considered divorce or separation a social disgrace." These comments reflect this ethical conflict:

"Divorce is a personal failure."

"I believed you married forever."

"I wanted to make it because of family pressure."

"I have two boys; I'm afraid of them becoming feminine."

"I would never leave my children under any circumstances."

Battered women expressed concern about the negative status of being divorced and about the social stigma associated with being a divorcée. Some churches and communities tend to condemn divorce and to hold negative attitudes toward remarriage. In fact, many religions hold that divorce is a sin. Most religious groups extol the virtues of the family unit—a father, mother, and children (not a single parent and her children)—and center most of their activities around family events. As one would expect, the stigma of divorce affects a battered woman's decision to stay (Truniger, 1971).

Case History: Amanda and Ray

Amanda had three children under the age of 5. She was the devout Christian wife of a devout Christian batterer. She asked for church counseling after Ray broke her nose. Her husband went with her. He explained that he had been angry and that she had been "nagging" him. She said she had been pushing him to do some chores around the house. He explained that he had no intention of hurting her and how sorry he was. She said she believed him. The pastor prayed with them. He admonished Ray and Amanda about the importance of maintaining a Christian home for the children.

By the time Amanda contacted the shelter hot line at the advice of a friend, she had received pastoral counseling on two additional occasions and had appeared before a board of elders. She was also spending three nights a week in her car with her children to avoid an incident. She was very concerned about receiving censure from the church and losing that very significant support group in her life. The church was not only a spiritual and emotional support but also a possible source of financial assistance for her and the children. Amanda did not believe she could maintain her resolve to leave the relationship if her wish for peace and safety conflicted with her moral obligations.

Shelter staff agreed to intervene and they scheduled a meeting with the church bishop, the board of elders, and Amanda. With reassurance from her advocates, Amanda was able to tell her story in more complete detail. Church members were appalled and agreed that Amanda and her children needed to be at the shelter. Censure was applied to Ray, not to Amanda, and Amanda was able to leave because she had clergy support.

* * *

The Failure of Institutional Responses

Gondolf (1990) along with others (e.g., Lenore Walker) in attendance at the International Institute on Victimology (Onati, Spain, May 23-27, 1989) concluded that victimization of women and children ultimately stems from the patriarchal nature of society (as suggested previously by Pagelow, 1981b). Lester (1980) established an inverse relationship between the status of women in 71 different world societies and wife beating. Worldwide, societies have sanctioned victimization of women by such practices as genital mutilation, foot binding, dowry death, selective malnourishment, female infanticide, forced prostitution, and violent pornography (Heise, 1989). In most countries, wife beating is an acceptable form of control whether legal or illegal.

Justice and the System

A number of researchers have cited the inadequacy or lack of institutional response as a factor in battered women's decision to stay (Gelles, 1976; Hodson, 1982; Pagelow, 1981c). According to Pope (quoted in M. Beck, Springer, & Foote, 1992, p. 54): "In our society, we tend to deny and downplay those types of abuses in which males are the perpetrators." Male-to-female violence has recently become an issue of national importance. Senate Judiciary Committee Chairman Joseph R. Biden, Jr., noted: "Today it is easier to convict a car thief than a rapist. Police officers are more likely to arrest a man for parking tickets than for beating his wife; and lawyers still put victims of vicious assaults on the stand to ask what clothes they were wearing at the time of the attack." Senator Biden has announced legislation to ensure tougher prosecution against individuals who commit crimes against women ("Bill on Violence," 1991, p. 7). His bill would make gender-based assault a violation of civil rights, specifying women as victims of hate crimes. As Hirschel, Hutchison, Dean, and Mills (1992, p. 276) have asserted, "Spouse abuse is probably the only area of criminal behavior in which it has been considered necessary to justify the arrest of offenders on the grounds that such arrests will serve as a deterrent."

Availability of victim compensation, especially for victims of domestic violence, has been problematic ("Victim Agencies Struggle," 1992). Although the 1988 amendments to the 1984 Victims of Crime Act mandated inclusion of battered women, alternative requirements have perplexed agencies charged with interpretation and enactment. For example, contributory misconduct regulations prevent compensation for victims who may have used "fighting words" or obscene gestures, acted in a negligent manner, or failed to withdraw from a threatening situation. Although agency staff who were interviewed unanimously agreed that one intention of the laws was to prevent payment to individuals in a stereotypical barroom brawl, victims of such fights made up a large portion of their caseloads.

Furthermore, all of the states require that victims cooperate with local law enforcement agencies (i.e., make an official complaint). But a victim of battering may choose not to prosecute for a variety of reasons. Another prerequisite is that there be no "unjust enrichment" of a perpetrator. Because battered women may choose to stay with their abuser, they may not qualify for compensation under this clause. That is, the batterer cannot benefit from her remuneration.

The police and domestic violence. Police departments and social agencies traditionally have viewed family violence as noncriminal, noninjurious, inconsequential, and primarily verbal (Fields, 1978; Waaland & Keeley, 1985). Police in general have been reluctant to get involved in "family" problems for reasons rooted in myth, misogyny, and misinformation: (a) If he beats her and she stays, there are no real victims (Waaland & Keeley, 1985); (b) it may be her fault; (c) it is not the best solution to the problem (Saunders & Size, 1986); and (d) it is too dangerous for police to intervene.

FBI statistics for the 10-year period from 1973 to 1982 revealed that "Responding to Disturbance Calls" was the single most frequent category of felonious assaults on officers (FBI, 1984). A later reclassification of the 1973-1982 data indicated that, next to traffic calls, disturbance calls were the least dangerous (see Garner & Clemmer, 1986).

It is ironic that, on the one hand, the police tended to dismiss domestic disturbances as family "spats" that a woman could handle on her own and, on the other hand, have judged themselves to be in such probable danger that it was extremely risky to interfere. Browne (1983) used these same FBI statistics to point out that a woman's chances of being assaulted at home by her mate are greater than those of a police office being assaulted on the job.

A New York Committee on Domestic Violence (STEPS to End Family Violence, 1987) concluded that the criminal justice system fails to support battered women. Although spouse abuse is condemned in theory, the law still allows it to continue in practice (Waits, 1985). For example, Pagelow (1981c) maintained that the police ignored 61% of the requests to arrest made by battered women, and Dutton (1988) estimated that the police arrested suspected batterers in only 21.2% of the cases, even with prima facie evidence of assault.

Case History: Rachel and Abe

Rachel had two children, a temporary restraining order, and an abusive husband who violated it regularly. The order had not been difficult to get, but enforcement was a joke. The first few times Abe violated the order, the police did not arrive until he was long gone. The next few times, the police demanded that he leave the premises. They finally arrested him, but he was out of jail within 24 hours. It was only after four more arrests and court appearances for violating the restraining order that a judge sentenced him to 8 months in jail. The judge was finally persuaded by Abe's continued threats on Rachel's life ("I'll kill the bitch") in the judge's presence, despite the judge's demands that Abe "stop threatening her or I will have to incarcerate you."

*   *   *

The impact of logical consequences. The case history of Rachel and Abe illustrates a considerable amount of activity by the criminal justice system, but little substantive support. Because battering men are aware of police officers' attitudes and behavior, they are likely to perceive that their abusive behavior has no adverse consequences. Dutton (1987) estimated that the possibility of any penalty for wife assault was only 38%.

In one study, only 1% of the batterers received jail time beyond the time served at arrest (often just a few hours; Hirschel, Hutchison, Dean, & Mills, 1992). Carmody and Williams (1987) surveyed 1,626 men, 174 of whom were physically assaultive, concerning their views about the certainty and severity of the sanctions for battering. Possible sanctions included retaliatory force by the wife, arrest, wife-instigated separation or divorce, and social condemnation by friends and associates. Findings revealed that 52% of both assaultive and nonassaultive men perceived no possibility of arrest. Similarly, Williams and Hawkins (1989) reported that 494 male subjects, including 146 spouse abusers, generally did not perceive loss of their partner as very likely. Rather, they saw their marital relationship as quite resilient.

Some police officers simply decide that no crime has been committed (Hirschel, Hutchison, Dean, & Mills, 1992). Others apply consequences only to the woman. According to Hamberger and Arnold (1991), police in a midsized community of 85,000 evidenced a 12-fold increase in arrests of women and a 2-fold increase in arrests of men over the previous year. Upon further investigation, most of the women arrested (67%) had acted violently, but in self-defense.

The Bureau of Justice Statistics (Lanagan & Innes, 1986) reported that only 19% of *arrested* batterers reoffend compared with 37% of batterers simply advised by the police to desist and 33% of batterers ordered to leave. Many researchers, however, have not replicated these findings. In fact, Sherman et al. (1991) maintained that the superiority of deterrence effects of arrest lasted only 30 days. On the basis of a Dade County study, Sherman (1992) finally concluded that the deterrent effect was limited to employed offenders. Taken together with previous research, arrest might even escalate violence in unemployed men.

Taking a different approach, Dunford, Huizinga, and Elliott (1990) found that the effects of three different police dispositions (mediation, separation, or arrest) did not produce different rates of recidivism 6 months later. Reoffending was less likely, however, in contrast with the 247 cases where the offender was not arrested because he was absent. Hirschel, Hutchison, and Dean (1992) compared three types of police response to domestic violence calls: (a) advising, and possibly separating the couple; (b) issuing a citation to the offender; and (c) arresting the offender. Results showed conclusively that arrest was not superior to the other treatments in terms of recidivism or in terms of the victim's evaluations. There may have been several reasons for the failure to find a difference between the three methods: (a) Because the majority (69.4%) of the male offenders had had a previous criminal history, being incarcerated was not a new experience; (b) incarceration length was very short, averaging 9.4 hours; (c) the offender was prosecuted in only 35.5% of the cases; and (d) fewer than 1% of the offenders spent additional time in jail beyond the original arrest period. The researchers concluded that "the dynamics of domestic violence in general, and the abuse of female spouses in particular, are so complex and intertwined with historical, traditional, psychological, political, and social forces that it may be unreasonable to expect any short-term action by the criminal justice system to have a significant deterrent effect" (p. 31).

Syers and Edleson (1992) pinpointed two crucial variables affecting recidivism: number of previous arrests and duration of court-ordered counseling. In this study, men arrested the first time the police visited the residence, and those mandated into counseling programs for a longer period of time, were significantly less likely to violently revictimize their female partners than their counterparts. Gamache, Edleson, and Schock (1988) also called attention to lowered recidivism rates brought about by community intervention projects that coordinated the various components within the criminal justice system.

Jaffe, Wolfe, Telford, and Austin (1986) pinpointed several positive consequences of mandatory arrest policies. Their data revealed a 2,500% increase in police-made charges (from 12 to 298 cases) accompanied by a dramatic decrease in victim-laid charges (92 to

22 cases). Most important, a significant reduction in police calls resulted, along with a decline in victim-reported violence. Battered women felt safer and continued to call for help when they needed it.

Police departments with mandatory arrest policies do not uniformly adhere to the stated guidelines but use discretion. For example, Ferraro (1989) established that officers made arrests in only 18% of assaults involving intimate partners. One crucial determinant in Ferraro's study was the failure of the police chief to implement the directives. Buzawa (1988, p. 175) quoted one New England police chief who "could not recall a 'genuine' call for domestic violence in his numerous years as an administrator." Other factors (Ferraro, 1989) were more situational and included such matters as citizen complaints about police behavior. Balos and Trotzky (1988) documented an arrest rate of only 22% for a violation of a protection order, even *after* the legislature had passed a mandatory arrest law. Stubbing (1990), however, cited at least two cities where domestic homicides dropped following a change in police policies, one from 9 a year to 2 in four years and the other from 13 to 8 a year. Stubbing claims that family homicide is one of the most preventable crimes, not one of the least.

Although it may be preventable, it is not easily predictable. An early study in Kansas City (Police Foundation, 1977) helped to shape public opinion about the possibility of predicting domestic homicides. The Crime Control Institute (1990), however, was unable to identify any predictors or patterns of predictors in domestic homicide. In more than 15,000 cases of domestic violence in Milwaukee during a 22-month period, only 1 of 33 domestic murderers had a police record of domestic violence, and, in 1,000 cases in which police were called repeatedly, no murders occurred. Even events such as a prior death threat accompanied by pointing a gun at a spouse did not predict homicide. Overall, scientific attempts to predict domestic homicide may be no better than battered women's.

Positive police action can demonstrate to a battered woman that the system is behind her. Negative police response demonstrates the reverse. Stith (1990) attempted to predict the responses of police officers to 100 domestic violence scenarios on the basis of several individual differences, such as level of marital stress. She found that, the higher the officer's stress level, the more likely he was to use violence in his own marriage. The greater the use of violence in the officer's own marriage, the less likely he was to report that he would arrest the abuser in the scenario. In addition, the lower his belief in sex-role equality, the higher his acceptance of marital violence. The higher the officer's approval of marital violence and the lower his acceptance of sex-role equality, the more likely he was to make an antivictim response (e.g., discouraging arrest of the abuser, arresting the woman). Other studies have disclosed that police officers resent the loss of discretion (Balos & Trotzky, 1988) and express negative attitudes about such policies, even when the outcomes are beneficial (Jaffe et al., 1986).

Eigenberg and Moriarty (1991) examined law enforcement personnel (in Texas) to estimate their "domestic violence IQ." With training, almost three fourths of the 64 officers knew that Texas law required officers to inform domestic violence victims about social services such as shelters. Most knew that they were legally allowed to make a warrantless arrest of a perpetrator, even if they had not witnessed the assault and even if they saw no visible injuries. Shelters in major metropolitan areas (Austin, Houston, San Antonio) noted greater support and responsiveness to their clients. Police officers had instituted a more aggressive arrest policy if there was some sign of injury or a woman reported feeling pain as the result of a domestic assault. The training that is mandated or encouraged for police officers has not been imposed on attorneys and judges.

The Impact of Legal Reforms

New spouse abuse laws have been written and older laws modified. In this country, every state has at least one statute pertaining to battered women (Myers, Tikosh, & Paxson, 1992). Caringella-MacDonald (1988) has offered a number of vital analyses of the aftermath of legal reforms for sexual assault, marital rape, and domestic violence victims. Although some progress has occurred, discretionary arrest and prosecution and the inadequacy of some laws have limited the degree of positive outcomes envisioned by feminist reformers. Unfortunately, the arrest of battered women as perpetrators has demanded further advocacy efforts by women's groups ("Alternatives to Incarceration," 1992).

Brygger (quoted in Youngstrom, 1992) notes that a number of recent laws, such as mediation during a divorce or child custody dispute, have backfired against battered women. The assumption that the woman is free to speak at such sessions does not reflect the reality of the situation. Mandatory arrest laws, in particular, have led to a large number of arrests of women who were violent in self-defense. Hamberger (cited in T. Adler, 1991) noted that the new Wisconsin laws on mandatory arrest have created a new criminal, the "battering wife." His research, however, has revealed that two thirds of the women arrested were actually battered women fighting back. Hamberger does not believe that the women arrested are true batterers. Asher (1990) says that the police do not always know who to arrest, who is the violent party.

In some cases, mutual restraining orders have been issued against both spouses, giving the false impression that the victim has been violent as well. It is critical to gather information from the battered woman that would allow shelter workers and others to determine the potential lethality of her abusive partner and the probable efficacy of a restraining order (see also Campbell, 1986). Brygger (quoted in Youngstrom, 1992) says that restraining orders are effective "only if the batterer has had no contact with the criminal justice system and 'fears the consequences' of violating the order" (p. 45). Fortunately, many perpetrators of intimate violence fall into that category.

Case History: Omar

Omar's wife obtained a restraining order. What she did not know, however, was that Omar was violating it on a regular basis, "after hours," usually between midnight and 2:00 a.m. He would "just check up on her" by driving around the house or by stopping and looking through her windows. One night at about midnight, as Omar was peeking through her bedroom window, the police pulled up and arrested him. He spent the night in jail, where his shoelaces were stolen. Omar had a "religious" experience; he did not violate the order again.

* * *

Summary

A number of institutional forces have routinely erected barriers that prevent battered women from obtaining sufficient help. First, patriarchal practices within society, the church, and the criminal justice system have created a gender imbalance and removed power from the hands of women. Ordinarily, women do not have a "level playing field" to compete in the marketplace. They cannot usually find equal employment opportunities even with equivalent educational backgrounds and, as a rule, will not receive comparable pay.

Following a divorce, the legal system does not uniformly enforce existing laws or compel men to assume financial responsibility for their children. The financial and caretaker burden placed upon women creates havoc in their lives and in the lives of their children. On the whole, society allows men to vent their anger and frustration upon wives, ex-wives, other intimates, and their own children, without fear of reprisal. If a battered woman tries to escape, there may be no place for her to go. She may even become homeless. Despite newer mandates to police departments to protect her, she cannot count on being safe.

What would you do if you had several young children and no job? Call your clergyman? Call the police? Call your member of Congress?

3

● **Living With Fear:**
The Force That Holds,
Molds, and Controls

Case History: 911

Woman: I'm Robin Prunty calling on Donald Prunty. I'm at work at
 Smitty's and he's stalking the parking lot at Smitty's. He's
 supposed to be wanted in Chandler, and they haven't picked
 him up yet, and he's breaking the order. I have an order of
 protection.
Dispatcher: You said your name is Donna?
Woman: My name is Robin Prunty, P–R–U–N–T–Y.
Dispatcher: Has he already been served?
Woman: Yes, he has. It's been a good month now.

 (Pause: . . . 16 seconds of confusion, muffled sound)

Dispatcher: Is he there shooting?
Woman: I'm supposed to be safe . . . Oh my God . . .
Man's Voice: Get over here, get up, get up right now. C'mere.
 C'mon out here.

(Loud Bang)

Dispatcher: I think there's a shooting going on . . .

(" 'I'm Supposed to Be Safe,' " 1992, p. A6)

* * *

Robin's call was the prelude to a shooting spree. Her estranged husband burst into the coffee shop where she worked. Before he shot himself, he had killed Robin's pregnant friend, who had given her refuge, and a stranger who was having his morning coffee. Robin was seriously wounded but survived.

Chapter Overview

Fear, both emotional and physical, is a significant feature in battering families. Its functions include control and entrapment. A discussion of male-to-female injury and homicide clarifies the tangible nature of men's threats of aggression. Laboratory research, clinical impressions, and case studies substantiate the development of fear as a learned response. Denial and minimization are consequences of escalating fear that allow a woman to remain in her violent home and make it difficult to see the "forest for the trees." Gender dissimilarities in the motivations for aggression as well as the experience of fear provide a context for understanding "why she stays." The pervasive nature of apprehension affects not only the family who experiences it but also those involved peripherally.

Marital Violence

Weitzman and Dreen (1982) have used the term "violence-prone interaction setting" to describe the family context. Other investigators (Flynn, 1987; Gelles, 1979; Laner & Thompson, 1982) have cited reasons for this terminology: (a) the frequency, diversity, and intensity of relationship interactions and (b) relational interdependence leading to stress.

To a certain extent, violence is in the "eye of the beholder." For example, Sedlak's (1988a) study demonstrated that perceptions of intimate abuse depended on the nature of the observer's own personal history with aggression. Both male and female subjects who had experienced violence in their own relationships did not recognize battering in the test cases. Baumeister, Stillwell, and Wotman (1990) revealed that perpetrators describe their own violent behavior as comprehensible and as an isolated event, while victims portray the perpetrator's behavior as arbitrary, incomprehensible, and as the last in a series of provocations. Males may be more likely than females to perceive aggression as mutual (Laner & Thompson, 1982). In a study of dating violence, Laner (1990) noted that couples seem to believe that becoming jealous, upset, and subsequently violent is not unusual. Similarly, society has generally regarded hitting a spouse as acceptable and a private matter (R. P. Dobash & R. E. Dobash, 1991), even though the same actions perpetrated by strangers would be termed violent if not criminal.

The Subjective and Objective Nature of Fear

Fear is a powerful element in producing behaviors that are characteristic of victims in general and battered women specifically. Safety issues are a primary concern for both battered women and the individuals who work with them. In the 1985 study of battered women by Barnett and Lopez-Real (1985), fear (specifically, "fear of revenge") was the second most frequently given reason by women for remaining in their violent relationships. ("Hoped partner would change" was first.) Women in this study listed some of the following concerns:

> "He kept seeking me out and finding me."
> "I felt other people would die if I left."
> "He was suicidal; I feared he would come after me."
> "I have left and still have trouble getting out from under abuse and fears and threats. My ex-partner is continuing abuse anyway he can. I now see why it truly is hard to get out and why it took me so long."

"I remember feeling many times afraid to go and afraid to stay. That very real fear of revenge is so powerful a deterrent to doing anything constructive."

"I think that police protection should be questioned a lot."

These findings echoed those identified by Truniger (1971), who found that fear of retaliation caused battered women to remain in their violent situations. Painter and Dutton (1985) believe that a combination of hope and fear entraps battered women. Hanson, Sawyer, Hilton, and Davis (1992) studied death anxiety in three groups of women. They identified a significant elevation of death anxiety in a group of battered women attending college in contrast with nonbattered college women and battered women living in a shelter. The following case manifests a battered woman's worst nightmare.

Case History: Betty and Henry

Betty and Henry were married and had a 14-month-old daughter, Melissa. Henry was self-employed but unmotivated. He was also possessive, controlling, and insecure. When Betty's independence got the better of him, he became abusive. Betty had gone to work on numerous occasions with bruises on her face and arms. For the most part, nobody talked about what was happening. (It is often easier for friends and family to deny abuse, to minimize the severity of discord, and to ignore evidence.)

Betty's friends and financial security were a threat to Henry. He became more controlling, and he threatened to kill her if she tried to leave. His obsession culminated in Betty's 2-week "confinement." He stayed at home to watch her. Eventually, he needed money and took her to the bank to make a withdrawal from her savings account. Betty and Melissa escaped to the Long Beach Battered Women's Shelter.

Henry threatened to sue Betty for custody of the baby unless he was allowed to visit her. A third-party visitation was set up by the shelter through her attorney. No one at the shelter felt good about this arrangement, but everyone felt compelled to go ahead with the plan because of the legal ramifications of noncompliance. Betty and the baby were to go to her attorney's office accompanied by a male friend of Betty's (the father of one of her friends). While they were in the parking lot, Henry grabbed the baby and told Betty to get into his car or she would never see Melissa again.

Betty's body was not discovered for several months. Henry was charged with murder. He had taken Betty to an isolated spot in the desert where he beat and shot her. Her body had to be identified by her dental records. Melissa had been in the car.

At Henry's trial, one of his previous wives admitted to the abuse she had experienced at his hands. She was still afraid of him. Henry was eventually convicted of second-degree murder. Betty's last words to one of the authors (AL) as she left to meet Henry were: "If I don't come back, it is because he killed me."

* * *

Battered women in the Barnett and Lopez-Real (1985) study reported that, in addition to being physically assaulted, they were threatened. Of the 43 women in the study, 41 reported that their husbands had threatened to kill or injure them. The men also threatened to harm other family members and coworkers or to further intimidate their wives by actions such as destroying property or taking all the money. In a study by Stahly, Ousler, and Tanako (1988), battered women indicated their reasons for staying in an abusive relationship. One of the most commonly designated reasons was fear of losing their children, a fear based on their batterer's threats.

In a subsequent study, Barnett (1990) corroborated the frequency of male-to-female threats with questionnaire responses by 87 abusive males who admitted their own intimidating behavior. Relative to two comparison groups of nonviolent men who were happily or unhappily married, the abusive men more often threatened their wives that they would (a) destroy property, (b) hurt a child, (c) lock their wives in or out of the house or room, (d) take all the money in the house, (e) leave their wives, (f) hurt or kill their wives, and (g) kill themselves.

Threats engender fear and have a long-term effect. It is common-place to hear battering men talk about their behavior as occurring "in the past." Over the course of the relationship, most men expect their partners to ignore the threats and not to take them seriously. Abusive men also expect their wives to believe that they will never really hurt them, that they will know when to stop. Tinsley, Critelli, and Ee (1992) verified this type of gender discrepancy in an investigation of sexual aggression. Women victims gave significantly higher appraisals of intimidation or force employed, resistance offered, and offensiveness of the experiences compared with assessments given by male perpetrators. Males were unaware of or unconvinced by the fear reactions of females; they either ignored or discounted them.

We assert that, in battering relationships, nothing is really left in the past. The past keeps happening over and over again. Despite the promises of change, change rarely happens, and if it does, it does not seem to last. We also assert that leaving and safety are not synonymous. Some abusive men will continue to harass and intimidate their intimates even after they leave. The National Crime Survey (cited in Okun, 1983) revealed that 29% of reported wife assaults were perpetrated by ex-husbands. In a comprehensive study of family and intimate assault, Saltzman et al. (1990) sampled police incident reports in Atlanta, Georgia. About a fourth of such reports involved prior or estranged partners.

A recent Kentucky study ("Homicides Followed by Suicide," 1991) reported on situations where one person killed him- or herself as well as one or more other people. Of these homicide/suicide clusters, 85% involved family members. In 37 clusters, the perpetrator was the current husband; in 7 clusters, the boyfriend. In 18 of the 37 cases, the couple had previously filed for divorce or were separated. In 7 clusters, the wife had obtained a domestic violence protective order or restraining order from a court. It is common to hear threats made by men who either do not follow through with them or follow through at a lesser level. For some abusers, however, "till death do us part" is taken quite literally.

Case History: Rosita and Poncho

Leaving Poncho became the most dangerous action Rosita could take. Her husband had threatened to hunt her down if she ever left. He told her repeatedly that no other man could ever have her and that if she ever left he would kill her or "mess up her face so that no man would ever look at her again." He also threatened to kidnap the children if she did not stay.

Rosita knew that he was not making idle threats. The judge would award him visitation, and he would always be able to find her. Rosita reasoned that, if she stayed, she would at least know what he was doing and have some control over what would happen. Her "paranoia" was really an accurate perception of reality.

* * *

Stout (1988) analyzed the *Uniform Crime Reports—Supplemental Homicide Report,* 1980-1982, prepared by the Federal Bureau of Investigation. Her results disclosed that male intimates killed 4,189 women. Of these women, 57.7% (2,415) were killed by their husbands, 24.9% (1,041) by their boyfriends, 7.9% (332) by common-law husbands, 4.9% (205) by their ex-husbands, and 4.7% (196) by male friends. The weapon of choice was a gun (67.9%) followed by a knife (14.4%) or personal weapons (hands, feet; 8%).

Learning to Fear

Watson and Baby Albert. Fear is a powerful emotion capable of creating behavioral and psychological change. To clarify how emotions such as fear are learned, Watson and Raynor (1920) applied Pavlov's conditioning procedure to an infant named "Baby Albert." (The mental health of Albert's parents remains questionable at best, given that they consented to this research.) Watson showed Albert a white rat (that Albert previously liked and did not fear) and then made a loud sound behind the baby's head. After Watson repeated the process a number of times, Baby Albert began to cry and act startled whenever he saw the white rat, whether or not the sound occurred. It did not take long for Albert to demonstrate a fear response. Albert had learned to anticipate a noxious event when he caught sight of the rat, and the anticipation created fear.

Women's chronic low-level fear. According to C. Smith (1988), women in general experience a chronic, low-level fear of being victimized. Men and women may experience fear somewhat differently, and they also may fear different things. For instance, a man walking alone down an empty street at night might not experience fear at the sight of three unarmed women walking toward him. The reverse is probably not true.

In a study on fear in 37 professional women, Rozee-Koker, Wynne, and Mizrahi (1989) recognized that women took a staggering number of precautions to ensure their safety. Respondents reported walking to their cars with someone else whenever possible, keeping their keys between their fingers, and carefully checking the back seat of their cars before they got in. Half of the women had taken self-defense classes, and more than three quarters had planned rape-prevention strategies. This pilot study also indicated that women tend to cope with fear in one of three ways: denial, flooding (overexposure to fear cues or thinking), or reasoning.

Fear in abused women. Russell, Lipov, Phillips, and White (1989) noted that, clinically, abused women were more fearful than other women. Battered women learn that their spouses may be quiescent for a time (like the Kilauea volcano), but sooner or later there is an eruption. For women caught in a battering cycle, there is a nonviolent time, but not necessarily a time of feeling safe. Battered women learn to anticipate punishment, much as the subject of experimental conditioning learns to anticipate shock. The implied construct in both situations is fear.

Several important factors emerge given the content, quality, and quantity of violence-elicited fear in most battering relationships. First, there is the fear of another beating. Aversive cues such as yelling, breaking things, and particular facial expressions can precede a fight. Even though a physical assault is less common, the possibility of its appearance is always present. Thus it serves to intimidate (Edleson & Brygger, 1986). Although a batterer may believe that his mate should feel safe because he says he "won't really hurt her," she does not.

Case Histories: Becky and Annie

Becky: He used to smile at me in this funny kind of way when he was really angry, and then all hell would break loose. I still get scared when I see that smile, and I stop whatever I am doing.

Annie: I'd go home and he'd be quiet. It was a very loud quiet. I'd always say, "Are you OK? Is anything wrong?" He'd always say everything was OK, but I knew I was in trouble. Sometimes the quiet would last a while, two, three days, a week. And sometimes it would end quickly with an ugly remark or yelling or worse. But that quiet was like the "quiet before the storm," a signal telling me I had been bad and would be punished.

* * *

Veronen and Resnick (1988) describe the typical fight/flight response generated in humans and animals when they encounter danger. For battered women, the opportunity to flee is not generally available during an assault. Cues associated with the assault become conditioned (discriminative) stimuli that bring about intense fear when encountered again. Learned fear has a way of mushrooming and spreading into new areas (generalization). Because stimulus generalization occurs, events that are similar to the "punished situations" may come to trigger a fear response. As a result, cues that seem totally nonthreatening to most people may come to elicit self-defensive responses in battered women. When safety depends on reading significant cues accurately, people become speed readers.

Back to Baby Albert: After he became permanently traumatized by the sight of the white rat, similar objects such as a fur coat or Santa Claus's beard also evoked a fear reaction. Baby Albert had learned to generalize (Watson & Raynor, 1920).

Case History: Cheryl

Cheryl didn't risk much anymore. She knew that her husband got angry when she visited friends and family. She knew he didn't like her to change plans. She also knew that, even though he said she was crazy, he wouldn't like her going to therapy for help.

Cheryl visited her family sometimes, and she took one night class, but her fear of his response restricted her activities. She was afraid to make new friends, to get a job, or to go out after class with other students. Her fear had generalized to almost everything.

Even though her husband told her she needed a "shrink," she feared contacting a counselor. Cheryl's sister called a therapist specializing in spouse abuse and drove Cheryl to her first few appointments. Cheryl was never able to tell her husband that she was going to therapy, and she paid for it in cash so that her check register could not give her away.

*   *   *

Punishment Effects and Fear

Laboratory research can provide a model for understanding learned responses brought on by aggression. Violence in an abusive home is analogous to punishment in a "Skinner box." Punishment is the presentation of an event that *reduces* (suppresses) responses. Commonly used punishers are shocks for animals or spankings for children. Experiments demonstrate that a number of variables such as intensity and timing of punishers modify their effectiveness. Severe punishment can function to greatly suppress behavior. (See Appendix A, sections 1C and 1D.) The following case history illustrates the long-term effects of intense punishment.

Case History: Julie and Mickey

Julie and Mickey were high school sweethearts. He was a popular football star. Although she also was well liked, she thought she was lucky to have Mickey. They married because she was pregnant. Julie believed her love would mold Mickey into the perfect husband.

He did not hit her until after they got married. Julie says she will never forget the incident. "He balled up his fist and hit me in the mouth. My lip and chin opened and there was blood all over my face. I remember seeing stars and thinking: 'This is what happens to Popeye in the cartoons.' I went numb. You never forget it when someone hits you that hard, and you never have to be hit that hard again to continue to be afraid. In fact, I don't think he ever hit me that hard again. But in the following years that we were together, I was always afraid that he would, and it kept me in line."

*   *   *

Punishment intensity. A number of investigators uncovered a relationship between severity of abuse and the decision to leave (Butehorn, 1985; Ferraro & Johnson, 1984; Frisch & MacKenzie, 1991; Gelles, 1976; Gondolf, 1988a). Women who returned to their violent mates were those who had reported less intense violence than women who did not return.

Two studies, however, have provided contradictory results. Data from 293 shelter residents in the Pagelow (1981a) study indicated that, the more severe a woman's injuries were, the longer she remained in the relationship. This was true even though severity, frequency, and degree of pain suffered from the beatings increased over the duration of the relationship. When Schwartz (1988) studied the extent of injury in married, divorced, or separated women, he found that injury level did not predict which women left. The severity of injury tolerable to women varied individually.

To survive in a battering relationship, one must adapt and develop survival behaviors and, in fact, that is what battered women do (Campbell, 1987; Gondolf, 1988a). Some people think that leaving is easy and that abused women must like to be hit or they would not stay. There is no indication that abused women enjoy a good beating. There was nothing about laboratory experiments that indicated that animals "liked" to be punished to obtain food. They just liked to eat! (See Appendix B, sections 1 and 3, for relevant experiments.)

Intermittent punishment and the cycle of violence. Punishment variables other than intensity affect battered women's decision making. Long and McNamara (1989) pointed out how animal studies on intermittent punishment and punishment plus reinforcement (Azrin, Holz, & Hake, 1963) formed a foundation to explain battered women's persistence in the relationship. Interpreting "battering followed by contrition" as "punishment followed by reinforcement," they theorized that the battering cycle actually increases the female partner's love and dependency. Dutton and Painter (1981) hypothesized that intermittent punishment, along with power imbalances, lead to traumatic bonding, which in turn leads to the woman's inability to leave. See Dinsmoor (1952) and Holz and Azrin (1961; also in Appendix B, section 3), Rosenblum and Harlow

(1963; also in Appendix B, section 4), and Azrin et al. (1963; also in Appendix B, section 5).

Escalation. Animal research has established that the gradual buildup of punishment leads to continued responses rather than to suppression. Along the same lines, an initial intense shock followed by shocks of decreasing intensity will continue to suppress behavior (Sandler, Davidson, Greene, & Holzschuh, 1966). (See Appendix B, section 6, for a summary of this experiment.) Extrapolation of these findings to humans suggests that battered women subjected to escalation of abuse will "adapt" and remain in the relationship. Those initially severely beaten will limit (suppress) their activities and be controlled by the abuse. Warren and Lanning (1992) showed that battered women, in fact, tolerate more controlling behavior than nonbattered women.

Although the evidence addressing the escalation of abuse in battering relationships has been inconsistent, there is sufficient experimental and clinical support to indicate a gradual buildup of violence in a large number of battering relationships. The notion of a gradual buildup of violence emerged primarily from anecdotal reports offered by shelter workers and Walker's (1979) "Cycle of Violence" theory. Indeed, a number of scientific studies have shown that maritally abusive behavior increases over time (R. E. Dobash & R. P. Dobash, 1979; Pagelow, 1981b; Roy, 1977; Walker, 1979). Pagelow (1981b), for example, reported that, in a sample of 293 shelter residents, both the frequency and the severity of abuse increased over time. Follingstad, Hause, Rutledge, and Polek (1992) substantiated this pattern of intensification in a sample of 234 abused women. Stout (1988) cites a government study (Fields, 1978) showing that the severity of violence escalates even after the intimate relationship has ended.

On the other hand, two studies have questioned the uniformity of increased aggression. In a longitudinal study extending over 36 months, O'Leary et al. (1989) classified 42% of a sample as demonstrating unstable levels of aggression (cf. Follingstad et al., 1992). Lloyd's (1989) data also failed to support an inevitable progression of violence over time, but it did indicate that nonviolence is constant over time. Differences in the participants sampled and data collection methods may have caused these inconsistencies.

Other interpretations of nonescalation are credible: (a) Severe abuse early in a relationship may make later abuse unnecessary to obtain the same effects (see Church's [1969] animal research showing the effectiveness of prior shock); (b) abuse is triggered sporadically by factors such as unemployment and stress (Shainess, 1977); (c) victims have perfected their denial and minimization (Adams, 1986); and (d) escalation may characterize only one kind of abusive relationship but does not preclude other patterns. By and large, the battered woman does not leave a relationship the first time her partner pushes, slaps, or hits her (Campbell & Sheridan, 1989; Follingstad et al., 1992).

Another supposition that seems likely is that the batterer is also affected by the gradual buildup of so-called punishment (the battered woman's reactions) directed back at him. The responsive "punishments" that he receives for his violent behavior probably start out mildly also. Her initial reaction to his abuse may include anger, shock, and withdrawal. Over time, she may add depression, silent suffering, her own angry outbursts, and leaving temporarily. Her behavior will probably occur along a continuum of increasing intensity over a period of time. This is not battering. With gradual, subtle changes in his aggression and her response, adjustment occurs. (See Appendix B, section 6, for an explanatory animal study by Sandler et al., 1966.) They stop believing each other. They begin to accept the fact that he is not going to stop and she is not going to leave.

H. Douglas (1991) asserted that violent couples think of the aggression in their relationship as an aberration and the noncrisis period as the norm and the true state of their marriage. The gradual buildup of intermittent punishment allows the partners (and children) in a violent family the opportunity to recuperate. With the subtle adjustments, what was once severe punishment could begin to look like mild punishment as the increase becomes obscured by more violent outbursts and repetition. The once severe punishment may become the new baseline.

Case History: Kathy

"The first time I heard him say he felt like cutting my heart out with a knife, I was stunned. Nobody had ever said anything like that to me before. I had never been threatened before this relationship. I guess it just stopped meaning anything after I heard it over and over. It fell into the category of 'that's just the way he talks,' and then he beat me up. As I look back on it, the physical threats should have taken on new meaning, a greater significance, but they didn't. I couldn't sort it out or make it important. It was just one more thing."

* * *

The Nature of Gender Violence

The road to extreme violence and homicide is paved with denial. In a study of gender homicide, Wolfgang (1957) reported that, in 87% of the cases in which women kill their husbands, the men had actually provoked the attack by striking the first blow. Application of the concept of victim provocation to marital violence, however, sparked a controversy: Are women hapless victims of male abuse (e.g., Walker, 1979) or mutual combatants (e.g., Pizzey & Shapiro, 1981)? When Straus et al. (1981) provided evidence that frequency levels of spouse abuse for each sex were about equal, Steinmetz (1977) extended the contention further by postulating a "battered husband syndrome."

Research, however, had failed to take into account the outcomes and motivations for the abuse (Straus et al., 1981) and whether the reports by the respondents were equally valid for each sex (Jouriles & O'Leary, 1985). Research has indicated that women report more fully than men (Edleson & Brygger, 1986; Szinovacz, 1983), and perpetrators purposely conceal undesirable aggression (Riggs et al., 1989). According to Marshall and Rose (1990), gender differences highlight one of the problems with most available measures of physical abuse: "The actions by a person of one sex cannot be considered the equivalent of the other sex engaging in the behavior" (p. 60). Browne (1990) called attention to the failure of current surveys to take into account the context of abuse.

Findings of other studies contradicted any assumption of gender equality. Not only are wives more seriously injured than husbands, but wives also less frequently use severe violence (Browning & Dutton, 1986; Brush, 1990; Gaquin, 1977-1978; Makepeace, 1986;

Margolin, 1987; Saunders, 1989; Straus, 1980; Szinovacz, 1983). Emery, Lloyd, and Castleton (1989) and Saunders (1989) also showed that men usually initiate the violence and are more likely to engage in multiple acts of assault. Campbell and Humphreys (1984) estimated that husband battering accounts for only 2% to 5% of all domestic violence. In a search of criminal justice records, R. A. Berk et al. (1983) found an injury rate of 43% for women and 7% for men.

Sexual assault in battering relationships. Sexual assault and rape occur frequently in married populations. For example, Campbell (1989b) reported that, in a sample of 97 battered women, 44.3% also experienced sexual abuse (see also Finkelhor & Yllo, 1982; Pagelow, 1980; Shields & Hanneke, 1983b). Sexually abused women more frequently seek medical care and the cost has been documented. In a study (Koss, Koss, & Woodruff, 1991) of women referred to a multidisciplinary pain center, 53% were either physically or sexually abused, or both.

Women's motivation for abuse. In hypothesizing rationales for female-to-male aggression, the most frequently alleged impetus has been self-defense (e.g., Bowker, 1983; Browne, 1987; Makepeace, 1986; Margolin, 1987; Saunders, 1988; Walker, 1979). Both Laner and Thompson (1982) and Marshall and Rose (1990) contend that, when women react violently, it is more situational than when men react violently. Violence perpetrated by women is more likely a reflection of what is done to them rather than a stable personality trait.

Saunders (1986) asked 56 battered women whether they used violence and, if so, under what circumstances. The women judged the percentage (0% to 100%) of time that their violent responses were self-defensive, retaliatory, and the first strike. Results revealed that self-defense was the most common motive for both severe and nonsevere violence. (See Appendix B, section 7, for an account of the "matching law" [Herrnstein, 1970]; extrapolate it to the use of negative reinforcers to obtain an idea of a self-defensive buildup of aggression.)

Barnett, Keyson, and Thelen (1992) compared one group of battered women with two groups of nonbattered women to determine the nature and extent of their use of marital aggression. The groups differed in the frequencies of abuse except for verbal abuse (see also Russell et al., 1989). Primarily, the battered women, significantly more than the nonbattered, reported that their abuse was "self-defensive" (see also Hamberger, 1991). A major conclusion of the study was that battered women's violence in no way creates a "battered husband syndrome."

In animal research, punishment leads to increased aggression. A punished monkey will attack objects, other organisms, or even itself (Ulrich, Wolff, & Azrin, 1964). Humans will become aggressive when shocked as well (Berkowitz & LePage, 1967). Not only can this research explain battered women's self-defensive aggression, but it also would predict other outbursts of aggression as well. From this perspective, battered women's aggression toward their children may occur as a result of elicited aggression. Another possibility is Freudian displacement of aggression—the "trickle-down" theory. No one is suggesting that violent females do not exist and that there are no assaulted men. A truly "battered" male, however, in the physical sense is rare, and hitting and battering are not identical (Campbell & Humphreys, 1984).

Emotional reactions to abuse. Anger and fear emerge as the two predominant reactions to assault. In one English study (Shepherd, 1990), 62% of crime victims reported feeling angry because of their victimization. Feindler's (1988) study of battered women disclosed similar results. Shelter women had significantly higher anger arousal and intensity than a comparison group of nonbattered women. Anger was highest in the group of severely battered women. Russell et al. (1989) detected clinically elevated anger scores in battered women (see also Edleson & Brygger, 1986). In terms of fear, Russell et al. (1989) found that battered women had a significantly higher level than that of nonbattered women. Shepherd (1990) established that helplessness was the most immediate feeling of assault victims, while depression and anxiety usually set in later. Some victims suffered from flashbacks.

Several researchers (Blackman, 1988; Walker, 1984) have recognized this combination of emotions in victims, and the legal system has partially accepted it. Saunders (1986) believes that the motives of self-defense (fear motivated) and retaliation (anger motivated) become blended together for some battered women. Schneider and

Jordan (1978) reported that self-defense pleas in homicide cases do not become nullified when extreme terror becomes mixed with extreme rage, because it is reasonable to combine anger and fear when attacked. Anger is an emotion of self-protection as well as retaliation.

Male motivation for abuse. Almost uniformly, professionals in the field have proposed some variation of a control theme to explain male-to-female aggression. A number of researchers have pointed to factors such as patriarchal norms and the economic dependence of women as contributing to male-to-female-violence (e.g., Bograd, 1990; R. E. Dobash & R. P. Dobash, 1979; Straus & Hotaling, 1980). Breines and Gordon (1983) hold that battering is a form of personal and social control. Gondolf and Russell (1986) say that it is a sexist need to control women rather than a psychological, anger-derived behavior. Adams and Penn (1981) implicate culturally imposed traits, such as compulsive masculinity (a combination of such traits as aggressiveness, competitiveness, emotional detachment, hostility toward women, and violence). Along the same lines, researchers (e.g., Bograd, 1990; Saunders, 1988) have contended that gender and unequal power distribution must be applied as explanatory variables.

Other rationales for battering. Some researchers have cited individual differences in the need for power (Dutton & Strachan, 1987) and in communication skills, especially assertion deficits (Rosenbaum & O'Leary, 1981), as contributing factors. Another approach (Barnett & Hamberger, 1992; Hamberger & Hastings, 1986) has focused on batterer personality differences or psychopathology as a basic determinant. A further explanation has been the batterers' propensity to formulate and externalize blame (Sapiente, 1988; Shields & Hanneke, 1983a). Most likely, a combination of factors are at work, but, regardless of its origin, the abuse perpetrated by these men serves to enforce power and maintain control.

Even the definition of battering requires clarification. One reason that battered women do not leave is that they do not conceptualize occasional physical abuse as battering (see Sedlak, 1988a). Ordinarily, researchers have operationally defined battering as repeated physical violence, but grass-roots shelter workers and other investigators have called for the inclusion of other forms of abuse such as verbal abuse and threats (see Barnett & Wilshire, 1987; Follingstad, Rutledge, Berg, Hause, & Polek, 1990; Stets, 1991). Adams (1986) specifies intimidation and pressure, withholding of financial or emotional support, issuing ultimatums and accusations, and using children as confederates against the woman as part of a system of behaviors used to establish and maintain power and control over another person (see also Stets, 1991).

Generally, very little systematic investigation has emerged on the motives or outcomes of interpartner aggression. Barnett and Thelen (1992) divided marital abuse into five areas: (a) verbal (e.g., name-calling and ridiculing), (b) psychological (e.g., destroying property and hiding a partner's belongings), (c) threats (e.g., "to take all the money in the house" and "to hurt" their partner), (d) physical (e.g., kicking, pushing, slapping, hair-pulling), and (e) sexual.

A comparison of 30 battered women's responses with those of 34 court-mandated batterers revealed that the motivations for abusive behaviors differed substantially. As predicted, battered women's primary motive was "self-protection." Findings were compatible with Laner and Thompson's (1982) contention that reciprocity is evident in female violence. Given the objective nature of the external threat facing battered women, their actions are appropriate (e.g., Bograd, 1990). To "let out their violent feelings," the women became more abusive than nonbattered women (Barnett, Keyson, & Thelen, 1992), but not more than men.

In contrast, the men's predominant incentive for abuse was "showing her who was the boss" (gaining control). These results coincide with the conception of battering as a goal-oriented (Felson, 1992) mechanism to maintain an imbalance of power between the batterer and battered woman (as in Schecter, 1982). The findings also are consonant with those previously reported by Dutton and Strachan (1987) showing that assaultive men generate higher need-for-power themes than nonassaultive men. From a behavioral learning perspective, a batterer's ability to gain control, to feel powerful, and to be sexually aroused through intimidation is reinforcing (as in Dutton, Fehr, & McEwen, 1982), and therefore the aggression will increase. Similarly, Berg and Brennan (cited in Follingstad et al.,

1992) posited that reinforcers for violence could include enhancement of the perpetrator's sense of mastery and self-esteem as well as the victim's compliance.

Two other motives, "unaware of intentions" and "trying to get other's attention," revealed higher scores for batterers than for battered women. The endorsement of these rationales suggests that other, more obvious ones (e.g., "trying to hurt the other physically") have been minimized (Ganley, 1981), disguised, or underreported (O'Leary & Arias, 1984). For example, one of the authors (OB) listened to a man in group therapy describe his "simply reaching across the car and slapping his wife once." Records indicated that he had knocked her unconscious, necessitating the services of paramedics. For the batterers, the two most consistent outcomes were to "frighten her" and "to get their own way." According to Frisch and MacKenzie (1991), chronically abused women who did not escape reported feeling substantially more controlled by outside forces on Levenson's (1973) Locus of Control Scale than formerly abused women who had escaped. In actuality, outside forces probably control battered women.

In the Carmody and Williams (1987) study, men predicted that retaliatory physical assault by their wives was very unlikely, and they further judged the severity of her assault as very low. Men also reported that they can easily protect themselves: "She was easy to stop"; "I just pushed her away"; or "I restrained her." As Campbell and Humphreys (1984) previously alleged, very few men fit into the category of "battered." One important reason is that, unless their mates have used an equalizer, the men just are not afraid. Unfortunately, even self-defensive violence may not bring safety for a battered woman, because it tends to contribute to an escalation of the man's violence (e.g., Bowker, 1983; Feld & Straus, 1989). Feld and Straus (1989) concluded that "hitting was the least effective strategy for discouraging subsequent assaults." A laboratory study of aggression with humans (Goldstein, Davis, Kernis, & Cohn, 1981) failed to identify any method capable of curbing the escalation of violence (see Appendix B, section 7).

It is important to note that physical abuse is more often in the "less severe" range (Barnett & Wilshire, 1987). These episodes include hitting, throwing things, slapping, and pushing. Injuries are usually cuts and bruises and rarely require hospitalization. Physical abuse is also less frequent than the psychological and verbal abuse, and both are intermittent (Willet & Barnett, 1987). The gradual buildup, the intermittent and nonsevere nature of the early abuse, the lowering of self-esteem, and the buildup of emotional dependency work together to entrap women.

Effects of Fear

The level of abuse does not necessarily correlate with the amount of fear women experience. A number of patterns composed of objective and subjective fear can exist. There can be mild physical abuse mixed with threats, or extreme physical abuse with no threats, or emotional and verbal intimidation. Once fear is a part of the relationship, however, the relationship changes.

Emotional abuse (e.g., verbal outbursts, withdrawal, jealousy), rather than physical abuse, generates much of the fear in a battering relationship. Because emotional abuse seems less potent, it is difficult to justify making major changes in one's life, such as giving up a home, financial security, intimacy, social support, and a job. In this light, leaving because of emotional abuse, a known stressor, may seem disproportionate in view of the enormity and unknown quality of the change.

The combination of sporadic violence interspersed with kindness (as in the Stockholm Syndrome) contributes to the development of hope and allows the battered woman to deny the side of the abuser that terrifies her (Ott, Graham, & Rawlings, 1990). If she denies his violent side, she can deny that she is in danger. Indeed, Ferraro and Johnson (1984) detected denial and rationalization as the basic mechanisms used by battered women to cope with battering. That is, battered women deny that their mates either intended to or actually did harm them. In fact, sometimes they deny being victimized altogether. Batterers deny the abusive nature of their behavior as well (Edleson & Brygger, 1986). One of the authors (OB) encountered a man who characterized himself as unhappily married, but nonviolent. Later inspection of his test data uncovered that he had admitted to having "choked her" "several times a year"!

Reality is something that you rise above.

Liza Minelli

Fear and denial in helping professionals. Fear and denial also occur in persons who work with battered women and batterers. These professionals learn to deny and minimize the severity of abuse, the potential of lethal interaction, or the possibility that they may be in some danger themselves. One of the authors (AL) thinks that it takes a sort of "adolescent omnipotence" to work in the field of family violence. At a theoretical level, workers know that anything is possible, but, at an emotional level, they cannot afford to accept the danger. Professionals hear the threats, see the injuries, and somehow go on with their work.

Case History: Keith

Keith called his therapist early in the morning. She was already gone, but he talked to another therapist in the office. She had no previous connection with Keith, but the conversation put her on edge and angered her. When Keith's therapist returned, she got an urgent message from her associate to call Keith. Her previous experience with Keith and his impulsive anger created a strong emotional response of uneasiness and apprehension.

Keith was furious when his therapist called. He thanked her for her "help" and then said that he was "leaving to kill his wife." Needless to say, the therapist was hooked; she believed that Keith would carry out his threat. The therapist worried that, as in the past, the criminal justice system would be unable to protect Keith's wife but that she could effectively intervene. The therapist also hoped that Keith had called so that he wouldn't harm his wife.

The therapist was unable to calm him down and, in fact, felt an escalation of fear and anxiety in herself. She called Keith's probation officer to warn her and to have her call Keith's wife. The probation officer and Keith's wife lived 6 hours away.

What ensued were 2 hours of calls involving the therapist, the client, the probation officer, and the estranged spouse. The client's rage produced rapid results. The therapist and the probation officer contacted the ex-wife and acted as intermediaries. The ex-wife made contacts with Keith and a negotiation followed that concluded with positive results; Keith's anger dissolved. His wife was safe, and the problem was resolved, at least for the time.

It is interesting to observe the behavior of those involved in this particular situation and to hear about their reactions. First of all, everyone responded to the rage by moving in the direction that seemed most productive but also in the direction pushed by the batterer, toward contact with his ex-wife. The threats produced immediate results, once again *reinforcing the notion that violence works*. The probation officer and the therapist talked about feeling manipulated, emotionally battered, and unable to slow down until the problem was resolved.

Keith sent the counselor a "thank you" card and an apology. He talked about feeling appreciative of her efforts. The air was cleared; communication was open and honest. They had been through a crisis together and had come out of it with a positive resolution. A residue of misgiving and distrust remained, even though good feelings returned. Let the loving respite begin!

* * *

If peripherally involved individuals react with fear to their minimal involvement with a batterer by changing their behaviors, why should one be surprised by the extreme behavior changes undergone by battered women?

Summary

This chapter has pointed out that wife beating accounts for a large number of injuries to women and for the murder of men, women, and other family members. Assaults are costly to society in terms of medical, legal, and criminal justice services. Normal responses to assault include fear and anger.

Learning experiments on animals have provided a number of human analogues that furnish a useful framework for understanding the behavior of battered women. Learning theory offers information about a number of learned reactions: (a) the generalization of fear to other cues in the environment, (b) the effects of punishment variables on the extent of suppression of behavior (e.g., intermittent punishment), (c) the effects of a gradual buildup or decline of assault, and (d) the creation of an atmosphere typified by chronic anxiety.

Research also portrayed women's aggression as primarily self-defensive, while men's was power oriented. Furthermore, men's aggression successfully intimidated women, while women's assaultive behavior did not usually frighten men. Men showed little worry about criminal justice sanctions, which is one of the many factors suggesting the patriarchal nature of male-to-female violence. Some researchers and societal agents have implied gender equality in spousal violence and even gone so far as to suggest a "battered husband syndrome." Research has clearly contradicted this assumption. Given the broad nature of learning principles and their applicability to behavior in general, becoming a battered women could happen to anyone.

4

• Victimization:
Betrayed by the Tie That Binds

Experiencing violence transforms people into victims and changes their lives forever. Once victimized, one can never again feel quite as invulnerable.

KOSS (1990, p. 374)

Chapter Overview

IT IS IMPORTANT to address the question of whether victims are different than other people. Researchers who study female victims (battered women, adult survivors of incest, rape survivors) have often attempted to describe them in terms of their presumed deviance, that is, the characteristics that distinguish them from "normal" people. The underlying assumption seemed to be that victims arc to blame for their own victimization and that they are inherently provocative by nature or behavior. The concept of victim provocation formed a framework for understanding all victims. Observation of victimization phenomena brought on by captivity and extreme trauma, however, began to challenge earlier beliefs. This chapter explores victims, the myths surrounding them, and forms of victimization.

69

Case History: Zari and Ahmed

Zari sat in the office shaking and confused. She had nothing left. She had given up her friends and family, a Fifth Avenue apartment, and a lucrative job as a media consultant to help Ahmed start his business. She had been in other relationships and had maintained friendships with those other men. Ahmed was different. At first, he did everything she liked to do. They jogged and worked out together, went to plays, and socialized with her friends. He said that he wanted children and that was very attractive to her.

"Mr. Hyde" did not appear for some time. The negative behavior started with criticism of her appearance and her friends. Over time, he began to follow her and read her diary. For a long time, she didn't notice that cash was missing from her drawer. When she saw Ahmed searching through her dresser, she told him to leave. Ahmed, however, hung on, trying to get her to take him back. He called her friends and family and had his therapist call her to plead his case. She took him back.

Criticisms and put-downs began again after they had gotten back together and moved across the country. He began to break her things. She hadn't realized the extent of her dependence, isolation, and humiliation until most of her furniture had been destroyed. She realized that, in helping him start his business, she had lost her independent source of income and her support group. Although he didn't pay her a salary, he did pay her expenses. She felt like a child dependent upon her parents for her allowance. She felt imprisoned.

He started pushing her around, and he accused her of being crazy and breaking his things. It was only when he choked her and threw her into his glass coffee table, which shattered and cut her leg, that Zari escaped.

The police took pictures of her injuries and wanted her to press charges. She found out that Ahmed had previous charges against him for stalking and terrorizing a business associate. Although he was gone, her freedom did not restore her self-confidence and security. She had escaped from her captor, but she hadn't stopped feeling controlled and intimidated. She wondered if she would look in her rearview mirror one day and see Ahmed's eyes staring at her. She wondered if he would ever stop following her.

* * *

People still want to know if battered women like Zari are somehow different than other people. The real, underlying questions appear to be whether battered women come from poor, nonwhite families with no education or have some psychological maladjustments that predispose them to provoke their mates, behave in "sick" ways, or look for men who will eventually batter them. In other words, "If I am different than battered women, I will not be battered."

Victim Characteristics

Race. Researchers (e.g., Schulman, 1979) have probed statistical data to determine whether race differentiates battered from nonbattered women. Three studies on intimate violence have failed to make a racial distinction. Rouse (1988) investigated possible differences between African American, Anglo, and Hispanic university students who had experienced abuse in their dating relationships. Sorenson and Telles (1991) examined marital violence rates for Caucasian women, Mexican American women born in Mexico, and Hispanic women born in this country. Gondolf, Fisher, and McFerron (1988) analyzed data from more than 5,700 intake interviews with battered women. Overall, research supports the position that marital violence is color-blind but does not occur in equal numbers in each racial group (as in Hirschel, Hutchison, Dean, & Mills, 1992).

Socioeconomic status. Two studies based upon large, national, representative samples have provided evidence that battering is more prevalent in blue-collar and lower-class families. The National Family Violence Survey (cited in Straus, Gelles, & Steinmetz, 1981) estimated that families living at or below the poverty line had a marital violence rate that was 500% greater than families above the poverty line. (See also the National Crime Survey—Klaus & Rand, 1984—of 60,000 households.) In a review article of most extant studies, however, Hotaling and Sugarman (1990) judged socioeconomic status to be relevant for only the most severely assaulted. As Hirschel, Hutchison, Dean, and Mills (1992) have asserted, "It is clear that spouse abuse is not characteristic of any particular group.

It is less clear whether all groups are truly equal in both prevalence and incidence of abusive behavior" (p. 256).

Nonetheless, prevalence rates remain controversial for two main reasons. First, family violence studies usually employ small samples from shelters and funded community-based programs that generally serve people with the fewest resources (finances, family, friends). Women with more resources usually have more options. Second, statistics based on police arrest records may overrepresent minorities and the poor because of differential arrest policies (Black, 1980). In other words, fewer people from Beverly Hills and Scarsdale may be included in arrest and prosecution data (see also Bowker, 1984). The importance of racial and economic status emerges in trials of battered women who kill, when the jurors have formed an impression of "prototypical" battering as occurring only in certain racial and economic groups (Schuller & Vidmar, 1992).

Shelter workers have long contended that spouse abuse crosses all socioeconomic levels somewhat equitably, based on hot line calls and contacts with battered women who participate in nonresidential shelter services. Evidence obtained from the Orange County probation department in California (K. Miller, 1992) concurs with this supposition. These statistics revealed the following socioeconomic information regarding individuals charged with domestic violence and placed on probation or diversion for 1989: (a) 37% were white collar; 46% were blue collar; (c) 8% were unemployed or disabled; and (d) 9% were service personnel (e.g., restaurant workers, housekeepers). Further data on upper-class battered women may yet come to light through other samples.

Physical abuse during childhood. Some researchers and helping professionals have attempted to establish a link connecting the abuse of young girls to their later abuse as women. Gelles (1976) formulated several hypotheses to establish an association between childhood exposure to violence and later tolerance of abuse: (a) The more an individual is exposed to violence as a child (both as an observer and a victim), the more violent he or she is as an adult; (b) the more a girl was struck by her parents, the more inclined she is to stay with an abusive husband. Kalmuss (1984) identified a strong, non-gender-specific relationship between observing one's father hit one's mother and later perpetration of or victimization by severe marital aggression.

Fantuzzo and Lindquist (1989) identified physical health problems, mental health problems, and increased alcohol and drug use as correlates of exposure to parental violence. Whether abused women have suffered more childhood abuse than nonbattered women has become an issue. As a baseline, Straus (1991) maintained that corporal punishment of children is so pervasive that differences in consequences are difficult to specify. He also estimated that at least a third of American children have witnessed violence between their parents.

A study of 426 shelter residents disclosed a childhood abuse rate of 53% (I. M. Johnson, 1988). Because 47% of the residents claimed that they were raised in nonviolent homes, the difference between groups did not confirm child abuse as a precursor to adult victimization. Landenburger (1989) also reported that only one sixth of the women in her study had experienced physical abuse as children, and an even smaller percentage had observed parental violence. Shelter residents in one study described their childhood homes as "secure" (although not necessarily nonabusive; Pagelow, 1981a). Astin, Ogland-Hand, Coleman, and Foy (1991) found no significant differences between battered and nonbattered women on an experimenter-designed test to assess childhood physical and sexual abuse.

From a slightly different standpoint, Gelles (1976) hypothesized that battered women's exposure to childhood abuse influenced their decisions to stay. I. M. Johnson (1988), however, was unable to substantiate such a relationship. As a final word, Hotaling and Sugarman (1990), in a comprehensive review, noted no differences between groups when other risk markers (predictors) were taken into account.

Sexual abuse during childhood. Researchers and clinicians have also inquired into the effects of childhood sexual abuse on later intimate victimization. As a standard for comparison, Susan Burnett (cited in "Sex Abuse," 1990) asserted that 25% to 33% of women in the general population were molested as children. The percentages uncovered in four studies using small samples of battered women were not substantially different than Burnett's findings (see also Back, Post, & D'Arcy, 1982; Bergman, Larsson, Brismar, & Klang, 1988; Hamberger, 1991; Landenburger, 1989). Finally, Astin et al. (1991) detected no difference in childhood sexual abuse between a group of battered women and a comparison group of maritally distressed women. All in all, the incidence of childhood sexual abuse in battered women does not appear to differentiate them from women in the general population.

Personality. While some researchers focused on race, socio-economics, and child abuse as precursors to adult battering, other social scientists explored individual idiosyncracies. M. A. Douglas and A. Colantuono (1987) explored possible personality problems in battered women by evaluating their MMPI scores. Analyses revealed that the personality profiles of battered women differed substantially from one another, thus supporting Walker and Browne's (1985) contention that battered women do not fit a particular personality profile or fall within a singular diagnostic category such as borderline or schizophrenic. Rhodes's (1992) study using a comparison group of nonbattered women from a clinical population, however, yielded discrepant findings. Battered women scored substantially higher on the Psychopathic Deviate score of the MMPI. Taken together with findings from other studies (e.g., Scott & Stone, 1986), score elevation most probably represents the effects of victimization.

One popular assertion has been that battered women's failure to leave a violent relationship is a consequence of their low self-esteem (Mills, 1985). Gold (1986) contends that women abused in childhood, especially those who have been sexually victimized, tend to suffer characterological self-blame when abuse occurs later in life. Most researchers have reported incompatible findings. Russell, Lipov, Phillips, and White (1989) reported that battered women did not have lower self-esteem than nonbattered women, and Hotaling and Sugarman's (1990) review reached the same conclusion.

Several researchers maintained that battered women's low self-esteem, when exhibited, represented an outcome of chronic victimization and was not a precursor to it (Hartik, 1979; E. Stark et al., 1981; Telch & Lindquist, 1984). In a sample of severely battered women, Cascardi and O'Leary (1992) ascertained that, as the frequency, form, and consequences of physical aggression increased, the level of self-esteem decreased. Being abused can lower self-esteem by creating or adding to a sense of personal defectiveness (E. Stark et al., 1981). Some excerpts from survey articles (Hotaling & Sugarman, 1986) emphasize the misplaced focus on women as the provocateurs of marital violence: "Very little heuristic value can be gained by focusing primarily on the victim in the assessment of risk to wife assault" (p. 12). "What is surprising is the enormous effort to explain male behavior by examining the characteristics of women" (Hotaling & Sugarman, 1986, p. 120). Overall, research lends credence to a "just like anybody else" viewpoint about battered women.

In an English study of male and female victims of violent assaults, including battered women, behavioral changes were apparent in two thirds of the population sample immediately after the assault. These changes remained for at least 6 months in one quarter of the victims (Shepherd, 1990). The most common behavioral change was avoidance of the location where the attack had occurred. Other symptoms were physical problems and emotional distress. A study of rape victims revealed that fear was the major symptom, even a year postrape (Kilpatrick, Veronen, & Resick, 1979).

Researchers have established that a number of factors mediate a victim's response to trauma. For example, factors that affect rape victims include the victim's level of life stress (Ruch, Chandler, & Harter, 1980), her general ability to cope (Burgess & Holstrom, 1979), and her level of self-blame and feelings of responsibility (Janoff-Bulman, 1979). Other factors include the duration, frequency, and intensity of catastrophic events.

Victim Blaming

In tune with the search for distinctive victim characteristics, most early writers who described battered women failed to ascribe the violence to the perpetrator. They frequently said or implied that the battered woman was to blame; it was something about her that caused him to be violent. Quite often, members of society blame the victim without regard to the context. They blame people who are robbed for leaving their doors unlocked, and they blame battered women for nagging. They even blame rape victims for having their "turtlenecks cut too low." Golda Meir, former prime minister of Israel, highlighted this lopsided point of view. When her male cabinet members concluded that they should impose a 10:00 p.m. curfew on women to reduce the incidence of rape, she opposed them. Because men did the raping, why not subject them to the curfew? She was overruled.

Ewing and Aubrey (1987) demonstrated that public opinion about battered women rests upon widely held and false assumptions. A random selection of 216 community members completed a questionnaire after reading a scenario about a violent couple. More than 60% of the respondents agreed that, if a battered woman were really afraid, she would simply leave. More than 40% decided that she must have been at least partly to blame for her husband's assaults, even though the story provided no rationale for such a belief. There was some tendency for respondents to believe that the woman must have been masochistic or emotionally disturbed if she stayed, that the couple had serious marital problems, and that the woman could avoid the beatings if she entered counseling. By and large, people seemed reluctant to place all of the blame on the perpetrator. Most of the sample, however, did not believe that the police or the courts could be counted upon to protect her. Although most people hold a man accountable for beating a stranger, they do not apply the same standard when he beats his wife (Shotland & Straw, 1976).

Unfortunately, victim-blaming attitudes are also present in the police department. Police officers make decisions based on extra-legal information that parallels the misinformation used by the public (Kalmuss, 1979). Waaland and Keeley (1985), using a paper-and-pencil test, examined police officers' use of legal and extralegal factors in assigning blame or in making an arrest in a hypothetical case of domestic disturbance. Extralegal information, such as the victim's housekeeping skills, sobriety, and demeanor, greatly affected their attributions of responsibility. Officers judged the female victim's use of alcohol as more important in assigning blame than the male perpetrator's drinking. Concurrently, the police discounted the male abuser's prior history of arrests for domestic assault.

Lack of social support. Social support theory assumes that exposure to environmental duress leads to personal stress and that social support may act as a "buffer" after the event occurs (Thoits, 1982). Shepherd (1990) indicated that, although social support was extremely important to recovery, gender differences occurred in kinds and levels of support offered victims. Whereas the male victims in his study generally found their bosses sympathetic and their colleagues jokingly accepting, battered women experienced pay suspensions and bosses who were characteristically unsympathetic and victim-blaming. Lack of support, both personal (Aguirre, 1985; Butehorn, 1985; Hendricks-Matthews, 1982) and social (Alsdurf, 1985; R. E. Dobash & R. P. Dobash, 1979; Gelles & Harrop, 1989), creates a dilemma for battered women that ensnares them in their relationships.

Pitts, Barnett, Deatherage, and LaViolette (1991) assessed battered women's perceptions of their social support contrasted with two nonbattered comparison groups. Battered women reported receiving less social support than the other groups, results consistent with those obtained by Mitchell and Hodson (1983). Pitts et al. (1991) also reported that younger women received less social support than older women.

Most people seem to be looking for someone or something to blame in their attempts to explain wife beating. Violent couples and observers alike are prone to allege that alcohol is the major factor precipitating a violent episode. Battered women, in particular, have clung to the "demon rum" hypothesis (Fojtik, 1977-1978; LaBell, 1979; Sapiente, 1988). Nonetheless, alcohol is probably not the causal agent it is assumed to be. Bard and Zacker (1974) and Rounsaville (1978) reported relatively infrequent drinking in males before violent episodes, and Barnett and Fagan (1993) indicated that drinking was much more likely to be a consequence, rather than a precursor, of abuse. In addition, most men who batter when they are drinking also batter when they are not. Both batterers and battered women use denial and minimization to blame some agent other than the abuser for the aggression.

A. Adler (1927), in a discussion about causalistic thinking, asserted that one of the major outcomes of victim blaming is that it excuses the perpetrator from responsibility. For instance, when people blame social conditions for criminal behavior, offenders lose accountability for their actions (and victims seem to acquire it).

Victims of aggression usually also search for explanations of the question: "Why me?" Although a number of reactions are possible, some victims blame themselves for either causing the violence or being the victim of it. For example, rape victims may blame themselves for not having done more to avoid being assaulted (e.g., Janoff-Bulman, 1979). Battered women, however, need to explain the very existence and cause of the violence, not just its occurrence. Some common rationalizations given by battered women are that his aggression happened when he was "not himself" and was "temporarily out of control," that he was a "victim of child abuse," "an alcoholic," or "unemployed." When a battered woman says, "it is my fault," she is simultaneously absolving or partially absolving her assailant.

Attributions in Violent Relationships

An *attribution* is an idea or thought generated to explain the source or cause of behavior. *Dispositional attributions* involve ascribing behavior to factors within the individual, such as his personality traits, his attitudes, or his motives. *Situational attributions* involve attributing actions to situational or environmental factors that are external to the person. Attribution theory deals with the guidelines that people use to infer these causes.

D. T. Miller and C. A. Porter (1983) point out that victims of negative events often exaggerate or misconstrue the extent to which they are responsible for their own victimization. Gilbert and Webster (1982) detected a common theme emerging from interviews with women who had experienced assaults at the hands of men (rape, incest, battering): They (a) blamed themselves, (b) denied the magnitude of the events, (c) denied their anger and wish to retaliate, (d) felt unable to set limits or fight back, and (e) found it difficult to indict the men who injured them, wanting instead to protect them. The inability of women to condemn the aggression directed at them by a loved partner seems directly proportional to their level of involvement in the relationship.

A common attribution made by battered woman is that they somehow provoke the violence. Therefore they can or should be able to prevent or eliminate it by changing their own behavior (Prange, 1985). Painter and Dutton (1985) speculated that this belief, along with the contradictory belief that they are powerless, leads to enmeshment in the relationship. Prange (1985) found that women who returned to their abusers made "internal attributions" about their physical abuse, that is, that something was wrong with them. Attributions made by battered women about being assaulted are important determinants of the degree of blame they personally accept.

Behavioral versus characterological blame. Manley (1982) discussed two types of self-blame. *Behavioral* blame is the identification of specific controllable actions that led to the occurrence of the negative events. Behavioral blame presumably facilitates a perception of control and thus contributes to efficient adjustment. *Characterological* blame, in contrast, is the identification of an enduring quality or trait that caused the hurtful events. This type of blame leads to feelings of depression and helplessness.

Case History: Laura

Laura didn't want to argue with her husband anymore. They fought about everything from religion to his job. He said that he was tired of her nagging and that he wouldn't have to hit her if she'd just shut up. Laura began to see her behavior as provocative and tried to change it. She even began to believe that it must be her responsibility to change his behavior. At that point, her husband told her that she was a sick woman and making him crazy; and, at that point, she was convinced.

* * *

Prototypes and levels of self-blame. Barnett et al. (1991) compared 31 battered women with two nonbattered comparisons groups comprising 62 women. Battered women had significantly higher levels of self-blame. Results validated the actuality of two major dimensions of blame, behavioral and characterological. Battered women blamed themselves more on the behavioral questions than on the characterological items. Especially poignant was the self-blame regardless of their actions. The following statements exemplify this "damned if you do, damned if you don't" predicament.

> "You tolerated the abuse."
> "You were too afraid to leave."

> "You did not protect the children from his abuse."
> "You might deprive the children of two parents."

> "You loved him, but you knew better."
> "You stopped loving him."

> "You did not contribute financially."
> "You worked, had a job."

Endorsement of the behavioral items suggests that battered women consider themselves to be "deficient" in fulfilling their parental and marital roles. Their agreement with characterological items corresponds with perceived "deficiency" in emotional or mental stability.

Barnett and Lopez-Real (1985) reported that battered women in their study felt that they were "to blame" more than any other feeling listed in the survey (e.g., anxious, angry, powerful). Women in this study blamed themselves, as reflected in these comments:

> "I'm to blame because I was not strong enough."
> "I felt I could have helped the situation better."
> "He said I provoked his attacks. Now I realize it took very little to provoke him."

The women also reported an increase in blame correlated with the belief that their "efforts to escape were unsuccessful."

Although most family violence experts have speculated that battered women feel to blame (i.e., responsible) for being victimized (Frieze, 1979; Gilbert & Webster, 1982; Hendricks-Matthews, 1982), some take exception to this supposition. For example,

Holtzworth-Munroe (1988) states that "abused women generally do not blame themselves for their husband's violence" (p. 331). In a study that made use of a comparison group of nonbattered women, Campbell (1990) disclosed that only 20% of the battered women in her sample reported feeling that they were to blame.

Landenburger (1989) proposed that battered women may either blame themselves for causing the abuse or blame themselves for tolerating it. In either case, blame is the end result and blame tends to produce guilt. As Erica Jong so cleverly phrased it, "Show me a woman who doesn't feel guilty and I'll show you a man."

Self-blame in relationship to other processes. Current theories of depression contend that self-blame both causes and maintains depression (Peterson & Seligman, 1984). Andrews and Brewin (1990) studied depression in 286 British victims of violence. Of the women who had suffered interpartner assault, 53% currently involved with the perpetrator experienced self-blame for causing the violence compared with 35% of those who were no longer in the relationship. Within the self-blaming group, 68% blamed their behavior, while 32% blamed their characters. Characterological self-blame was significantly correlated with previous childhood physical and sexual abuse, lack of social support, and level of depression after leaving the relationship (see Sato & Heiby, 1992).

Do self-blame levels remain constant over time? In the Andrews and Brewin (1990) study, women who were abused early in the relationship blamed themselves more than those abused later. Some researchers (e.g., Walker, 1984) have observed a decrease in the level of battered women's self-blame (or perhaps an increase in depression) over time as they realize that nothing they do makes a difference (also see Cascardi & O'Leary, 1992).

In passing, also I would like to say that the first time Adam had a chance he laid the blame on women.

Nancy Astor (British politician)

According to Finkelhor (1983), the literature on domestic violence consistently portrays abuse as occurring in the context of psychological exploitation. Batterers use their power to manipulate victims' perceptions of reality. Furthermore, men who blame women for being battered hold more patriarchal views than men who do not blame women (Coller & Resick, 1987; Kristiansen & Giuletti, 1990; Saunders, Lynch, Grayson, & Linz, 1987). Analogously, some investigators (e.g., Walker, 1981) have ascertained that battered women's sex-role scores reflect a highly feminine or even undifferentiated orientation that may make them more vulnerable to male dominance (Warren & Lanning, 1992).

Battering coupled with self-blame diminishes a battered woman's belief in herself, erodes her self-esteem, and reduces her integrity. She feels demeaned as she responds to the demands of her batterer, both overt and unspoken. She may jeopardize her relationships with her children, other family members, friends, and community contacts. The more extensive her compromise, the greater the erosion of her self-respect.

Effects of Captivity

Investigators ("Abusive Relationships," 1991) have pointed to parallels between women in abusive relationships and hostages. Battered women exhibit hostage-like behaviors such as praising their abuser, denying the battering, and blaming themselves. These behaviors may in actuality represent a struggle for survival.

Many victims of violent crimes or impending violence identify with the person or persons who seem to have control over their well-being. As perceived power differences intensify, the person with less authority generally forms a more negative self-appraisal and feels less capable of taking care of herself. Thus the person with less power becomes more dependent on the person with greater power (A. Freud, 1942). This phenomenon is called *identification with the aggressor* and became manifest in "brainwashing," for example, the Stockholm and POW syndromes.

The term *brainwashing* came into being during the Korean War when imprisoned American soldiers denounced the United States or supplied information to the enemy. Patty Hearst, a wealthy socialite-turned-bank robber, provided another alleged example of this phenomenon. People condemned the Korean prisoners as traitors, and the courts sent Patty Hearst to prison. It seems that those who sat in judgment went on with their lives believing that the "brainwashed" were innately weak and completely culpable.

Stockholm Syndrome. One of the most dramatic examples of identification with the aggressor occurred in 1974 in Stockholm during a bank robbery. Three tellers were held hostage for a period of 10 days. For the first few days, the robbers intermittently threatened them, held them at gunpoint, and pushed them around. At first, the robbers also denied food and bathroom privileges to the tellers. After the initial intimidation, a period of "normalcy" ensued. The robbers-turned-kidnappers were "kind" to the hostages, letting them go to the bathroom and walk around. Captors and hostages had conversations with each other and began the process of getting acquainted. Think about what you might do to survive in this situation. Forming a bond, becoming a real person to your captors, could save your life.

After 10 days, the ordeal ended with the release of the hostages and the incarceration of the hostage-takers. During the trial, two of the three tellers testified in defense of their assailants. Indeed, one of the tellers married her former captor after he was released from prison. In other rare cases, hostages have been known to post bail or to have emotional relationships with their captors (Strentz, 1979).

These strange occurrences have become known as the Stockholm Syndrome (Lang, 1974) and have come to represent a specific combination of emotional responses and behaviors that can occur when someone is held hostage. There are three primary indicators of its development: (a) The hostage feels negative about the people working for his or her release, (b) the hostage has positive feelings about the captor, and (c) the captor feels positive about the hostage (Kuleshnyk, 1984).

Graham, Rawlings, and Rimini (1988) have successfully applied the Stockholm Syndrome to the psychological processes undergone by battered women. Ott et al. (1990) analyzed data from the Stockholm Syndrome Questionnaire for Battered Women provided by 164 emotionally abused but not physically abused women. A second questionnaire contained four hypothesized precursors to the development of the syndrome: Threat to Survival (emotional violence), Isolation, Inability to Escape, and Kindness. Results indicated that Threat to Survival was the most important variable and that Isolation was the second best variable for predicting the Stockholm Syndrome on the Battered Women scale.

Even before the application of the Stockholm Syndrome to battered women, Walker (1979) theorized that kindness, after abuse, reinforced the bond between the battered woman and her abuser, and Browne (1987) subsequently postulated that abused women ultimately consider the cessation of abuse as kindness. The kindness displayed by the abuser gives the battered woman hope, allowing her to deny the other side of the abuser that terrifies her.

Case History: Jane and Lewis

Jane and her husband Lewis have been married for 9 years. Both are professionals and working in the same field. They share many of the same interests, own a home together, are involved with their families, participate in the same organizations, and share an abusive relationship.

Lewis is a soft-spoken and shy man. Rage doesn't appear to fit him well; it is confusing. His temper tantrums are usually verbal in form. He rants, he raves, he threatens and demeans. Sporadically, there is an accompanying physical outburst.

Over time, Lewis's verbal outbursts have diminished Jane's sense of self-worth. Some of the attacks were subtle, questioning her decision making at work, wondering if this or that person really liked her, commenting on the quality of her performance, and then jumping to her defense if her family insulted her or her boss didn't appreciate her. He was concurrently her best friend and her biggest critic.

Jane became focused on obtaining Lewis's approval and obtaining his emotional support. She poured her emotional energy into analyzing their relationship, leaving her with little energy to maintain other emotional attachments. Her job performance nose-dived, and she questioned her abilities, even her abilities to contribute to her profession. As her self-confidence waned, her conduct as friend, family member, coworker, and wife suffered. The feedback she received began to support her diminished self-appraisal, but Lewis remained steadfast, her loyal friend and her avowed enemy.

Currently, Jane's emotional dependence on the relationship has increased. She supports her own negative self-view with "quotes" from her husband. She fears that, without Lewis, she is nothing. She has been brainwashed.

* * *

Treblinka. In Steiner's (1966) book *Treblinka,* he describes the victimization of inmates existing in the extermination camp. He asks and tries to answer a number of questions: (a) How do inmates in a death camp stay alive at all? (b) What did living under such conditions do to their souls and to their sense of themselves as humans? (c) Why did they go on when it was easier to die? At Treblinka, the commanding officers of the SS morally disarmed the camp inhabitants by creating an environment replete with panic and uncertainty. Moral disarmament forces a victim to make minor concessions that lead to others and eventually leads to humiliation, self-hatred, and submission. The strategy was to make victims accomplices in their own victimization. The SS removed vestiges of humanity by dividing families and by removing social life. The notion of time and space were lost. The commandant of Treblinka committed random acts of violence, including verbal threats, beatings, and executions. This intermittent punishment caused fear and helplessness. The unpredictability of his attacks made his authority seem mystical. Prisoners felt the exaggerated presence of a permanent menace. With a gun and a few guards, the SS controlled 600 captives and created a psychosis of fear.

Case History: Melinda and Jason

As the headlights made a path into the driveway, the three children and their mother in the house stopped laughing. By the time the key turned and the door was pushed open, the children were quietly doing their homework, and Melinda was ladling soup into bowls. As Jason came in the front door and went upstairs, he didn't say anything except "Hi." No one could read his mood. The atmosphere screamed with tension, but the house was silent.

The older boy was afraid that Dad had had a bad day; he worried about what would happen when Dad found out that his report card wasn't good. The younger boy sat in a corner and tried to make himself invisible. The little girl was afraid that Dad could read her mind and would know that she hated him. She knew that he would hurt her when she figured out what she was thinking.

Melinda didn't do much outside of the home. It was almost as if *he* knew when she saw family or friends during the day. She wondered if he had friends around who "told" on her, because his anger seemed to intensify in direct proportion to her happiness. Two weeks before, he had chased the boys around the house, screaming about the need for discipline, and had finally beaten them with a belt. She used to intervene, but it never worked; she could not even protect herself, much less the children. She felt confused, paralyzed, and disoriented.

Jason came down to dinner. His mood seemed calm. He began to talk. Everyone listened. In a while, the whole group was talking and more relaxed. They eased into laughter, but they wondered when everything would change. Mom never quite joined in. Her eyes were a little dull. You never saw much excitement or change of emotion from Mom. In time, the four prisoners finished their meals and went to bed.

*   *   *

Battered women as prisoners.

Until someone is physically abused, they could never know: the humiliation—the damage that is done to your self-respect. To become diminished—to feel less than a human being. To be debased— to be lowered in character, dignity, and value. Emotional scars that never heal.

Hearing transcript (cited in Nerney, 1987, p. 9)

As a battering relationship continues, there is an exaggerated belief on the part of a battered woman that her batterer is omnipresent. She becomes less able to see the connection between her behavior and the nature or rationale behind her batterer's aggression. Although his violence may occur randomly, the odds are better than 600 to 1 (as in Treblinka) that she will be the target of his abuse.

Dutton and Painter (1981) pointed out some features of imbalanced relationships that resemble the experiences of captivity. In all cases, the maltreated person is dominated by the other person, and abuse is intermittent. Dutton and Painter termed "traumatic bonding" the process of forming strong emotional ties in a relationship where one person intermittently abuses, harasses, threatens, beats, or intimidates the other. In one study, McCleary (1979) described traumatic bonding in juveniles. He found that delinquents were "poignantly loyal to their [abusive] parents and cruelly tortured by any thought of separation" (p. 262).

Forced institutionalization. Examination of data gathered from battered women living in an Israeli shelter convinced Avni (1991b) to apply the concept of institutionalization to circumstances in a battering relationship. Her deduction rested upon several comparisons: (a) In an institution, the staff make all the rules and punish noncompliance. In the home, the batterer makes all the rules and punishes noncompliance. (b) In an institution, the inmates suffer from constant exposure to the staff. In the violent home, the battered woman suffers from constant exposure to her husband's surveillance. (c) In an institution, mortification of the self occurs by such procedures as strip searches and shaving the head. In the violent home, mortification occurs as a result of the husband's suspicion and humiliating attacks.

Battered women in Avni's study said that they felt like prisoners. Indeed, a number of the women reported being locked in their homes. In one case, a spouse plastered the door shut before he left for work. In another, a batterer locked his wife inside the house, even though she was 9 months' pregnant. The isolation experienced by these women led to greater dependence on their abusers. The suspicious climate in their homes led to hypervigilance and, for at least one woman who was repeatedly interrogated about alleged infidelity, total self-doubt about her sanity: "Maybe I really did it without being aware of it. I was going crazy" (Avni, 1991b, p. 145).

Case History: Sandy and Jim

Jim: "My wife, Sandy, is a teacher and I'm self-employed. I don't fit
in with her friends at work and I don't like to go to her parties. One night, I let her go with a friend and I'll never do
that again. Two guys took their clothes off and jumped into
a hot tub. They were drunk and acting crazy. When my wife

told me what happened, I went off. I threw her against the wall and grilled her about what she did. Then I beat her up like she was a man. I don't tolerate infidelity. I've only had sex with prostitutes, never an affair."

Sandy: Jim never trusts me. He thinks I'm flirting with everyone and that I dress up for other men. I was surprised when he said I could go to the party and relieved at his attitude. Sometimes he literally questions me for hours. It feels like a police interrogation. Sometimes I wonder if he's right. Am I trying to attract other men? When he beat me up after the party, I wondered what I had done to encourage these guys to strip and jump into the hot tub.

* * *

Romero (1985) theorized that the strategies of control and coercion used on prisoners of war were comparable to those used on battered women: (a) psychological abuse occurring in the context of violence, (b) the employment of emotional dependency created through intermittent reinforcement, and (c) isolation from the victim's support system (also see Adams & McCormick, 1982). Edleson, Eisikovits, Guttman, and Sela-Amit (1991) offered a similar conjecture, that the use of violence coerces a battered woman into compliance and enhances the perpetrator's sense of control over her.

Conformity and Obedience

Syndromes do not describe the behavior of all individuals subjected to terror or captivity, but they do portray what happens for most. Even under circumstances less trying than life at Treblinka or institutionalization, individuals exhibit a propensity to conform to authority. In one of the most influential studies ever conducted by a psychologist, Stanley Milgram (1963) explored the extent to which people will obey an authority figure. Before conducting his research, Milgram asked psychiatrists to predict the percentage of individuals who would shock another person simply at the request of an authority figure. Psychiatrists estimated an obedience rate of under 1%.

In this experiment, the investigator requested the teacher-subjects to shock learner-subjects whenever they made a mistake in a verbal learning experiment and to increase the shock level with every successive error. The experiment was designed so that the learner, who was sitting behind a screen out of sight, appeared to cry out in pain and to beg the "teacher" to stop. Most teachers stopped at the request of the learner and informed the experimenter that they did not wish to continue. Amazingly, however, the experimenter had only to issue a directive phrase, such as "you have no other choice" or "the experiment must go on," to encourage them to continue. Every teacher conformed to some degree. The unexpected result was that 65% of the participants were willing to administer shocks at a level marked "dangerous" to obviously suffering human subjects.

The outcome of this research was so startling that other scientists tended to doubt its authenticity. Replications, however, demonstrated its validity. For example, Hofling, Brotzman, Darlymple, Graves, and Pierce (1966) devised a real-life experiment in which a doctor, unfamiliar to a nurse, ordered her to give an extremely large dose of an unusual medicine to a hospitalized patient without the required written prescription. Even though the doctor ordered administration of an amount of medicine that was twice the maximum dosage printed on the label, 95% of the nurses tried to obey the order before being interrupted by a confederate of the experimenter.

Summary

Women entering relationships that eventually become abusive do not appear to differ from their nonbattered counterparts in terms of demographic variables, histories of childhood abuse, and other psychological attributes. Society, nonetheless, is inclined to place the blame on them rather than on the perpetrators, where it belongs. These proclivities, along with a batterer's tendency to manipulate his partner's feelings, add to the probability that a battered woman will blame herself for being beaten or for her failure to escape.

Victimization is a profoundly negative experience with long-lasting effects. Phenomena like the Stockholm Syndrome and the events at Treblinka demonstrate how individuals who are seemingly normal can become psychologically entrapped. An extrapolation of these processes helps to clarify battering relationships and to make sense of the battered woman's emotional quandary. Compliance with the demands of individuals in positions of authority is well understood by anyone with a healthy fear of consequences. Although conformity is an everyday occurrence, the effects of conformity as evidenced by Milgram's research are no less significant than the behaviors resulting from captivity. Conformity experiments reflect these dramatic effects on people, in general, and on battered women, in particular. Given the nature of victim-blaming and the process, becoming trapped in a battering relationship "could happen to anyone."

5

● Meltdown:
The Impact of Stress and
Learned Helplessness

*She has lost her faith in the world's essential predictability,
fairness and safety, and approaches even ordinary routines
like driving with the hesitancy of an outsider, a foreigner in
a hostile land.*

JAY (1991, p. 23)

Chapter Overview

STRESS IS PART OF EVERYDAY LIFE and can result from either positive or
negative events. Apparently, most individuals do not handle stress
productively and pay a heavy price both physically and psychologically for chronic mismanagement. Post-traumatic stress disorder
(PTSD) is a psychological manifestation of chronic abuse seen in
both battered women and abused children. Learned helplessness
is also a significant condition brought about by violence or, more
specifically, by the inability to stop it. Effects of PTSD and learned
helplessness may eventually culminate in a cluster of cognitions,
feelings, and behavior that constitute the battered woman syn-

drome. The core of fear and paralysis typifying this syndrome help to explain the unexplainable: why battered women stay or why they kill.

Violence-Induced Stress

In humans, a moderate amount of stress is essential to growth and development, but prolonged, intense stress debilitates the body and the soul. The concept of stress incorporates psychological reactions to stress(ors) as well as physiological ones. Loss of a job constitutes a "negative" stressor, while going on vacation constitutes a "positive" stressor. Psychological reactions to stress include cognitive impairment (e.g., confusion and poor test performance) and emotional responses (e.g., anxiety, anger, aggression, and depression). (For readers who enjoyed the movies *Willard* and *Ben,* an early experiment on stress in rats conducted by Selye, 1946, appears in Appendix B, section 8.)

Case History: Nicole and Tom

To describe Nicole now is to describe her life with Tom, a successful businessman. Tom was obsessed with Nicole's life prior to their relationship. In particular, he wanted open disclosure of previous sexual experiences. His interrogation would sometimes last for hours. He read her private papers and journals and went through her picture album. He found pictures of her standing next to male friends and relatives. These pictures served as a basis for his distrust, even though he was aware that she had had no prior sexual experience. She had come to this relationship as a virgin.

When she married Tom, she had not anticipated how much he would mistrust and control her. She had nearly earned her doctorate, and she wanted to keep things at home on an even keel until her qualifying exams were completed. She recognized that she had given up some important things to keep her relationship together. She had given up her friends and family, but only for a time, to make it easier for her husband to feel secure.

Nicole had known that Tom was jealous, but she expected it to diminish over time. She understood his jealousy and fear so well, in fact, that his frenzied fantasies of her infidelities became real to her.

She began to wonder if she had repressed the memories of affairs she had never had. His reality had become hers. Her ability to define herself apart from him became obscured.

Nicole didn't understand why she cried a lot or why she was unable to concentrate. She didn't know why she shook when she talked or why she was afraid. Physical abuse had not been that severe or frequent. She had no idea how she had gotten from there to here or when the change had begun, only that it seemed complete.

* * *

Researchers, experimentally, and clinicians, anecdotally, have documented the physiological toll of chronic anticipation. Generally, the women in the Follingstad, Brennan, Hause, Polek, and Rutledge (1991) study reported that their physical and emotional health had been better both before and after the violent relationship. Similarly, Barnett, Lopez-Real, Carter, and Hedayat (1985) found that battered women reported feeling physically ill as a consequence of violence-induced stress.

Case History: Mei

"I started having stomach pains the second year that we lived together, after the violence began. It was weird. I would be visiting a friend, and after I'd been there a few hours, I'd get a stabbing pain in my abdomen and feel sick. It was like the alarm ringing in the morning telling me that it was time to get up and go, and I would get up and go because I knew if I didn't, something bad would happen when I got home."

* * *

Unpredictable stress. Adams and McCormick (1982) allege that when batterers assault and abuse their partners, their unpredictable behavior helps them to maintain control. Campbell (1990) noted that not being able to predict the aggression is conducive to feeling helpless, and Cole and Sapp (1988) found that, the lower the level of internal control, the greater the level of stress. It seems that, when a batterer gains control, the battered woman loses even the illusion of it.

Although some battered women may be able to predict the *timing* of cyclical violence to some degree, most cannot (Hilberman & Munson, 1978; Walker, 1979). Nonetheless, Follingstad et al. (1991) showed that women who knew that physical abuse was inevitable, but did not know its exact timing, experienced less anxiety than those who were able to determine its onset. This finding was contrary to their original hypothesis but consonant with the Cycle of Violence theory. It seems to us that the group of battered women who can foresee a violent assault are so entrenched in the cycle that their greater exposure and familiarity have made them both more fearful and more accurate in predicting that abuse will recur. They can never predict, however, the "when and the how" with total precision. It is like being told that you have terminal cancer but not how long you might live.

In an animal experiment, Seligman (1968) was able to demonstrate that rats given unpredictable shocks developed a chronic state of fear and ulcers (Seligman & Meyer, 1970). To understand the effects of stress, Geer and Maisel (1972) conducted a study in which college students viewed graphic photographs of crime scenes. Some subjects could control the timing of the presentations; others had no control. Individuals who had control reported much less stress than those who did not. Similarly, subjects from other studies reported that predictable shocks were less aversive and less stressful than identical shocks that were unpredictable (Katz & Wykes, 1985). Knowing what to expect seems to provide a comfort zone or illusion of control. Experimental results of this type lay the groundwork for understanding the development of chronic apprehension as depicted in the battered woman syndrome. (See the description of the Abbot, Schoen, & Badia, 1984, animal experiment in Appendix B, section 9.)

Post-Traumatic Stress Disorder (PTSD)

Traumatic events are the most obvious source of negative stress for anyone. Experiences such as earthquakes, nuclear accidents, plane crashes, and physical assaults produce severe stress reactions in everyone, sometimes called disaster syndromes (Atkinson, Atkinson, Smith, & Bem, 1990). A disaster syndrome encompasses three psychological stages: (a) shock, disorientation, and bewilderment; (b) passivity and lack of capacity to initiate tasks, accompanied by the inability to follow orders; and (c) anxiety and concentration difficulties. When a traumatic event has a prolonged reaction, the resulting condition is called post-traumatic stress disorder (PTSD), a diagnosis first applied to Vietnam veterans. Recent psychiatric studies undertaken by the Veterans Administration (see Bower, 1992) found evidence suggesting that soldiers physically or sexually abused as children had a greater sensitivity to developing PTSD in response to trauma than nonabused soldiers.

PTSD received medical status in 1979 (American Psychiatric Association, 1980). Similar symptoms, however, have been associated with war for more than a century. These symptoms had been classified, depending on the war they were associated with, as "nostalgia," "shell shock," and "battle fatigue." Prior to the Vietnam war, medical professionals and others suspected that an individual who did not "get over" a traumatic experience in a reasonable amount of time was inherently disturbed or pathological. "Reasonable" was usually defined by the individuals who had a significant investment in the victim's "moving on" emotionally.

Recognition of an external stressor as the precursor to PTSD produced a radical contrast to the "innate character defects" theory. "In short, the diagnosis tacitly recognizes that the world can drive a normal person crazy" (Jay, 1991, p. 22). One significant consequence of the PTSD diagnosis in war veterans has been the provision of an appropriate status for all trauma victims.

PTSD is an anxiety disorder produced by an uncommon, extremely stressful event (e.g., assault, rape, military combat, death camp) and characterized by (a) reexperiencing the trauma in painful recollections or recurrent dreams; (b) diminished responsiveness (numbing), with disinterest in significant activities and with feelings of detachment and estrangement from others; and (c) such symptoms as exaggerated startle response, disturbed sleep, difficulty in concentrating or remembering, guilt about surviving when others did not, and avoidance of activities that call the traumatic event to mind (Goldenson, 1984).

T. Adler (1990) studied identical twins as a method for clarifying assessment of PTSD symptomatology. Because identical twins have the same genetic inheritance, environmental forces affecting only one sibling are easier to evaluate. Investigators are more easily able to rule out individual idiosyncrasies. This study supported external causation of PTSD. Because the symptoms most clearly associated with environmental determinants are those described by Goldenson (1984), his definition is well founded.

Living in a war zone caused PTSD in about 15% of Vietnam veterans (American Psychiatric Association, 1980). Susan Solomon, chief of the Violence and Traumatic Stress Research Branch of the National Insititute of Mental Health (NIMH), reported that 39.1% of a group of 1,000 young adults in Detroit had suffered a traumatic event in their lifetime such as a natural disaster, a serious accident, an assault, exposure to violence, and sudden loss of a loved one. Of these, 23.6% developed PTSD ("High Prevalence for Post-Traumatic Stress," 1991).

Other studies have estimated even higher percentages of PTSD symptomatology: (a) 24 of 30 rape victims (80%; Kramer & Green, 1991); (b) 24 of 25 adult incest victims (96%; Donaldson & Gardner, 1985); and (c) 66% of family survivors of homicide victims (Amick-McMullen, Kilpatrick, Veronen, & Smith, 1989). Some experts (Foa, Olasov, & Steketee, 1987) consider female victims of sexual assault and other assault victims to be the largest major group of PTSD victims. Riggs, Kilpatrick, and Resnick (1992) established that levels of PTSD symptomatology in women raped or assaulted by a husband were comparable to levels in women raped or assaulted by strangers. Astin, Lawrence, Pincus, and Foy (1990) demonstrated a significant relationship between childhood sexual victimization and PTSD. In the Amick-McMullen et al. (1989) study of homicide victims' relatives, the more dissatisfied family members were with the criminal justice system (e.g., charges against the perpetrator were reduced), the worse their PTSD symptoms.

One correlate of stress-related illness is having a network of close friends from whom the victim feels she or he must hide a "shameful" trauma. In other words, the traumatized individual is actively inhibiting disclosure (Pennebaker & Susman, 1988). According to Jay (1991, p. 22), there is a "relentless external pressure on the victim to maintain the breach between the private, ravaged self and the public, acquiescent persona." Listening to trauma victims tell their stories creates stress, because the listener sees the pain and empathizes with the fear (Kessler, McLeod, & Wethington, 1985).

Trauma, once or twice removed, still shakes the security of those peripherally involved in the world of the traumatized. For example, 8 weeks after the Loma Prieta earthquake in San Francisco, a study revealed that victims were still thinking about it, but they had stopped talking about it, because others did not want to listen. In another study, parents bereaved by a child's death discovered that many of their friends and relatives avoided them, thus reducing opportunities for them to talk out their feelings and sending a strong message that implied that the time for being sad and the time for being heard were over (Pennebaker, 1991).

PTSD and the Violent Home

In an effort to make an analogy between the experience of combat soldiers and those of battered women, we have inserted parallel wording in a quotation from Goodwin's (1987, p. 8) description of PTSD victims:

> Due to circumstances of war [her married life], extended grieving was unproductive [and not allowed] and could become a liability [exacerbating his guilt, leading to increased anger]. Grief was handled as quickly as possible [to make way for the honeymoon stage]. Many soldiers [battered women] reported feeling numb. They felt depressed and unable to tell anyone. "How can I tell my wife [neighbor/friend/family member/pastor], she'd [he'd] never understand?" they ask. "How can anyone who has not been there understand?"
>
> Essentially, Vietnam-style combat [home-style combat] held no final resolution of conflict for anyone. Regardless of how one might respond, the overall outcome seemed to be an endless production of casualties with no perceivable positive results. They found little support from their friends and neighbors back home, the people in whose name so many people were drafted into military service [a battering relationship]. They felt helpless. They returned to the United States trying to put some positive resolution to this episode in their lives, but the atmosphere at home was hopeless. They were still helpless.

This analogy seems reasonable as a number of investigators have diagnosed PTSD in battered women. Houskamp and Foy (1991) indicated that 45% of their sample met full criteria in the DSM-III-R for PTSD (see also Astin et al., 1991; Kemp, Rawlings, & Green, 1991). Prior to the research documenting PTSD, Painter and Dutton (1985, p. 366) described some abused women as having suffered an "emotional collapse indicative of extreme aversive, prolonged arousal similar to that experienced by disaster victims" (also see Gondolf, 1988a; Walker, 1983).

Houskamp and Foy (1991) showed that the extent and severity of exposure to violence, as judged by the revised Conflict Tactics Scale, was significantly correlated with severity of PTSD symptomatology in battered women. Sustained contact with the batterer through such events as court appearances along with his continuing threats are "likely to have significant influence on symptomatology" (p. 374). Kemp et al. (1991) established that subjective abuse-related stress and actual assault level correlated positively with PTSD, anxiety, and depression. For the most part, the more severe and more chronic the trauma, the more extreme the symptoms (see Astin et al., 1990; Houskamp & Foy, 1991).

Case History: Ginger and Fernando

Ginger went to counseling because her supervisor told her that "whatever it was that was bothering her was negatively affecting her work." Ginger's symptoms included emotional anesthesia (diminished responsiveness), inability to concentrate or complete projects she had started, difficulty in getting to sleep, and nightmares when she finally did sleep. She was a nurse and earned substantially more money than Fernando, who worked in a restaurant. They had been married for 5 years.

The beatings had been going on for the past 3 years, but the humiliation and emotional assaults had gone on longer than that. One night while she was making dinner, she heard Fernando muttering in the living room. She knew that he was angry. Then she heard something break. When she looked in the living room, her new coffee table had been flattened and her crystal bowl was flying into the wall. Ginger tried to calm him, but he stormed out of the apartment. She cleaned up the mess one more time.

On one occasion, Fernando screamed at her in front of her sister because "she thought she was too important to do his laundry and was too busy with her important job to cook and clean for him." He called her *gorda* (fat) and told her she was ugly and disgusting, and no one would want her. Then a week later, he beat her for "coming on" to a neighbor in the elevator.

The ultimate humiliation for Ginger was coming home from work and finding Fernando in bed with a prostitute. This time she did the screaming and this time he beat her for embarrassing him. Later, he suggested that they both be tested for HIV.

Ginger closed herself off from friends and family. She lost interest in her life and avoided any situation that could "put her in jeopardy." In fact, Ginger appeared more depressed and anxious than many of her clients in the psychiatric unit in the hospital. Ginger's therapeutic diagnosis was PTSD.

* * *

Avoidance and PTSD. Avoidance behavior is a central feature of PTSD and a basic coping strategy employed by Ginger and other battered women. In one study of battered women, hypersensitivity was the most common symptom manifested; avoidance symptoms were second; intrusive thoughts, third; and depression, fourth. The levels of stress suffered by the women were actually higher than those found for a community sample of Vietnam veterans (Green, Lindy, Grace, & Glese, 1989).

Avoidance learning experiments with animals offer an explanation for some of the PTSD-associated behaviors of battered women. Rats in a Skinner box learn to press a bar to escape from or to avoid a shock. In escape and avoidance learning, the animal must learn to make a response (press the bar) to escape or avoid pain. (See Appendix B, sections 10 and 11, for a learning explanation of avoidance behavior.)

A battered woman might learn to avoid battering through *self-protective* actions. For example, if she is talking to a friend on the phone when the threats occur, she may hang up and start dinner, move to what she considers to be a safe area of the house, or leave the area entirely. Use of more avoidant coping was particularly true of women who held traditional sex-role beliefs and who had few resources (Hodson, 1982). An investigation of the effects of abuse on attachment styles of battered women (Justice & Hirt, 1992) uncovered two results. Compared with nonabused women, abused women scored significantly higher on Emotional Detachment, specifically on the factors of Angry Withdrawal and Availability. Angry Withdrawal reflects an avoidance coping style, while Availability refers to the expectation that responses to one's needs will not be positive. PTSD in battered women represents a combination of high arousal, high avoidance, intrusive memories, memory loss, and cognitive confusion.

Maintenance of PTSD symptoms. Amick-McMullen et al. (1989) introduced a learning conceptualization (two-process avoidance theory) to explain the occurrence and maintenance of PTSD. In this theory, two processes occur: classical conditioning (fear) and operant conditioning (avoidance response, e.g., run to a safe location; Mowrer, 1947; Rescorla & Solomon, 1967). In the first process, an organism becomes classically conditioned to fear a stimulus such as the ringing of the phone paired with an aversive message (e.g., "your brother has been killed"). In the second process, the organism becomes operantly conditioned to respond by not answering the phone to avoid the fear generated by the stimulus of the phone message.

Preventing the fear associated with such a message is reinforcing and therefore maintains the avoidance behavior. Unfortunately, one core feature of PTSD is the constant cognitive reexperiencing of the stressful event. This recurrence helps to maintain a high level of anxiety. To counteract the anxiety generated by the mental replays, an individual must repeatedly monitor his or her actions. Even when someone is feeling less stressed, the occurrence of a very similar event can elicit the fear all over again. In learning terms, the reappearance of the fear (the learned response) is called "spontaneous recovery." (Refer to Appendix B, section 12.)

Case History: Wanda and Paul

Wanda paid a high price for having fun. Paul went through her closet, removed her fancy dresses, and ripped them to shreds. He wanted to punish her for dancing with other men at her cousin's wedding. Actually, this was not the first time that she had been punished for "indiscretions." He had slapped her and had broken the phone because she had talked with her sister, twice in one week.

Wanda spent a lot of time questioning her behavior. Activities that used to seem normal became distorted in her own mind: "Maybe I do spend too much time on the phone or with my family." "I shouldn't have danced with other men at my cousin's wedding."

A little at a time, Wanda withdrew and avoided contact with people who upset Paul. If she was on the phone, and Paul entered the room, she jumped. She forgot what life before Paul was like, and that she used to be happy.

* * *

Frustration and Problem Solving

For a battered woman, her desire to be close to her partner and to have a happy home is countered by the reality of his violence. Frustration generated by this approach-avoidance conflict may cause a problem-solving deficit.

Animals caught in an approach-avoidance situation tend to develop frustration when a problem leading to a reward becomes unsolvable and attempts at solution are painful and presumably create fear. Some of the consequences for the laboratory animals were the development of inflexible, rigid behavior, refusal to behave, and unsuccessful attempts to escape. (Turn to Appendix B, section 14, for an explanation of the N. R. F. Maier [1949] animal experiment on frustration.)

How is this animal research relevant to human behavior? Maguire and Corbett (1987) found that crime victims (of robbery and assault) experienced severe symptoms including an inability to perform ordinary tasks. Launius and Jensen (1987) studied problem solving in three different groups of women. One group of women was not battered but was in therapy for anxiety and depression; the second group was not in therapy, nor were they in violent relationships; and the last group consisted solely of battered women. All three groups received everyday problems to solve, such as this one: "You are in a long line in the theater and two people cut in ahead of you. You don't appreciate this. What can you do?"

Battered women chose fewer effective solutions to the situations presented than did the other groups, and they generated both fewer total problem-solving options and fewer effective options. In a test involving a hypothetical abuse situation, however, they showed no deficit. In fact, Campbell's (1989a) data indicated that battered women solved a higher number of relationship problems than did nonbattered women. Nonetheless, in situations with their male partners, they were more passive and less assertive than the other women. Claerhout, Elder, and Janes (1982) obtained comparable results.

Problem-solving deficits seem to be situation specific and an outcome of the cognitive distortions associated with PTSD. Survival mandates a focus of attention on the person who controls the situation. From this perspective, the battered woman's attention and problem-solving abilities seem to be pointed in the practical direction (Campbell, 1989a). Trimpey (1989) speculates that a battered woman's inability to effectively generate solutions to some problems is caused by the anxiety brought on by pervasive physical and psychological violence. Russell et al. (1989) found that the abused women were significantly more anxious, confused, and fatigued than the nonbattered women.

Finn (1985) and Maertz (1990) demonstrated that the problem-solving deficits were not solely a consequence of the abuse but also an outcome of the stress induced by unsuccessful problem-solving attempts during the test (see Morrison, Van Hasselt, & Bellack, 1987). Negative effects of extreme stress are not limited to battered women. Depressed and anxious subjects in other populations also manifest problem-solving deficits (Gotlib & Asarnow, 1979; Nezu & Ronan, 1986).

Effects of frustration vary, however, depending upon the design of the experiment. Amsel and Rousel (1972) rewarded rats twice, first after a short run and again after another run. After the animals adjusted to that pattern, the researchers removed the first reward. The animals began to run faster. In other words, the rats performed more to get less. Researchers interpreted this outcome as increased performance motivated by frustration. Increased performance as a consequences of frustration sharply contrasts with apathy and rigid responding as outcomes.

It seems to us that the differences in the consequences (inflexibility versus increased motivation) of the two types of frustration experiments arise from tangential differences generated by the dissimilarity in experimental procedures. That is, inflexibility (as in N. R. F. Maier, 1949) arises from the frustration accompanied by pain and fear, while increased motivation (as in Amsel & Rousel, 1972) emanates from frustration without fear and pain. Applying the findings of both these studies to abusive relationships, the more a battered woman is frustrated by her inability to improve her relationship and to end the violence, the more motivated she is to continue trying (Amsel & Rousel, 1972). Nonetheless, as fear increases, active problem-solving behavior diminishes (N. R. F. Maier, 1949). (Appendix B, sections 14 and 15, more fully review the animal research.)

Learned Helplessness

Additional theoretical rationales help complete the picture of why battered women stay. Learned helplessness is the most significant and widely used of these concepts. Gerow (1989, p. 193) defines *learned helplessness* as "a condition in which a subject does not attempt to escape from a painful or noxious situation after learning in a previous, similar situation that escape is not possible." (See Appendix B, section 15, for a more detailed description of the original animal experiment by S. F. Maier & M. E. P. Seligman, 1976.)

According to Martin Seligman (1975), there are *three components to learned helplessness*: (a) motivational impairment (passivity), (b) intellectual impairment (poor problem-solving ability), and (c) emotional trauma (increased feelings of helplessness, incompetence, frustration, and depression). Seligman particularly emphasized the similarity between learned helplessness and clinical depression (Peterson & Seligman, 1984).

Hiroto (1974) studied learned helplessness using three groups of human subjects: (a) One group experienced uncontrollable noise; (b) a second group was given noise controllable by pushing a button four times; and (c) a third, normative group was not given either. For the second stage, each subject had to move his or her finger from one side to the other in a box to escape the noxious sound. As predicted, the subjects who had previously received uncontrollable noise in the button-pushing experiment failed to learn the second task. They were unable to escape or avoid the noise.

When the concept of learned helplessness is extended to humans, the relationship between uncontrollable shock and learned helplessness is less direct. The uncontrollability of aversive events is not sufficient to produce helplessness. The way someone's behavior changes as a result of an aversive event depends on how the person interprets the causes of the events (Abramson, Garber, & Seligman, 1978; Peterson & Seligman, 1984).

There are two kinds of helplessness: personal and universal. Universal helplessness develops when the individual sees no relationship between what he is doing and the outcome (external causality). Personal helplessness develops when the individual associates an unsatisfactory outcome with his own behavior (personal causality; Abramson, 1977).

Internal-external locus of control. The constructs of Internal-External Locus of Control reflect the degree to which an individual believes that the occurrence of rewards is dependent upon his or her own behavior. This level of belief is a correlate of helplessness. External control is the perception that outcomes and reinforcements are dependent on forces outside of the individual (beyond one's control) such as God, luck, fate, chance, or powerful others. Internal control represents the perception that reinforcements depend on some quality or trait of the individual such as his or her skill or interpersonal behaviors (Rotter, 1954).

Walker (1979) was the first researcher to extrapolate the original learned helplessness findings to battered women. The learned helplessness model became a popular concept used to explain battered women's entrapment in abusive relationships. Walker (1979) and Hendricks-Matthews (1982) suggested that learned helplessness causes battered women to make causal attributions that tend to keep them entrapped in the relationship. For example, a battered woman is likely to blame herself for the violence as though she has done something to provoke the attacks. Unfortunately, society tends to reinforce this view.

Carlisle-Frank (1991), making use of the reformulated learned helplessness model, conjectured that battered women might have internal beliefs about controlling the violence in their homes while having external beliefs about their ability to escape (see Hendricks-Matthews, 1982). In fact, battered women may have learned that they could not escape by actually having tried to do so, a type of "learned externality."

Individuals who are prone to make attributions that the causes of aversive events are self-generated, unchangeable, and widespread are especially likely to feel helpless and depressed. The battered women who believe that their beatings occur in multiple situations (not related to any particular event or action), and think that they are to blame and that the situation will not change, are most likely to experience a feeling of personal helplessness. In line with learned helplessness theory, a number of researchers have documented clinical depression in battered women (e.g., Riggs et al., 1992; Rounsaville & Weissman, 1978; Sato & Heiby, 1992).

Learned helplessness controversy. There has been some disagreement over the appropriateness of applying the learned helplessness model to battered women (as in Carlisle-Frank, 1991). In addition to depression, investigators testing the model have examined locus of control, coping styles, and help-seeking behavior. Walker (1984) used the Levenson Locus of Control Scale (Levenson, 1973) to measure three different types of control (Internal, Powerful Others, and Chance) in battered women. She tested the hypothesis that battered women would score high on the powerful others and chance dimensions. The women, however, scored high on all three scales. From these data, Walker suggested that battered women believe that they have a great amount of control over their lives and that they will eventually be able to change their batterer's behavior, a sort of learned hopefulness, as described previously. Along the same lines, Follingstad et al. (1992) reported that battered women believed that their own sanctions (e.g., threatening divorce) against abusers were responsible for terminating the violence. Walker (1984) surmised that the battered woman may interpret her own focus on her batterer's happiness and her use of coping strategies as actually being in control of the battering (an illusion of control).

Two investigations have established that battered women's coping strategies were deficient compared with nonbattered samples of women (Finn, 1985; Hodson, 1982). Battered women were less apt to use active coping strategies (obtaining social support, reframing stressful events, and seeking spiritual support) but significantly more apt to use passive strategies such as fantasizing (McCubbin, Larsen, & Olson, 1982). Similarly, Walker (1984) conjectured that active coping styles such as confrontation might escalate the abuse (see also O'Leary, Curley, Rosenbaum, & Clarke, 1985). Gellen, Hoffman, Jones, and Stone (1984) thought that elevations in battered women's MMPI scales indicated elements reflective of learned helplessness. A correlational analysis between stress and coping revealed that, as stress levels increased, effective coping strategies decreased. Finn (1985) judged these findings to be consistent with learned helplessness theory.

Wauchope (1988) attempted to use the relationship between help-seeking behavior and severity of violence as a test of learned helplessness theory. Her findings indicated that, as the severity of violence increased, women were more likely, rather than less likely, to seek help. She interpreted her findings as failing to support learned helplessness theory. Other researchers have corroborated her findings (Barnett & Lopez-Real, 1985; Campbell, 1989a; Sullivan, 1991).

On the basis of research portraying battered women as active help-seekers, Gondolf (1988a) formulated a "survivor theory" to describe battered women's attempts to obtain help. He viewed the active, energized behavior of help seeking as opposite to the behavior implied by learned helplessness theory. Battered women in his study averaged six help-seeking behaviors before they entered a shelter. The women finally left only when it was clear to them that their batterers would not change or that the danger of remaining was too great. Gelles and Harrop (1989), using a large sample, identified the most powerful predictor of help seeking as the frequency of severe abuse.

Despite the contradictory evidence from studies of help-seeking activity, the weight of evidence is consistent with learned helplessness as a factor contributing to battered women's behavior (Kuhl, 1985). It seems probable that, like problem-solving deficits, learned helplessness may be situation specific, a finding consistent with the animal studies (S. Maier & Seligman, 1976) and with one study using college students (Hiroto, 1974). A battered woman may have learned helplessness regarding certain areas of her life, but not all. Another possibility is that, as the abuse occurs more frequently and the severity escalates (as in Gelles & Harrop, 1989), the learned helplessness generalizes. Consider the cases of battered women who believe that homicide or suicide are their only viable options.

Battered women are very focused on the abuse and the abuser. It becomes the predominant theme of family life and the pivotal feature around which everything else revolves. It would make sense that generalized problem solving and coping might be impaired as energy goes to problem solving and coping with the abuser. For the most part, the behavior of the battered woman has little long-term effect on what happens within the relationship. If she stops talking to friends on the phone because it upsets him, sooner or later something else will trigger the controlling behavior or the violent episode. Even her effective problem solving may only delay the abuse; it will not stop it.

According to the model of social support provided by Dunkel-Schetter, Folkman, and Lazarus (1987), people need to have social support systems already in place, including a network of individuals who can function appropriately in times of stress. Seeking help is easier if there is someone tangible to provide it. A number of battered women lack adequate and available social support systems. Unfortunately, having a "support network" in place may be a "double-edged sword." For example, a friend might listen with concern to a neighbor's story of abuse but then insist that the neighbor's only answer is an immediate divorce. This theory of social obstruction, set forth by Gurley (1989), proposes that help-fulness and harmfulness are independent dimensions that may coexist.

The Battered Woman Syndrome

While the law specifically, and society in general, have offered little help to the battered wife, and indeed may be partially responsible for the actions of those who strike back violently, many of these women now face homicide charges brought by the same society and its legal system.

Anonymous (cited in Nerney, 1987, p. 21)

Definition. There has been confusion concerning the definition of the battered woman syndrome (BWS). Some authors (see Campbell, 1990) use the abusive acts committed against the woman as the defining aspects of BWS (e.g., severity and frequency of assaults). Walker (1985b), in contrast, conceptualizes the syndrome as a severe stress reaction, a subcategory of PTSD. Basic personality components include fear, depression, guilt, passivity, and low self-esteem (M. A. Douglas, 1987).

BWS expands the concept of legal self-defense. This defense holds that a battered woman is virtually held hostage in a violent household by a man who isolates and terrorizes her, convincing her that if she leaves he will track her down and kill her. DePaul (1992, p. 5) describes the syndrome as "the situation of a long-time victim of physical, sexual, and psychological abuse who loses self-confidence, feels trapped, and eventually strikes back, assaulting or killing the abuser." Only six states currently have passed laws recognizing the battered woman syndrome (Mones, 1992).

The American Psychiatric Association (1980) conceptualizes BWS as the development of a set of personality attributes brought on by abuse that render the victim more able to survive in the relationship and less able to escape it. The battered woman's belief that escape is impossible and the depression that accompanies this belief lead to her entrapment in the relationship. The three components of the syndrome are as follows: (a) behaviors brought on by victimization, (b) learned helplessness behavior, and (c) self-destructive coping behaviors.

Although it is possible that battered women's behavioral repertoires included these elements before the battering, it is more likely that the fear engendered by the violence produced or exacerbated the conditions. Schneider (1986) fears, however, that use of BWS may reinforce the sentiment that women are helpless beings and may create a new category of mental incapacity. According to DePaul (1992, p. 5), "Without expert testimony to explain how women come to feel so dependent or fearful that they cannot leave an abusive relationship, juries often are left to wonder why the woman did not walk out long before she felt compelled to retaliate."

Greene, Raitz, and Lindblad (1989) studied the level of juror's knowledge about the experiences of battered women. Jurors were relatively informed about the findings of empirical research on a number of issues: violence escalates in a relationship; women are anxious, depressed, feel helpless, and suffer in many ways; battered women are afraid that their spouses might kill them; and leaving the batterer may lead to further harm. Jurors have much less information about other factors: Battered women blame themselves, feel dependent upon their husbands, accept their spouses' promises to change, can predict when the violence will occur, even occasionally provoke an assault to end the buildup of tension, and come to believe that they must use deadly force to stay alive.

Veronen and Resnick (1988) point out that it is a mistake to focus on battered women's traits during the trial. Battered and nonbattered women are not significantly different (see M. A. Douglas & Colantuono, 1987). Instead, expert testimony should focus on the impact of violence and the woman's perception of threat. To accomplish this goal, expert testimony may need to include a description of the woman's conditioning history—for example, which cues have become classically conditioned to elicit fear. A woman whose husband informed her that after his nap he was going to torture her in his new underground torture chamber might think the time has come to prevent his ever waking up.

Jurik and Winn (1990) wanted to determine whether homicide by females has been affected by women's liberation and whether gender differences were still relevant. Their sample included 108 male-perpetrated homicides and 50 female-perpetrated homicides. Results indicated that, when women kill, they generally kill in their own homes during domestic conflict. They are prone to kill male partners, within a context of economic dependence, past attacks, and victim-initiated violence. In contrast, men are more likely to kill someone away from the home, and they usually initiate the violence when they kill (see also Goetting, 1991).

Although in absolute numbers more men kill women than the reverse, Greenfeld and Minor-Harper (1991) documented that violent female offenders were more likely to have murdered a male (61.49%) than male offenders were to have murdered a female (52.70%). Women almost always kill a spouse or an intimate in an intimate setting.

In one study of more than 1,600 homicides, self-defense characterized almost all killings by females, but almost none by males. A number of other actions and motives typified male killers, but not females: (a) Men often hunt down and kill spouses who have left them; (b) men kill as part of a planned murder-suicide; (c) men kill in response to revelations of wifely infidelity, although men are generally more adulterous than women; (d) men kill after subjecting their wives to lengthy periods of coercive abuse and assaults; and (e) men perpetrate family massacres (M. I. Wilson & Daly, 1992).

The *Report of the Governor's Committee to Study Sentencing and Correctional Alternatives for Women Convicted of Crime, State of Maryland* (1988, cited in "Violence and Women Offenders," 1990) established that 43% of the women in prisons and jails in Maryland had been physically abused and 33% had been sexually abused. According to Sheila Kuehl (personal communication, April 16, 1992), who is working on the California Clemency Project for battered women who kill, 93% of the women imprisoned for homicide in California claim to have killed their batterers.

Barnard, Vera, Vera, and Newman (1982), in a study of men and women in Florida prisons for spousal homicide, asserted that 73% of the women reported being physically abused by their husbands. For men, the precipitating event was usually some form of perceived rejection. Barnard and his colleagues called these murders of wives by husbands "sex-role threat homicides." In contrast, the women killed in response to what they saw as an attack or threat by their partners. Bernard and his colleagues cited the physical abuse of wives as the major factor in their lethal actions against their spouses. In reality, most battered women who kill are no threat to society. Nonetheless, few women are acquitted at trials; most (72%-80%) are convicted or accept a plea bargain, and many receive very long sentences (Osthoff, 1992).

The 1987 Committee on Domestic Violence and Incarcerated Women recognized that the criminal justice system does not act effectively to protect women from being beaten ("Panel Says," 1987). A battered woman may not be able to obtain a restraining order or keep it in effect. She may be unable to obtain even temporary financial support for a 30-day period. The court will most likely allow her abuser visitation with the children. In the end, no one can guarantee her safety ("Domestic Violence in the Courts," 1989). The Committee determined that the criminal justice system's response was "inconsistent and inadequate," leaving some women with no option but to kill their abusers to end the violence ("Panel Says," 1987, p. 6).

A New York Committee on Domestic Violence (STEPS, 1987) has concluded that killing an assaultive male should not be the only option left to battered women. When leaving is more dangerous than staying (as in the cases of Tracy Thurman and Lisa Bianco), but staying amounts to living in daily terror, the battered woman's dilemma can reach its final, catastrophic climax.

Summary

A woman's acceptance of responsibility for the violence in her home, coupled with her inability to stop it, create confusion, frustration, and obstruct certain forms of effective problem solving. If she is unable to see any relationship between what she does and what happens to her, it is likely that she will feel helpless and depressed.

Results from learning experiments have explained and simplified the mechanisms underlying a battered woman's avoidance-motivated behaviors as well as the development of PTSD symptoms. While learned helplessness explains some aspects of her behavior such as her problem-solving deficits and ineffective coping styles, PTSD provides an expanded psychological and physiological framework for understanding her behavior in relation to other victims. PTSD more fully documents the experiences of individuals exposed to chronic and/or severe trauma such as battering. If a battered woman cannot stop the violence and perceives that she has no other options, a day may come when she makes a lethal choice: to kill herself or to kill her abuser.

6

• Catalysts for Change

The struggle to be free of violence . . . from men is a pre-requisite for women's freedom. This issue is still avoided by men; it is considered unimportant, secondary, irrelevant.

LEFCOURT (cited in Nerney, 1987, p. 1)

Chapter Overview

THIS CHAPTER IS DEDICATED to the community-change agents of the 1970s who uncovered a problem that had been buried and unnamed. That problem is the violence directed against women in their homes, the places that have been synonymous with women's safety. Without the feminist movement, battered wives would still be dead-bolted into their homes and manacled to their abusers. These grass-roots pioneers began organizing to create solutions. This chapter is about those solutions and the solutions for the future.

Importance of Prevention

According to an article in *Emergency Medicine* ("The Battered Woman," 1989, p. 104), "The progressive nature of domestic violence, along with such consequences as substance abuse, depression, and attempted suicide, underscores the importance of early recognition and intervention." Jaffe, Hastings, and Reitzel (1992) have documented that exposure to family violence has a number of profoundly negative effects on children, such as increased anxiety, low self-esteem, truancy, low school achievement, and other behavioral problems. Main and George (1985) established that toddlers as young as 3 were affected. Given the serious consequences to women, children, and society, steps to prevent battering are essential (Browne, 1987; Jurik & Winn, 1990).

Several advocates have ideas about how this should happen. For example, violence against women should garner attention from organizations devoted to human rights (Rosen, 1991). Adams and McCormick (1982, p. 171) emphasized that "men have a particular role to play in educating other men about the nature of abuse and how men can change." Murphy and Meyer (1991, p. 99) proposed that "treatment in the area of spousal violence should be part of a larger movement designed to alter the social factors that contribute to violence against women and that keep women trapped in abusive relationships." The old saying, "an ounce of prevention is worth a pound of cure," has particular relevance when considering the consequences to future generations.

Educational Strategies

Education is an essential piece of primary prevention programs and has the potential to reach across generational and cultural differences. There is a great need for education that conveys the message that family violence will not be tolerated (Kaci, 1990). Straus (1983) has expressed the need for education to address the prevention of even mild violence within couples because it can lead to more severe forms. Kaci (1990) reports that public service announcements and documentaries have been successful in that regard. In New Jersey, battered women's advocates have initiated a new program to offer information to battered women. The underlying philosophy is that information about domestic violence and the belief that "you are not alone" will crack through denial and isolation and reinforce action. Some doctors are allowing educational films to be shown in their waiting rooms and in hospital lobbies. These films inform the public about the causes and effects of spouse abuse, the legal consequences and remedies, including emergency protective orders, and local resources. For more information about these films, correspond with the New Jersey Coalition Against Domestic Violence.

Prevention programs are also available in some schools. The Southern California Coalition on Battered Women and Barrie Levy developed a curriculum for junior and senior high school called "Skills for Violence-Free Relationships" (Levy, 1984). One outgrowth of the program was the development at Jordan High School in Long Beach, California, of a *family support* group for students who lived in violent households or who had experienced dating violence.

Jaffe, Suderman, Reitzel, and Killip (1992) documented favorable changes in attitudes, behavior, and intentions following a large-scale, secondary school primary prevention program for violence in intimate relationships. Gender differences indicated that females had a greater sensitivity to domestic violence and women's equality than males.

King and Berrio (1992) used written vignettes to study empathy. Although instructions increased empathy for victims of interpersonal violence, the instructions had little effect on such perceptions as deservedness, abusiveness, and intention to harm. The researchers conjectured that use of videotaped stories may have heightened awareness more successfully.

Jaffe, Hastings, et al. (1992) make several recommendations for schools: (a) Train personnel to recognize the behavior of children exposed to domestic abuse; (b) teach children conflict-resolution skills; (c) establish a board to enlist agency services for referrals; and (d) develop a school protocol for handling disclosures. Stagg, Wills, and Howell (1989) also advocate greater attention to the children from violent homes through special spouse abuse classes. Because of mandatory child abuse reporting laws in every state, the school may intervene in spouse abuse because of the possibility of child endangerment.

The Church

Much of the intervention that occurs or must occur, however, does not happen at a primary level. Society must change its view of women as subordinate to men and change the structure that imposes that subordination. As discussed previously, the church is the first place many women turn to in a crisis (Pagelow, 1981b). The religious community has an opportunity to make important contributions in assisting couples caught up in the cycle of violence by taking a fresh look at the problem.

Thompson (1989) claims that clergy should help victims determine the best theological choices yet realistically offer them a number of possible options. She goes so far as to advise victims "to shop around and get second or third opinions from religious helpers in the community" (p. 38). A few religious organizations have taken a very active role in aiding spouse abuse victims by starting a shelter or by designing and conducting training programs for shelter staff and the religious community (S. E. Martin, 1989). Church-sponsored, problem-oriented focus groups where members are free to discuss issues such as alcoholism and child-rearing problems have spurred increased dialogue on and church recognition of these problems.

Some religious leaders have perceived spouse abuse as an issue that they do not know how to handle and have shown a willingness to seek help outside of the church family. They have come to view the secular shelter movement as an ally, not an adversary. With the support of some astute clergy, battering families are seeking help and receiving appropriate referrals.

S. E. Martin (1989) studied the responses of religious organizations to spouse abuse. She surveyed clergy from 143 churches and synagogues and found that more than half of the clerics acknowledged the need to address the problem but cited problems such as victim reticence and lack of information about state law and programs for abusers as factors hampering their response. Martin concluded that not only must the clergy actively encourage abuse victims to seek help, through sermons, dissemination of information, and other programs, but also organizations dedicated to aiding abused women ought to reach out to clergy as a source of information and support.

Economic Independence

Helping battered women achieve economic independence also plays a pivotal role in avoiding victimization. Programs geared to assist battered women find employment should be sensitive to their possible lack of self-confidence, job skills, and the effects of battering on work performance. "Connections must be made between battering and feminization of poverty as outcomes of domination that extend beyond the personal realm" (Shepard & Pence, 1988, p. 60).

M. N. Wilson et al. (1989) concluded that working away from home appears to be a crucial survival strategy, possibly because it lessens the battered woman's economic, social, and emotional dependence on her husband. Gelles (1976) contends that holding down a job helped reduce a battered woman's isolation, thus giving her a different perspective on the world. We think that dependence can be conceptualized as a form of helplessness and that working can provide a woman with the social and economic reinforcement, as well as the emotional strength, to end her dependence.

Taking a broader, long-term view of criminogenic home situations, Hackler (1991) advocated economic equality for battered women as a curative measure. When women leave their violent homes, they usually take their children with them. From Hackler's view, leaving is a prevention strategy for reducing future crime, because it removes the children from a violent environment.

Police Training

Police can also interrupt the intergenerational cycle of violence. Appropriate police response can provide critical relief for battered women. Most batterers have suffered no logical consequences, because they are seldom arrested, prosecuted, or punished. Improvement of police training is an initial step toward increasing arrest rates, hence effecting consequences. Buchanan and Perry (1985) have shown that domestic abuse training improves the attitudes of police cadets. In Hamberger's (1991) opinion, training of police should include their sensitization to the research on domestic violence, in particular, that violent women are rarely "husband beaters" or "mutual combatants." Officers need to improve their investigatory work and their comprehension of the psychosocial context of abuse.

Stubbing (1990), a police trainer and advocate for battered women, has promoted additional program components. Training included hearing battered women speak of their terror and inability to get out and listening to batterers describe their "out-of-control" behavior and how an arrest started to turn their lives around. Police trainees also heard the voices of children "praying" that the police would remove the batterer. According to one of the authors (AL), inclusion of battered women and children in police and probation training creates empathy, an effective tool for reaching the hearts of those who listen.

Volunteer protectors. Private citizens can also have a positive impact on law enforcement and engender tangible evidence that the community will not tolerate violence directed at women and children. Peter Van Sant on *Street Stories* (Bradley, 1992) presented a segment titled "Someone to Watch Over Me" about a new type of community volunteer organization in Milwaukee. The group, composed of both men and women who had some personal relationship to family violence, protected battered women stalked by abusive male partners. These brave, unarmed citizens worked with the police to enforce protection orders or to restrain a violent man until police arrived on the scene. They also escorted women to court and provided as much information about legal options as possible. Although they ordinarily charged a fee, they had never rejected a call for help.

The Courts

From a feminist perspective of wife beating: "The attitudes of the public, the court, and even many helping professionals condone a certain level of abuse in the home, and support the patriarchal structure of the family which perpetuates the abuse from generation to generation" (Maertz, 1990, pp. 48-49).

When battered wives ask the court for protection, the criminal justice process often victimizes them ("California Panel Urges,"

1990). The following is an excerpt from the testimony of a battered woman given before the Maryland Special Joint Committee on Gender Bias in the Courts ("Domestic Violence in the Courts," 1989, p. 3):

> The thing that has never left my mind from that point to now is what the judge said to me. He took a few minutes and he looked at me and he said, "I don't believe anything that you're saying." The reason I don't believe it is because I don't believe that anything like this could happen to me. If I was you and someone had threatened me with a gun, there is no way that I would continue to stay with them. There is no way that I could take that kind of abuse from them. Therefore, since I would not let that happen to me, I can't believe that it happened to you.
>
> I have just never forgotten those words. . . . When I left the court-room that day, I felt very defeated, and very powerless and very hopeless, because not only had I gone through an experience which I found to be very overwhelming, very trying and almost cost me my life, but to sit up in court and make myself open up and recount all my feelings and fear and then have it thrown back in my face as being totally untrue just because this big man would not allow anyone to do this to him, placed me in a state of shock which probably hasn't left me yet.

Under the leadership of Los Angeles Superior Court Judge David M. Rothman, the gender-bias committee forwarded a number of recommendations to the court involving the handling of domestic violence cases. Courts handling these cases should have metal detectors, secure waiting areas, and parking lot escort programs to protect victims. The panel further pointed out the need for curative legislation to find better ways of maintaining court protection of domestic violence victims when emergency protective orders expire as well as exemption of domestic violence cases from mandatory mediation in child custody and visitation disputes. In addition, legislation could mandate domestic violence training for judges and attorneys.

It is essential to continue the restoration of justice through clemency for battered women convicted of murdering their abusive spouses (Osthoff, 1992) and to make expert testimony acceptable everywhere. Jurors have a tendency to judge a battered woman who kills as "not guilty by reason of insanity or diminished capacity" rather than "not guilty by reason of self-defense" (Follingstad et al.,

1989). Good testimony explains the notion of chronic self-defense and explains that the "reasonable man" standard is unreasonable for women and children. Courts (*State v. Wanrow*, 1977) have recognized the need for juries to take women's size and social conditioning into account when rendering verdicts.

The multiplicity of courtroom practices in regard to acceptance of expert testimony on the battered woman syndrome and the outcomes when testimony is allowed show how essential it is to assess critically whether the testimony performs its intended functions (Schuller & Vidmar, 1992). According to Schuller (1992), the presentation of expert testimony on the battered woman syndrome does lead juries to make interpretations more favorable to the battered woman's claim of self-defense.

Legislation

Myers, Tikosh, and Paxson's (1992) summary of the variation in state statutes underscores the patchwork quality of laws governing domestic violence. As an example, only a few states have statutes limiting mutual orders of protection. Mutual orders of protection create several complications. The batterer will probably interpret the order to mean that he will not be held accountable for his violence or that the victim is as responsible for the violence as he is. Furthermore, the police may be less likely to intervene and the victim may be less likely to seek the order.

In our opinion, if men were being assaulted by women at the same rate as women by men, legislation to correct that situation would be passed without a filibuster. "Crimes against men" would be given the status of "real crimes," and violating a protective order would be a capital offense. Fortunately, the Senate Judiciary Committee approved legislation in July 1991 to increase the criminal justice system's sanctions for crimes against women (cited in "Judiciary Committee," 1991). One aspect of the legislation is to allow victims to sue for civil damages. For example, Patti Chiles ("Woman Sues Husband," 1988) won a judgment of $1.4 million in a civil suit against her husband after a divorce. The judge awarded $500,000 of the payment for emotional distress suffered at the hands of her abuser.

Support From the Medical Field

For some battered women, emergency room staff may be the first contact they may have regarding the abuse. If the staff (nurses, aides, doctors, and social workers) respond appropriately, they may provide the catalyst that will encourage a woman to take action. Certainly, the identification of battered women is a first step. McLeer and Anwar (1989) found that, upon development of an emergency room protocol for asking how women's injuries occurred, identification of battered women rose from 5.6% of cases to 30%.

Appleton (1980) found that, of 620 women seeking care at a general hospital, 35% reported in an anonymous questionnaire that they had been struck at least once by their intimate partner. Kurz and Stark (1988) and Kurz (1990) discovered in an observation of emergency room personnel that only 11% made a positive response (recorded the incident, discussed the abuse, assessed safety, or provided helpful information). Campbell and Sheridan (1989) emphasized the need for emergency room personnel to consider any trauma to a female patient as battering until it is ruled out.

Campbell and Alford (1989) also revealed that the sexual abuse of battered women was routinely ignored, and they concluded that doctors should regularly conduct examinations to detect possible infections, vaginal or rectal bleeding, and other pain-related symptoms. Approximately 46% of the battered women in Campbell and Alford's study had been raped immediately after discharge from the hospital (usually following childbirth).

One of the four emergency rooms surveyed in the previous study had a far better record of responding than the others. In this department, a physician's assistant had developed a medical index card for recording information about battered women and had given training sessions to the nurses. She was an advocate who conceptualized her role as understanding and dealing with domestic violence.

Campbell (1986) has devised a 15-item scale to be used in the emergency room for assessing the danger of homicide. Ideally, a nurse or hospital social worker stays with a battered woman while she completes the questionnaire. This type of intervention might increase a woman's awareness of the danger she encounters daily and motivate her to seek help. In addition, Shepherd (1990) recommends integration of emergency room personnel and victim support services offered by social workers. He says, "The more victims there are who can talk and receive support, the fewer there will be who need longer and more intensive help" (p. 331).

Hamberger (1991) noted that physicians also need training on how best to assist battered women. The primary areas of training ought to include development of the following skills: (a) understanding the dynamics of domestic violence, (b) observational skills, (c) interviewing skills, (d) risk assessment, (e) safety planning, (f) follow-up, and (g) documentation. A physician can exhibit support with an empathic attitude, nonjudgmental responses, and a good referral list.

Better Diagnosis by Helping Professionals

Tilden (1989) has clarified the need for closer scrutiny of psychiatric diagnoses applied to battered women. Andrea Jacobson (cited in "Assault Experiences," 1987) discovered that the admission charts of only 9 of 100 patients in a psychiatric setting contained assault history information. A diagnosis of depression, anxiety, or paranoia may later become influential in legal proceedings such as custody hearings. A diagnosis of post-traumatic stress disorder (PTSD) more accurately reflects the consequences of living with repeated, erratic violence (Tilden, 1989), and Riggs, Kilpatrick, and Resnick (1992) noted that therapists need to recognize it in battered women.

Furthermore, counselors need to be alert to the possibility that battered woman syndrome (BWS) may not be attributable to purely psychological causes such as post-traumatic stress disorder (PTSD). Lewis (1992) proposes that traumatic brain injuries (TBIs), as well as damage caused from self-medication with drugs and alcohol, may account for a number of the neuropsychological dysfunctions. He likens the brain damage sustained by battered women as similar to that sustained by boxers. Neurologists could use a test such as the Halstead-Reitan Test Battery for diagnosis of sequelae from so-called minor TBIs, sequelae that may not be readily detectable. Poteat, Grossnickle, Cope, and Wynne (1990) have developed a screening device that, taken together with other information, should alert psychotherapists to the potential for relationship abuse. Detection of this risk factor could contribute to the overall therapeutic treatment plan.

Role of Shelters

Other issues central to the maintenance of abusive home environments are the self-perpetuating nature of family violence and the isolation in which it thrives. Battered women's programs can effect change by intervening in these processes. Sedlak (1988b) conducted a small study of 20 battered women to determine the impact of shelter intervention on their rate of return to their abusers. After 3 weeks in the shelter, the women were significantly less depressed, were more hopeful, and had higher internal locus of control scores.

In our opinion, battered women in a shelter can improve by virtue of being separated from their abusers, feeling safe, having people to talk with about their problems, and working at a practical level to solve some of these problems. Gelles (1976) states that a shelter counseling program helps end a battered woman's feelings of isolation, which in turn allows her to evaluate her own situation differently (see also Schillinger, 1988; Weingourt, 1985). Dalto (1983) maintains that battered women who had formed close relationships with other shelter residents or shelter staff were more likely to leave their abusive relationships.

Counseling

For battered women who choose to stay in the relationship either temporarily or permanently, appropriate counseling needs to be part of the package for real change to occur (Dutton, 1986). Landenburger (1989) reported that many professionals see the woman's choice as one between "staying or leaving." A battered woman, on the other hand, often experiences the conflict in the following terms: "Don't help me end the relationship, help me end the abuse."

There are those who ask: "Where's the loss?" Most battered women, however, feel great deprivation and loss when their relationships end. Walker (1984), for instance, noted that battered women who had ended a relationship were more depressed than those who were still involved. Negating that loss does not help the women. Varvaro (1991) found that assessing battered women's losses and dealing with them in a support group enabled the women to develop a new sense of self-determination and to avoid the immobilizing effects of grief. According to Jillings (1985), awareness of one's grief enables individuals to resolve it, and empowerment is central in working with battered women.

Empowerment requires a positive self-appraisal. To critique oneself as responsible for the abuse is very damaging. A battered woman who stops blaming herself will feel better and begin to see alternatives, whether or not she decides to leave. Miller and Norman's (1979) reformulated theory of learned helplessness implies that, if a woman can find a reason outside of herself for the battering (external attribution), she will leave. Painter and Dutton (1985) contend that "as long as she continues to believe that she causes the violence, and that changes in her behavior might prevent the violent behavior from occurring, she is locked into the battering relationship" (p. 373).

Some of the most important work with battered women is the remaking of their belief systems (see Malloy, 1986). Wetzel and Ross (1983) pointed out that an important focus for shelters, therapists, and battered women's support groups is helping a battered woman make that change, to stop believing that she causes or can stop the abuse. There are several ways to accomplish an attitudinal shift: (a) breaking the silence and isolation by confiding in someone else (Vaughn, 1987), (b) getting education regarding sex roles and their relationship to domestic violence and power inequality, (c) building resources outside the relationship (M. N. Wilson et al., 1989), (d) developing empathy for other battered women and compassion for herself, and (e) grieving the loss of the relationship and her idealistic beliefs (Ferraro, 1979).

One effective approach to changing beliefs is cognitive reappraisal. In a study of rape recovery, Koss and Burkhart (1989) demonstrated that it is the victim's cognitive appraisal of the events that is likely to determine her adjustment. That is, her evaluation of the event moderates her ability to cope. She must make some cognitive readjustments along the lines of defining the meaning of the rape, what caused it, and what role it plays in her life now. Several cognitive-behavioral therapies that appear to be effective with battered women are D'Zurilla's Problem-Solving Therapy (D'Zurilla, 1986) and Beck's Cognitive Therapy (A. T. Beck, Rush, Shaw, & Emery, 1979).

Appropriate counseling should address the very real restrictions that women face in the world, in their relationships, and in stereo-typical roles. At a practical level, counselors can role-play job interviewing techniques, assertion skills, parenting skills, and even basic apartment- or house-hunting approaches. Holiman and Schilit (1991) considered using Gestalt techniques and other cognitive problem-solving strategies in a group setting to help abused women restore independent decision-making skills. They found that role-playing, expressing feelings, and problem sharing assisted the women in altering their feelings of powerlessness. Cummings (1990) believes that self-defense training for women is critical. Self-defense training can tap into a woman's physical power. It also offers her a constructive physical outlet for her emotions.

Counseling itself may contravene against the isolation that develops over time when battering is occurring and represent a start in obtaining support. Frisch and MacKenzie (1991) noted that formerly abused women who had counseling were significantly more likely to leave than women who did not. M. A. Douglas (1987) contends that therapy can help a battered woman to accept personal responsibility for her safety while rejecting personal responsibility for the violence. The next step is to evaluate both the costs and the benefits of staying in the relationship and the battered woman's personal reasons for remaining. The therapist can help the client to increase her self-efficacy and behavioral competence, to constructively use her anger, and to reduce the symptoms of her anxiety.

Social support. M. A. Douglas and A. Colantuono (1987) have pinpointed the importance of social support in recovery from chronic abuse. I. M. Johnson (1988) found that 63% of battered women who had little or no support returned to their abusers. In contrast, of those who had strong support systems, only 19%

returned. One of the great assets of 12-step and other self-help programs is the abundance and continuity of support that they provide. Cohen and McKay (1984) assert that having a strong social network when coping with a trauma is physically beneficial to the traumatized person (see also Bowker & Mauer, 1986). Chang (1989) has theorized that supportive involvement with others is critical in the transformation of a battered woman into a self-saver.

"Hard love." Kathleen Ferraro (1979) discusses the issue of loving your partner and not leaving in terms of "hard love." According to this philosophy, the fastest way to help your partner is to stop protecting him so that he will have to face the consequences of his behavior. If he gets into trouble or hits bottom, perhaps he will finally seek the assistance he needs to change his behavior.

The danger of couples' counseling. Seeking the help that *he* needs does not mean that *couples'* counseling is the best intervention. Hansen, Harway, and Cervantes (1991) underscored the need for counselors, psychotherapists, psychologists, and psychiatrists to give special consideration to the dangers inherent in providing family or couples' counseling to violent families. The primary issue is safety. A battered woman may be afraid to speak out about what has happened in front of her abuser, or she may feel safe in the therapist's office, speak out, and pay for it later. A second concern is that an individual issue (e.g., control and violence) may become confused with a family issue (e.g., communication and parenting). It is critical to recognize that a battering problem belongs to the person who batters.

Family therapists can also reject the tendency to legitimize a power imbalance in the family. When exploring interpersonal power and control issues, a therapist can too readily misperceive a battered woman's attempts at adaptation as a contest over power. From this position, it is a "short walk" to succumb to the familiar victim-blaming routine. Failure to address gender issues minimizes the support battered women need and deserve (LaViolette, 1991). The rationale for using systemic approaches may be to make violence seem more manageable than it is (Bograd, 1992).

Shelter staff and therapists working in this field should recommend group or individual counseling initially as a means of reducing isolation and establishing a level of physical safety. After a level of physical safety is established, battered women, in conjunction with their counselors, decide when and if it is safe to include their partners in therapy. Geffner (1990, p. 1) has attempted to alert the professional community by proposing that "the time has come to begin to establish minimum standards and credentials for practitioners in the family abuse field."

Abuser Counseling

For women who choose to stay with their abusers, help for these men becomes imperative. Violence also has an interrelational pattern. If a battered woman leaves her abusive mate, it only means that eventually he will move on to another woman and that woman will wish that he had received psychotherapy or antisexist education. The following quotation from *Newsweek* magazine ("Guns and Dolls," 1990) sums up the need to counteract the negative aspects of misogynous male socialization.

> Men's aggressive, powerful, domineering approach, their negative social attitudes toward women, and their belief in rape myths seem to have implicated men as perpetrators, while exonerating women. Perhaps the time has finally come for a new agenda. Women, after all, are not a big problem. Our society does not suffer from burdensome amounts of empathy and altruism, or a plague of nurturance. The problem is men—or more accurately, maleness. (p. 62)

And what is maleness? Adams and Penn (1981) describe compulsive masculinity as a combination of such traits as aggressiveness, competitiveness, emotional detachment, hostility toward women, and violence. Asher (1990, p. 7) says, "With the recent findings linking testosterone with aggressive behavior, the thought of dumping estrogen in the water supply certainly did come to mind."

The effectiveness of some court-sponsored programs has brought home the importance of abuser counseling. One outcome study (Chen, Bersani, Myers, & Denton, 1990) compared 120 court-referred abusers with a comparison group of 101 nonreferred abusers. Results indicated that, within the court-referred group, abusers who attended 75% or more of the counseling sessions reduced their recidivism rate on a experimenter-weighted scale. Sommer (1990) found that, after counseling, abusive men had been violence free for one year and had changed their misogynous and proviolence attitudes in a positive direction. For these reasons, Gene Fischer (1991), assistant director of the Family Service Center of the Marine Corps in San Diego, California, recommended that the Corps establish a model program to combat domestic violence. The model should be a dual-pronged, pro-prosecution, mandatory treatment.

Nonetheless, the effectiveness of abuser counseling with or without mandatory arrest remains debatable (Gondolf & Russell, 1986; Neidig, Friedman, & Collins, 1986; Pirog-Good & Stets, 1986). Criminal justice experts advise that diversion into a counseling program and out of the system should not occur before a plea is entered. As long as the abuser is under the control of the court, he can be sentenced without resetting the trial. According to the 1990 Family Violence Project (cited in Pagelow, 1992), without this leverage, a recalcitrant participant of a diversion program may be able to leave with no record at all.

By and large, researchers and other professionals specializing within the field of domestic violence (e.g., Gondolf, 1988b; Gondolf & Russell, 1986; Hart, 1988) have developed a pervasive skepticism about the quality and permanence of behavioral changes made by abusers as a consequence of psychotherapy. First, men who batter may use enrollment in a counseling program as a ploy to pressure their partners into a reconciliation, only to drop the program as soon as their female partner has returned (Bowker, 1983; Fagan, 1989). Second, recidivism rates are high. Last, outcome studies frequently base their findings on the number of men who actually complete the program. For example, in the Alternatives to Violence program (AL's program), calls to enter a program may number from 5 to 15 per day. Of that number, less than 50% show up for their first appointment. Of this 50%, less than half attend more than two sessions; 5%-10% actually complete a yearlong program. Extrapolation of findings about abuser counseling based upon such skewed samples contradicts statistical assumptions at the very least and, at the worst, may encourage battered women to persevere in dangerous relationships.

It is important to acknowledge, however, that counselors attempting to change chronic behaviors (e.g., substance abuse) and attitudes anticipate some form of recidivism. Many batterers' programs tend to take a "resocialization" stance, emphasizing attitudinal and belief change as well as behavioral change. These programs do not refer to cure but something more like recovery (G. Billingsbeck & K. Segal-Evans, personal communication, 1989).

Stress management in caretakers. Last, but not least, there must be support for the caregivers themselves. Directors of the National Organization for Victim Assistance (NOVA) have highlighted the essence and management of stressors specific to victim caregivers (NOVA, 1992). For example, in addition to typical stressors such as a low financial remuneration, many victim caregivers suffer the additional burden of working in underfunded agencies or in agencies with "roller coaster funding." Some representative stress reactions unique to caregivers include having ambiguous successes (e.g., counseling a battered woman who finally leaves a violent husband who subsequently kills her), feeling that a professional caregiver should not accept personal care and support, and reexperiencing a private trauma by listening to a victim recount his or her trauma.

Some restorative coping strategies are value clarification (i.e., contemplation of one's philosophy), identification of individual stressors (e.g., feeling unappreciated), and planning in advance how to deal with victimization (e.g., determining if working alone is better than working in a group). Acknowledgment, education, prevention, and amelioration of caregivers' stress is a high priority. Adequate salaries would generate reinforcement for what has been seen as undervalued "woman's work." Empowerment is a goal for both battered women and their caregivers.

Research Needs

Fagan (1988) called attention to the need to assimilate family violence research into criminal justice policy. Some research, such as outcome studies on mandatory arrest, has widely modified the criminal justice system. Other critical research remains unintegrated. In particular, knowledge about the limitations of criminal sanctions to terminate serious abuse and the need to emphasize victim protection have had little influence.

Government grants offer opportunities to garner new information and provide creative new alternatives. Some of the grants specified by the Victims and Violence Research Program within the National Institute of Mental Health (Department of Health and Human Services) address the following spouse abuse-related issues: (a) four grants focused on marital violence, psychological abuse, cognitive and physiological consequences, and emotional and communication issues; (b) two grants on spouse abuse treatment programs; (c) four grants on stress, such as child-rearing stress, need for social support, persistent/chronic reactions to rape and other forms of violence, and cognitive processing of traumatic victimization; (d) two grants on physical reactions (e.g., hormonal) to PTSD; (e) three additional grants related to PTSD—redefining a diagnostic category, cognitive processes, and treatment; (f) two grants on risk factors and predictors of sexual assault and PTSD; and (g) one grant on PTSD and depression.

A Multisystem Approach

When the systems work together, safety and support are the possible outcomes. Margaret's case demonstrates a successful coupling of social services and the criminal justice system.

Case History: Margaret and Joe

Margaret was a teacher, mother of four children, and wife of an abusive husband. Joe was the stepfather of the three older children. The youngest child was a product of Joe and Margaret's 7-year marriage. Margaret and the children became increasingly wary and fearful of Joe. His vicious verbal tirades had worsened over the years, and he had added hitting, choking, and throwing things to his repertoire.

Her impetus to take action came from her oldest daughter's school counselor. Margaret's daughter had been an outstanding student, member of the Pep Squad, and popular. The counselor was concerned because the girl was withdrawing from her friends, seemed depressed, and was failing in two classes. Did Margaret know of any reason for this? Was anything unusual happening at home? Margaret could truth-fully answer, "No." What was happening at home was not unusual.

Margaret made contact with a local battered woman's hot line. She decided she didn't need shelter, and she obtained a temporary restrain-ing order with an order for Joe to leave the house. Joe left, but not for long. He would park his car across the street and leave it there. Margaret and the kids were terrified. One night she came home from work to find the kids sitting in the living room very quietly. The lights were out. Joe came out of the shadows and pinned Margaret against the wall. "Where's your protection now? . . . Who's going to help you now?" Then he left.

Joe had intimidated Margaret and the kids before. It had worked. He was always able to return. This time, Margaret stood her ground. She again made contact with the local shelter. A shelter worker ad-vised her over the phone and agreed to advocate for her when she returned to court.

The shelter worker suggested that Margaret get written statements from her neighbors about seeing Joe, because he was wise enough to leave before the police could arrive. She also suggested that Margaret take a close-up picture of the car (when he parked it across the street) with a dated newspaper on it, and then take a picture of the car and newspaper in relation to her house. These photographs and written statements would substantiate Margaret's allegations that Joe was vio-lating the restraining order.

Armed with her evidence and her advocates, Margaret appeared in court. The judge issued a bench warrant for Joe's arrest and he was picked up. Joe has stopped harassing Margaret and the kids. She made the system work.

There is no single solution to battering. Sullivan (1991) suggests that those interested in helping battered women should focus their efforts less on therapy-oriented approaches and more on commu-nity-based strategies. A holistic community response would involve networking with all of the systems that have an impact on families. Altering social factors in the larger society requires altering attitudes present in traditional helping institutions. Piet (1989) argues that the most effective method for changing batterers' behavior is to combine criminal justice sanctions with therapeutic approaches and antisexist education. She essentially advocates the use of a multisystems approach as outlined by Tolman and Saunders (1988), in which community agencies help to coordinate all of the community resources to end domestic violence. To substantiate her contention, Piet (1989) points to failures in the systems when used independently and to successes when the two systems cooperate.

Workers in the battered women's movement have been able to see the potential of religious communities to become spiritual allies in assisting battered women and their families. The coalition of shelter workers, criminal justice personnel, therapists, and religious groups could be a formidable force in the prevention of spouse abuse.

Finally, according to Pleck (1987, p. 200), "The issue of wife abuse has always had a protean character, appealing to divergent groups for different reasons. And yet the modern coalition of social casework, feminism, and law and order proved to be more successful than any preceding effort."

7

● Voices of Hope:
Survivors Speak

*Heroism is not inherent in human nature. It is not their
initial helplessness that must astonish us, but the way they
finally overcame it.*

SIMONE DE BEAUVOIR
(cited in Steiner, 1966, p. xxii)

Case History: Gloria and Miles

Gloria is 44, has her bachelor's degree, three children, and is an R.N.
Her son will be graduating from Berkeley this year, and her daughters
are in high school. Gloria is a devout Catholic, a dedicated mother, and
an open-minded, free-thinking, and compassionate human being. She
is also a formerly battered woman who has spent the last decade pull-
ing her life back together.

Gloria married her high school sweetheart who was an athlete,
popular, jealous, and abusive. She was pregnant before they got married and had to deal with the shame that that engendered in her, but
she thought that getting married would end the jealousy and violence,
and the shame. Besides, she was in love.

They both attended college. He graduated, but didn't work regularly. She took early childhood education classes and worked in day-
care centers from the time she was 22 until she was 29 years old. She

supported the family much of the time, but turned the money over to Miles. Miles had an economic principle upon which he operated: His money was his, and so was hers.

The first time that she left Miles was 4 months after they married. Miles hit her and threw her around. He accused her of "coming on" to his friends, dressing like a "slut," not looking sexy enough, and on and on. The yelling, swearing, threats, name-calling, and beatings happened in front of their children. Gloria says that she never enjoyed being hit or thought it was sexually exciting. What she did feel was shame and hope. She thought that, if she could just change a little, things would get better. "If I could have cooked better, looked better, or did what he wanted more often, things would improve. I even tried smoking marijuana with him. Hope kept me going."

"It is also important to know that I was coming from knowing nothing about battered women." The first time that she read anything was an article about Francine Hughes (*The Burning Bed*). She learned that Francine was appearing on television and asked a neighbor to watch the kids because she knew she would be upset.

One night, Miles came home angry and drunk. There was an argument and he beat her with a pop bottle. "I don't know what I saw when I looked in the mirror afterward, but it scared me. I looked at the kids, looked in the mirror, and said to myself, 'I'm going to die if I don't do something.' "

She started writing letters about what was happening to her. She wrote to the YWCA, NOW, Catholic Social Services, and the Salvation Army. While she was waiting for answers to the letters, Gloria went to Parents Anonymous (she didn't know what it was, and she wasn't abusing the kids) and to a group called Recovery (for self-esteem). The only response that she received was from the YWCA, and they asked her to come in for a "talk." Later, Gloria found out that they wanted to know if she was crazy.

The YWCA took action. They set up three seminars on domestic violence to see who would show up. Of course, Gloria was there. From the meetings, a women's group evolved and she was part of that program. The group was empowering, and Gloria also felt proud about having been an impetus for the YWCA involvement. Gloria began making plans to leave months before she actually left. She made a wheel with "things to take care of a day at a time." One of the tasks was to write letters to everyone who had helped her. She put them in the mailbox on her way out of town.

Gloria and her children trekked (by car) across the country to a shelter for battered women. It was 1977. She started college again in 1978. She put herself through school on welfare and side jobs (AVON, college work study). She also went into therapy to get over Miles and the fantasies that she still had about building a life with him. She says that it's taken her 14 years to feel that she could be interested in another man, and she is still wary.

Gloria's son James went away to college and wrote his first sociology paper on domestic violence. It gave Gloria and James a real opportunity to talk. Her children are doing well and are proud of their mother. Gloria's daughter heard a lecture in school on spouse abuse. That evening she told her mother that she had lots of courage, that she was brave to leave. Gloria's eyes were full of emotion when she related that story.

Case History: Peggy

Peggy was married for 12½ years to the "All-American Boy." He was the guy other women wanted and he was the guy who was going to protect her from her abusive stepfather. He was the father of their four children, and he was also the man who blackened her eye on their honeymoon. Peggy's husband was an alcoholic who continued to abuse her throughout their marriage. When Peggy left him, her children ranged in age from 5 to 9. After he and Peggy separated, he neither supported the children financially nor visited them. Peggy's first husband had an alcoholic father who beat his mother.

Peggy's second husband was charming, romantic, and more brutal than the first. She lived with him for 4 months and left after a beating. He followed her, promising her that things would change and that life would be wonderful once again. He was extremely romantic and affectionate. But very quickly, he began drinking and using drugs again and Peggy left him in December 1975.

Peggy was terrified of her second husband, and, although she left him, it took her 5 years to gather the courage to divorce him. Peggy had undergone corrective ear surgery because her husband had battered her to the point of deafness. Peggy had been asked if she went to therapy. She replied, "No, I went to school and that saved my life."

Peggy supported herself and her four daughters by tending bar until the gradual loss of hearing became a total loss of hearing. The only sounds she heard were the phantom noises in her head, typical for people who experience hearing loss. She used state vocational aid, which paid for tuition, classes on deafness, sign language, and an interpreter. She also received Aid for Dependent Children. She completed her first semester with a 4.0 grade point average.

Peggy had a temporary restraining order, but her husband continued to harass her from the court-ordered distance. She changed her phone number and moved several times, but he would find her and drive around the neighborhood on his motorcycle. Peggy was often terrified but continued courageously to complete her schooling and to maintain a positive attitude.

Dr. Bud Martin of American River College in Sacramento was a major influence and source of support in Peggy's life during those difficult times. His class, Personal and Social Adjustment, was the beginning of her journey to healing. She wrote her first term paper in that class. It was an inspired autobiography called "A Case for the Battered Woman." She took every course Dr. Martin taught, and he encouraged her to finish school.

In February 1979, Peggy and her family suffered a great personal tragedy. Her 17-year-old daughter passed away as the result of a brain tumor. Peggy's determined voice still breaks as she recalls her daughter's last day. Peggy's resolve to graduate and to change her life probably also gave her the focus and resolve to complete her last semester.

Peggy became an expert in sign and received her Bachelor of Arts in Special Education and Deafness in January 1980. She graduated with an overall grade point average of 3.5. Peggy volunteered for the Long Beach Police Department Emergency translation team. In 1986, she began working for Su Casa, a battered women's shelter in Southern California.

In 1988, Peggy was recruited by the daytime drama *Days of Our Lives* as a consultant and later as a cast member. Peggy has become a national spokesperson for the problems of battered women and the double jeopardy experienced by battered women who are hearing impaired. Peggy was invited to sit on a panel at a conference at Gallaudet College (the only liberal arts college in the world for the deaf). Peggy spoke on deafness and domestic violence.

Case History: Christy and Dick

Christy is a vivacious woman in her late forties. Her sons are grown and her marriage is 32 years old. She finds it hard to believe that she is still married, and she doesn't recommend her path to other women.

She is happy now and feels in control of her life. That journey started a decade ago.

Christy met Dick when she was 18, and she married him when she was 20. They met in junior college. He was from a wealthy family and had attended a private high school. Christy's financial roots were much less auspicious. Her mother was a single parent. Both Christy and Dick came from abusive families. Christy calls herself a "classic case of the fifties." She had her children in rapid succession and became emotionally and financially dependent on her husband. Although she worked as a kindergarten teacher and supported her family for a year and a half, she stayed home as soon as Dick's career was established, and she gave everybody her best and took the leftovers.

Christy maintained friendships but says all her friends were like her—upper-middle-class, at-home moms, and abused. According to Christy, "What I have seen from other women is that they thought they were never good enough, because they were always told they weren't. We all believed it had to be perfect because it would make our husbands happy, but they're never happy, and it's never perfect. I used to plan a really fancy dinner and have it ready right when he got home, so he didn't have to wait and we could have a nice evening."

It took about 6 years for his rage to control her life, and it was about 15 before she had a word, other than "uncomfortable," to describe what was happening to her. Dick was very jealous. She had saved letters from a high school boyfriend and had them locked in a little box. On one occasion, he took the hinges off the box to read the letters. Dick was a drinker and, as he drank more, he became more verbally abusive and neglectful. He didn't hit Christy. He broke things that she liked, threw the coffee table, hit the walls, and told her what to do. She didn't always take it. She got angry, but didn't push him too far.

It wasn't until she started attending small seminars on mental health issues that she began to change. She started and stopped going to Alanon two or three times. At that time, nobody had heard of a battered women's group. And at 40, she began working as a fitness instructor, and she was very successful. Dick felt threatened, but she refused to stop moving forward. She was always searching to make her life better.

Christy told me that "recognition is an inside job." She found a wonderful support group through Alanon and has been a regular for more than 2 years. She said that there were several things that really made a difference to her, and she wanted to pass that information on to other women:

Networking: "I had to meet other women to get through my own denial and know that I wasn't alone."

Assertiveness programs: "I needed to know I had a choice. I didn't have to take whatever was in front of me."

Anger: "When I found out that I had a choice, I got angry and nasty because Dick had made me think I didn't have one. When I got angrier than I was fearful, he backed off. I have eventually found a middle road. Billy Joel's record *My Life* became my song. Remember that men who abuse women have a tremendous case of Alzheimer's disease. They don't want to remember how they've hurt you. Sometimes I remind him, but I actually like him now, and he respects and likes me. I know this couldn't happen in every case."

* * *

Do Women Remain in Abusive Relationships?

Lehnen and Skogan (1981), in analyzing data from the National Crime Survey, found that most victims at the time of their interview were divorced or separated. These data imply that "many or even most women leave abusive relationships" (p. 239). Generally, studies find that about a third of battered women fleeing to shelters return to their partners. Gondolf (1988b) discovered that 24% of shelter women planned to return, with an additional 7% undecided. Snyder and Scheer (1981) found a 33% return rate. In a study of 512 abused women living in a shelter, 74.2% had separated from their mates at least once, and some had separated more than 10 times (LaBell, 1979). According to Browne (1983), the average battering relationship lasts about 6 years, the same length of time as the average marriage.

Leaving an Abuser

What does it take for women to make a decision to take action? For the women interviewed here (by AL), breaking the isolation was a critical step. A second essential factor seemed to be the introduction of a person into the battered woman's life who was supportive and encouraging and who somehow convinced her that she was important. Once she has taken little steps, she has tangible evidence that she can take bigger ones. A battered woman needs a new mirror on reality, and other human beings can hold the looking glass.

Karen's Catalysts for Change

What were Karen Connell's "catalysts for change"? During the later 1970s and early 1980s, the system was basically unresponsive to battered women, so Karen's catalysts did not come from the system. Karen's leaving was influenced by several factors. She saw her son Ward changing from a decent, fairly happy little boy into a person who screamed and swore at her, a person like her husband. A friend gave Karen a shelter hot line number. Finally, on the day she made up her mind to leave, her husband Michael raped her.

For the last 3 years of her marriage, Michael had not worked. He stayed home and virtually held her hostage. Her time and actions were monitored and Michael placed a tap on the phone. Her "free" day was the morning she worked at Ward's co-op nursery. Karen planned her escape with a shelter advocate. On the day she worked at the co-op, she took Ward and went to the shelter. For the first time in years, she and Ward were safe. They never lived with Michael again.

Karen Revisited

We started our book with Karen Connell and it seems appropriate to end with an update. Karen's surgery saved her life and her voice. Although her vocal cords were cut, she has been miraculously able to tell her story. Karen's whispering voice has screamed the plight of battered women to millions of people through radio and television interviews and speaking engagements. She served on the staff of the Sojourn shelter for battered women in Santa Monica, California, and worked as a victim advocate for the Los Angeles City Attorneys' Domestic Violence Unit. Karen is currently self-employed as an accountant and financial planner. Ward continues to struggle with the abuse that he witnessed and directly experienced. In 1986, Karen received the Governor's Award for her work with survivors of spouse abuse.

General Learning Information

Understanding Divergence in Research Findings

In reading research results, one needs to bear in mind that a number of variables influence the findings. For example, the nature of the sample, the size of the sample, and the specific questions asked all determine the final outcome. Because investigators are prone to use different questionnaires and to focus on particular problems, their results are likely to differ. Sometimes, apparently divergent results may not vary as much as a superficial reading leads one to believe.

Learning Research

A few basic assumptions govern learning research: (a) A similarity exists between human behavior and animal behavior. (b) The results of laboratory experiments with animals using reinforcement and punishment can be extrapolated to describe human behavior. (c) It is necessary to postulate the effects of some nonobservable factors in humans, such as religious attitudes or beliefs in the traditional family, just as one postulates the existence of hunger as a motivation in food-deprived animals. Even when it is impossible to scientifically observe internal factors (e.g., sexist attitudes), it may be possible to verify them through empirically based research such as questionnaires. Furthermore, Follingstad et al. (1992)

139

asserted that "literature from the laboratory study of human aggression is particularly relevant for considering what happens in battering relationships" (p. 110).

This book incorporates several important experiments conducted on dogs and rats that have provided outcomes that seem to have significant applications for understanding why battered women may learn to stay with abusive husbands. Early researchers conducted a number of animal studies before enactment of newer guidelines governing animal research.

I. Classical Conditioning: Pavlov and His Dog

It is possible to condition emotional reactions. Laboratory experiments have demonstrated that human beings can learn to fear what they previously felt neutral about, liked, or even loved. The procedure used is called "classical conditioning." Classical conditioning is simply pairing two stimuli to produce a response such as in the famous case of Pavlov and his dog. Pavlov and his dog are the Jeff and Lassie of psychology. Pavlov sounded a tone, placed meat powder on the tongue of his hungry pet, and the dog salivated. After several pairings of the tone and the meat powder, the animal salivated after hearing the tone, before the meat powder arrived. That is, the dog salivated to the presentation of the tone by itself.

With classical conditioning, a reward (e.g., food) or aversive event (e.g., shock) occurs regardless of the subject's response. For example, Pavlov put the food in the dog's mouth whether or not the dog salivated. Pavlov, not the dog, controlled the presentation of the food.

II. Extinction and Spontaneous Recovery

Extinction refers to the decrease in responses when no reinforcement follows the designated response. Research has shown that, when learning takes place under intermittent reinforcement schedules (occasional rewards), it takes animals longer to stop responding (resistance to extinction).

Pavlov also noted an interesting side effect of his learning experiments. If he continued to sound the tone, but failed to present the food, the salivation diminished slowly; it was extinguished. If he waited a few days to present the tone (without the food) to the dog again, the dog once again salivated (spontaneous recovery). This pattern went on for days and did not seem to extinguish completely. The dog had to learn that the tone was no longer significant and did not mean food was on the way.

III. Operant Conditioning: Skinner and His Rat

Operant conditioning refers to a basic form of learning primarily covering voluntary behaviors such as driving a car or swimming. In contrast to classical, or Pavlovian, conditioning, operant conditioning requires the individual to earn a reward or to work to eliminate a painful circumstance. B. F. Skinner, the famous behaviorist, developed the operant paradigm. In Skinner's (1938) experiments, behavior is shaped by rewarding (reinforcing) responses in a step-by-step manner as the animal approximates (successive approximation) the desired behavior. Skinner's classic work involved putting a rat in a box containing a bar. Skinner has retained his immortality with psychology students not just for his research but because the box was given his name, the Skinner box.

In a Skinner box, the animal receives rewards (food pellets) as he slowly learns the desired behavior, the bar press. As the rat stands on his hind legs near the bar, a food pellet arrives in the food dish. When the rat touches the bar, another food pellet arrives and so on until the rat presses the bar and receives food regularly. This process is called "shaping." The animal learns that the reward is dependent upon his own behavior, that he has control over the outcome of his behavior. The consequences of behavior (getting food or avoiding pain) control the animal's rate of lever pressing.

1A. Reinforcement Definitions

Reinforcers: Reinforcers are events that increase responding.[1]

> *Positive reinforcer:* A positive reinforcer is any event that when added to a situation increases the probability that an organism will make a behavioral response.
>
> > *Animal Examples*
> >
> > > *Primary (unlearned) reinforcers*: food and water
> > > *Secondary (learned) reinforcers:* sound of a bell signifying food is coming (Secondary reinforcers have previously been paired with primary reinforcers.)
> >
> > *Human Examples*
> >
> > > *Primary (unlearned) reinforcers:* food and water
> > > *Secondary (learned) reinforcers:* smile, money, praise, approval, sexual contact, and affection
>
> *Negative reinforcer:* A negative reinforcer is any event that when taken away increases a behavioral response.
>
> > *Animal Examples*
> >
> > > *Primary (unlearned) negative reinforcer:* shock

Secondary (learned) negative reinforcer: sound of a bell signifying that a shock is coming

Human Examples

Primary (unlearned) negative reinforcer: shock

Secondary (learned) negative reinforcer: frown, criticism, name-calling

1B. Additional Facts About Reinforcement

1. Reinforcers greatly enhance learning, but learning can take place without reinforcement.
2. In general, the larger the reinforcer, the greater (or faster) the learning.
3. When reinforcement is not given after a response, the number of responses declines (extinction occurs).
4. Contingent (earned, dependent, or related) reinforcement produces much better learning than noncontingent reinforcement. A rat that must press the lever to earn food will learn to lever press far better than a rat who is given the food without having to lever press.
5. Delaying the presentation of the reinforcer retards learning.
6. Presenting the reinforcement on every trial in classical conditioning speeds up learning, while intermittent reinforcement (IR schedule) retards learning.
7. Presenting the reinforcement intermittently in operant conditioning will still induce learning, but the schedule of reinforcers (IR) will help maintain the behavior longer than if every trial is rewarded.
8. If motivation (e.g., hunger) is increased, learning occurs more rapidly.
9. Enjoyable activities (e.g., watching TV) can act as reinforcers as much as can stimuli such as food and water.
10. Behavior learned with intermittent reinforcement is more difficult to extinguish than behavior learned with reinforcement every time.

1C. Punishment Definitions

Punishers: Punishers are events that decrease responding.

Positive punisher: A positive punisher is any event that when added to a situation decreases a behavioral response.

Animal Examples

Primary (unlearned) positive punisher: bar slap–shock for pressing a bar to obtain food

Secondary (unlearned) positive punisher: a tone signifying bar slap will occur

Human Examples

Primary (unlearned) positive punisher: spanking or beating

Secondary (learned) positive punisher: pouting, disapproval, swearing

Negative punisher: A negative punisher is any event that when taken away decreases a behavioral response.

Animal Examples

Primary (unlearned) negative punisher: Water is removed when the animal eats.

Secondary (learned) negative punisher: Bell signaling food is turned off when the animal presses the bar for food.

Human Examples

Primary (unlearned) negative punisher: dessert taken away after a meal

Secondary (learned) negative punisher: deprivation of TV privilege; time-out (removal from others)

1D. Additional Facts About Punishment

1. Punishment is not the opposite of reinforcement. A noxious event like a shock does not always decrease responding (Skinner, 1938). "Punishment typically produces a change in behavior much more rapidly than other forms of instrumental conditioning, such as positive reinforcement or avoidance" (Domjan & Burkhard, 1989, p. 259).

2. The less intense and briefer the duration of the punishment, the less the suppression (Karsh, 1962). Mildly punished behaviors will recover (Appel, 1963).

3. Severity of punishment = duration × intensity.

4. If the first punishment is severe, but successive punishments are milder, the punished behavior will be inhibited (Sandler et al., 1966).

5. If the first punishment is mild, and successive punishments become more severe, behavioral suppression will usually not occur (Sandler et al., 1966). An animal continues to adjust and respond for the reward that is also present in the situation.

6. If punishment is discontinued, recovery may occur (Catania, 1984).

7. If the punishment is contingent upon the animal's behavior, the animal will learn to eliminate the responses (Camp, Raymond, & Church, 1967).

8. If the punishment is not contingent upon the organism's response, the organism will probably not learn to inhibit the undesirable responses (Hunt & Brady, 1955).

9. Punishment is more effective if given immediately after the undesirable behavior. If the punishment is delayed, the animal probably will not learn to suppress the undesirable behavior (Kamin, 1959).

10. The more consistent the punishment, the greater the decrement in the number of responses. Intermittent punishment does not maintain suppression of the punished behavior (Azrin et al., 1963). (Note that, in contrast, intermittent reinforcement schedules are very effective.)

11. If alternative, rewarded responses are available, the animal will inhibit the punished behavior more readily (Herman & Azrin, 1964).

12. A behavior that is both reinforced and punished is likely to recur (Azrin & Holz, 1966). If an animal both receives a mild shock and a pellet of food for a response, he will continue responding.

13. If a cue such as a light is used to signal forthcoming punishment, future presentations of the light will reduce behavior (Dinsmoor, 1952).

14. When punishment of a certain response is used as a discriminative stimulus (a signal) that a reinforcer will follow, the punished behavior will not be inhibited but probably will be increased (Azrin & Holz, 1961).

15. Higher levels of shock generally lead to more aggression by the punished organism toward objects or other people (Azrin, 1970; Ulrich et al., 1964) or toward oneself (Logan & Wallace, 1981).

16. Inescapable shock leads to a general inhibition of responding, which implies that the organism has developed a conditioned emotional response (CER) of "fear" (Estes & Skinner, 1941).

17. Inescapable punishment works proactively to prevent responding (Klee, 1944) and to reduce future problem solving. Dogs exposed to inescapable shock suffered from "learned helplessness" (S. F. Maier, Seligman, & Solomon, 1969).

18. Exposure to prior shock enhances the effects of mild punishment but decreases the effects of intense punishment (Church, 1969).

Note

1. These terms, examples, and definitions appear in Willet and Barnett (1987).

APPENDIX B

Specific Learning Experiments

1. The Use of Both Punishment and Reinforcement in Humans

Ayllon and Azrin (1966) conditioned schizophrenics to respond to a punishment (noxious noise) coupled with reinforcement (token) and not to respond to a no-punishment, no-reinforcement condition. When the time between reinforcements lengthened, schizophrenics continued to select a punished response even without the accompanying reinforcement.

2. Conflict in Animals

J. S. Brown (1948) and N. E. Miller (1959) used rats to demonstrate several different types of conflict (approach-approach, approach-avoidance, avoidance-avoidance, and double approach-avoidance). For example, one goal consists of water and shock while the other consists of food and shock. An animal faced with such a dilemma often runs halfway toward one of the goals and then retreats. Momentarily, he runs halfway toward the other goal and then returns. Presumably, his approach behavior represents his desire for the positive goal (food or water), while his avoidance behavior reflects his fear of the shock. The animal's degree of vacillation suggests his level of conflict or ambivalence.

146

3. Punishment as a Discriminative Cue for Reinforcement

When a cue (e.g., a tone) serves as a signal for forthcoming punishment, that same cue will reduce future behavior (Dinsmoor, 1952). Experiments by Holz and Azrin (1961) using pigeons indicated that, if punishment were necessary to obtain a reward, the animal would accept the punishment. Pigeons learned to respond on a (variable interval) to punishment (shock) coupled with reinforcement (food) and not to respond to punishment alone (extinction). Because getting food depended upon getting shocked, the pigeons increased their pecking even though they had to endure shocks. Punishment became a discriminative stimulus (cue) for a reward (signaled forthcoming food reinforcement).

4. Punishment-Facilitated Attachment

Rosenblum and Harlow (1963) detected significant variations between baby monkeys in attachment behavior with a monkey surrogate mother who differed in terms of her aversiveness. The babies given an opportunity to cling to a terry cloth "mother" in a situation involving the delivery of air blasts (punishment) spent more time with her than did a comparison group of monkeys given access to a "mother" without the punishment. These findings suggest that punishment enhances the baby's responsiveness to the mother.

5. Extinction Failure: Responses Fixated Through Punishment

When rats receive punishment that is not sufficient to suppress their behavior, their behavior may become almost impossible to extinguish (Azrin et al., 1963). In a human example, a child who is inconsistently punished for throwing tantrums may continue throwing the tantrums for a very long time even when the parents walk away (remove the reinforcement of attention). In other words, if a parent reacts to a child's tantrum by giving him or her attention such as by saying, "Don't cry. We are going to the park later. Come on, now, this is not worth crying about, and so forth," the attention serves as a reward for throwing the tantrum.

6. The Gradual Buildup of Punishment

Using an increasing level of shock to punish a rat for pressing a lever does not lead to suppression of lever pressing. Instead, the rat learns to adjust to the ever-increasing level of shock; he continues bar pressing (Sandler et al., 1966).

7. Matching Behavior

The Matching Law states that the relative frequency of responding on an alternative (e.g., choice A—highly rewarded—or B—less rewarded) matches the relative frequency of reinforcement for responses on that alternative. Interpreted, this statement implies that an animal will work harder on one alternative if it receives a higher reward (e.g., A) than he will for another alternative of lesser reward (e.g., B). That is, the animal matches his responses to the frequency (amount, value) of a reward. It may be possible to apply the matching behavior seen in animal experiments on making choices to the escalation of abuse in marital violence (Herrnstein, 1970). (In learning theory, noxious events such as electrical shocks for animals or physical violence for humans can be used either as punishers—to decrease behavior—or as negative reinforcers—to increase behavior through avoidance.) It may be possible to apply the idea of matching to the escalation of abuse in battering. First, assume that various forms of abuse, such as a "threats" or "swearing," function as negative reinforcers. Because negative reinforcers increase the probability of future responses, one abusive behavior (e.g., "swearing") might lead to responsive "threats" by the partner (a matching response), leading to "shoving" by the first partner (matching), and so forth. Each abuse (negative reinforcer) serves to increase the other partner's abusive response (which serves as a negative reinforcer), so that, overall, the abuse escalates.

8. Stress

Selye (1946) was the first to offer a relatively complete picture of the devastating effects of response-based stress on rats. Different stressors such as infection and heat caused a nonspecific response of the body that went through three stages: (a) alarm (the body mobilizes its defenses), pushing energy use to the limit; (b) resistance (the body returns to normal and copes with the stressor); and (c) exhaustion (the body can no longer adapt to the stressor; symptoms occur; death may follow). Human bodies may well go through similar stages when the stressor is emotional. If so, the experiments explain psychosomatic illnesses: real, physical illnesses whose origin lies in emotional stress.

9. Predictable and Unpredictable Shock

Abbot et al. (1984) gave rats a choice between a signaled and an unsignaled shock. The animals could not avoid the shock; they could only control their own ability to predict it. If the rat bar pressed at the beginning of a sequence of trials, he earned a warning tone before every shock. If he did not bar press at the beginning, he received no warning signal. All of the rats showed a marked preference for the signaled shock as reflected in their rapid learning of the bar press. The construct of control might be implied here.

10. Signaled Avoidance: Use of a Warning Signal

Bolles, Stokes, and Younger (1966) performed an experiment designed to examine escape and avoidance. In avoidance, rats learned to perform a task such as running to the other ("safe") side of a box at the sound of a tone (a learned signal) that signified that a shock was imminent. In escape, the animals could get away only after receiving the shock. They could not prevent it by performing a learned task (e.g., moving to the other side of a box).

11. Nonsignaled Avoidance: Use of Temporal Cues to Know When to Make an Avoidance Response

Work with laboratory animals in nonsignaled avoidance experiments also appears to be pertinent to the issue of control raised in battering relationships. In a series of studies, Sidman (1953) placed rats in precarious situations that required them to respond (almost continuously at certain points during the experiment) to avoid the pain of being shocked. In these experiments, there was no handy signal such as a tone to warn the animal of the forthcoming shock. To a certain extent, the rat had to estimate when a response was necessary by paying attention to time (temporal cues). A clock was set to deliver shocks to an animal provided it made no response. If the animal made an appropriate response (such as pressing a bar), the clock was reset, allowing the animal to rest before the clock was reactivated to deliver another shock. In other words, the rat could adjust his behavior to avoid or minimize the shock. Actually, Sidman used two clocks in his experiment. The Shock-Shock (S-S) clock's timer was set to control the interval between shocks (e.g., 2 seconds) if the animal made no response (e.g., pressing a lever). In other words, an animal who did nothing or did the *wrong* thing would receive a shock every 2 seconds ad infinitum until a power failure brought temporary relief. The other clock was called the Response-Shock (R-S) clock. This clock controlled the elapsed time between a response and delivery of a shock. To activate this clock, the animal had to make the appropriate response. If the R-S clock was set for 4-second intervals, the rat could "relax" for 4 seconds before responding again (pressing the lever). This behavior prevented the shock and reset the clock for another 4-second safe period. If the animal did not respond appropriately, the 2-second S-S clock took over again, and the animal was shocked every 2 seconds. Although there was no tangible cue that a shock was coming, no loud noise, light, or other event (conditioned stimulus) to warn the rats that shock was "just around the corner," they apparently learned to avoid shocks by attending to temporal cues, that is, to anticipate and to respond at specific time intervals. This procedure controlled by two clocks is one of the most demanding schedules ever devised by research psychologists. It required constant vigilance and rapid response. It also took a long time to learn. The animals virtually lived "on the edge." For animals tested over several days, fatigue made it impossible for them to avoid all shocks and, in fact, to attend to the time interval cues. The rats could learn to avoid shock, even most shocks, but the rats were never able to avoid *all shocks*.

12. A Warning Signal Generates Fear

J. S. Brown and A. Jacobs (1949) exposed rats to different fear experiences. The first group of rats received a warning signal that ended with a shock. The second group received the same "warning" signal, but no shock. Later, both groups experienced the opportunity to turn off the warning signal by crossing from one side of a shuttle box to the other. The light remained on until the rats crossed over. The results indicated that the first group—the group that received the warning signal followed by the shock— learned to make the shuttle response significantly faster than the second group. The researchers interpreted these findings as signifying that the first group learned the shuttle response to reduce the fear generated by the warning signal. The termination of fear is reinforcing.

13. Motivation Following Frustration by Nonreward

Amsel and Rousel (1972) allowed rats to run in a straight runway first to one goal box for food and then onward in the alley to a second goal box for additional food. After learning this procedure, the researchers frustrated the animals by not providing them with any food in the first goal box. When this occurred, the frustrated rats ran even faster than they had originally to the second goal box. They also ran faster than a control groups of rats that continued to receive the food reward in the first goal box. Apparently, frustration produced by the absence of anticipated reward in the first goal box intensified the rats' motivation to reach the second goal box.

14. Frustration and Its Consequences

Animals caught in an approach-avoidance situation develop "frustration" (N. R. F. Maier, 1949). One outcome of their frustration is stereotyped responses. For example, N. R. F. Maier, N. M. Glazer, and J. B. Klee (1940) trained rats to jump from a jumping stand into a slightly closed door. Food was behind the door as a reinforcer for jumping to the correct color (e.g., white rather than black). Later, after the jumping was well established, the problem was made insolvable. For a number of trials, the animals received reinforcement on half of their jumps to the formerly correct color (i.e., white) and on half of their jumps to the formerly incorrect color (i.e., black). After this frustration training, the animals exhibited a number of unusual behaviors: (a) rigid responses, for example, only jumping to the "right"; (b) apathy, refusal to jump at all; (c) peculiar postures that seemed catatonic; and (d) attempts to get out of the test situation altogether by jumping over the test apparatus into the laboratory area. One of the most fascinating occurrences was that the animals "walked" to the correct door if the experimenter placed a little bridge between the jumping stand and the door. If the bridge were removed and the door opened so that the animals could actually see the food, they still would not jump to obtain it. Their behavior was inflexible and self-defeating. The rats did not perform the correct response even when they knew what it was. This compulsive behavior is labeled "fixated."

15. Learned Helplessness in Dogs

Researchers using dogs for testing subjected one of three groups of dogs to inescapable shock trials (S. F. Maier & Seligman, 1976). A second group could escape, and a third comparison group received no shocks at all. Later, the experimenters tried to teach the dogs a new task, how to jump over a barrier to avoid a shock. The dogs given inescapable shocks were almost unable to learn the new task. The other two groups of dogs learned to avoid shocks in the new task quickly. The shocked dogs had apparently learned that "nothing I do makes a difference" (learned helplessness).

● References

Abbot, B. B., Schoen, L. S., & Badia, P. (1984). Predictable and unpredictable shock: Behavioral measures of aversion and physiological measures of stress. *Psychological Bulletin, 96,* 45-71.

Abramson, L. Y. (1977). *Universal versus personal helplessness: A experimental test of the reformulated theory of learned helplessness and depression.* Unpublished doctoral dissertation, University of Pennsylvania.

Abramson, L. Y., Garber, J., & Seligman, M. E. P. (1978). Learned helplessness in humans: Critique and reformulation. *Journal of Abnormal Psychology, 87,* 49-74.

Abusive relationships and Stockholm Syndrome. (1991, September 23). *Behavior Today, 22*(39), 6-7.

Adams, D. (1984, August). *Stages of anti-sexist awareness and change for men who batter.* Paper presented at the annual meeting of the American Psychological Association, Toronto.

Adams, D. (1986, August). *Counseling men who batter: A profeminist analysis of five treatment models.* Paper presented at the annual meeting of the American Psychological Association, Washington, DC.

Adams, D., & McCormick, A. J. (1982). Men unlearning violence: A group approach based on the collective model. In M. Roy (Ed.), *The abusive partner: An analysis of domestic battering* (pp. 170-197). New York: Van Nostrand Reinhold.

Adams, D., & Penn, I. (1981, April). *Men in groups: The socialization and resocialization of men who batter.* Paper presented at the annual meeting of the American Orthopsychiatric Association.

Adler, A. (1927). *Practice and theory of individual psychology.* New York: Harcourt, Brace & World.

Adler, T. (1990, May). PTSD linked to stress rather than character. *APA Monitor, 21*(5), 12.

Adler, T. (1991). Abuse within families emerging from the closet. *APA Monitor, 22*(12), 16.

Aguirre, B. E. (1985). Why do they return? Abused wives in shelters. *Social Work, 30,* 350-354.

Alsdurf, J. M. (1985). Wife abuse and the church: The response of pastors. *Response, 8*(1), 9-11.

Alternatives to incarceration. (1992, Spring). *Taking Steps, 5*(2), 1.

American Psychiatric Association. (1980). *Diagnostic and statistical manual of mental disorders* (3rd ed.) [DSM III]. Washington, DC: Author.

Amick-McMullen, A., Kilpatrick, D. G., Veronen, L. J., & Smith, S. (1989). Family survivors of homicide victims: Theoretical perspective and an exploratory study. *Journal of Traumatic Stress, 2,* 21-35.

Amsel, A., & Rousel, J. (1972). Behavioral habituation, counterconditioning, and a general theory of persistence. In A. H. Black & W. F. Prokasy (Eds.), *Classical conditioning II: Current research and theory* (pp. 409-426). New York: Appleton-Century-Crofts.

Andelin, H. B. (1963). *Fascinating womanhood.* New York: Bantam (Pacific Press ed.).

Andrews, B., & Brewin, C. R. (1990). Attributions of blame for marital violence: A study of antecedents and consequences. *Journal of Marriage and the Family, 52,* 757-767.

Appel, J. B. (1963). Punishment and shock intensity. *Science, 141,* 528-529.

Appleton, W. (1980). The battered wife syndrome. *Annals of Emergency Medicine, 9,* 84-91.

Arendell, T. J. (1987). Women and the economics of divorce in the contemporary United States. *Signs: Journal of Women in Culture and Society, 13,* 121-135.

Asher, S. J. (1990, August). *Primary, secondary, and tertiary prevention of violence against women.* Paper presented at the annual meeting of the American Psychological Association, Boston.

Assault experiences not always elicited during routine assessment. (1987, April 13). *Behavior Today, 18*(17), 6-7.

Astin, M. C., Lawrence, K. J., Pincus, G., & Foy, D. W. (1990, October). *Moderator variables of post-traumatic stress disorder among battered women.* Paper presented at the Society for Traumatic Stress Studies, New Orleans.

Astin, M. C., Ogland-Hand, S. M., Coleman, E. M., & Foy, D. W. (1991, August). *PTSD in battered women: Comparisons with maritally distressed controls.* Paper presented at the annual meeting of the American Psychological Association, San Francisco.

Atkinson, R. L., Atkinson, R. C., Smith, E. E., & Bem, D. J. (1990). *Introduction to psychology* (10th ed.). New York: Harcourt Brace Jovanovich.

Avni, N. (1991a). Battered wives: Characteristics of their courtship days. *Journal of Interpersonal Violence, 6,* 232-239.

Avni, N. (1991b). Battered wives: The home as a total institution. *Violence and Victims, 6,* 137-149.

Ayllon, T., & Azrin, N. H. (1966). Punishment as a discriminative stimulus and conditioned reinforcer with humans. *Journal of the Experimental Analysis of Behavior, 9,* 411-419.

Azrin, N. H. (1970). Punishment of elicited aggression. *Journal of Experimental Analysis of Behavior, 14,* 7-10.

Azrin, N. H., & Holz, W. C. (1961). Punishment during fixed-interval reinforcement. *Journal of Experimental Analysis of Behavior, 4*, 343-347.

Azrin, N. H., & Holz, W. C. (1966). Punishment. In W. R. Honig (Ed.), *Operant behavior: Areas of research and application* (pp. 380-447). New York: Appleton-Century-Crofts.

Azrin, N. H., Holz, W. C., & Hake, D. F. (1963). Fixed-ratio punishment. *Journal of Experimental Analysis of Behavior, 6*, 141-148.

Back, S. M., Post, R. D., & D'Arcy, G. (1982). A study of battered women in a psychiatric setting. *Women & Therapy, 1*(2), 13-26.

Balos, B., & Trotzky, K. (1988). Enforcement of domestic abuse act in Minnesota: A preliminary study. *Law and Inequality, 6*, 83-107.

Bandura, A. (1971). *Social learning theory.* Morristown, NJ: General Learning.

Bard, M., & Zacker, J. (1974). Assaultiveness and alcohol use in family disputes. *Criminology, 12*, 281-292.

Barnard, G. W., Vera, H., Vera, M., & Newman, G. (1982). Till death do us part: A study of spouse murder. *Bulletin of the American Academy of Psychiatry and Law, 10*(4), 271-280.

Barnett, O. W. (1990). *Forms and frequencies of abuse.* Unpublished manuscript, Pepperdine University, Malibu, CA.

Barnett, O. W., & Fagan, R. W. (1993). Alcohol use in male spouse abusers and their female partners. *Journal of Family Violence, 8*, 1-25.

Barnett, O. W., & Hamberger, L. K. (1992). The assessment of maritally violent men on the California Psychological Inventory. *Violence and Victims, 7*, 15-28.

Barnett, O. W., Haney-Martindale, D. J., Modzelewski, C. A., & Sheltra, E. M. (1991, April). *Reasons why battered women feel self-blame.* Paper presented at the annual meeting of the Western Psychological Association, San Francisco.

Barnett, O. W., Keyson, M., & Thelen, R. E. (1992, August). *Battered women's responsive violence.* Paper presented at the annual meeting of the American Psychological Association, Washington, DC.

Barnett, O. W., & Lopez-Real, D. I. (1985, November). *Women's reactions to battering and why they stay.* Paper presented at the annual meeting of the American Society of Criminology, San Diego, CA.

Barnett, O. W., Lopez-Real, D. I., Carter, M., & Hedayat, Z. Z. (1985, April). *Qualitative and quantitative aspects of battering.* Paper presented at the meeting of the Academy of Criminal Justice Sciences, Las Vegas, NV.

Barnett, O. W., & Thelen, R. E. (1992). *Gender differences in forms, outcomes, and motivations for marital abuse.* Manuscript submitted for publication.

Barnett, O. W., & Wilshire, T. W. (1987, July). *Forms and frequencies of wife abuse.* Paper presented at the Third National Conference of Domestic Violence Researchers, Durham, NH.

The battered woman: Breaking the cycle of abuse. (1989, June 15). *Emergency Medicine, 15*, 104-115.

Baumeister, R. F., Stillwell, A., & Wotman, S. R. (1990). Victim and perpetrator accounts of interpersonal conflict: Autobiographical narratives about anger. *Journal of Personality and Social Psychology, 59*, 994-1005.

Bauserman, S. K., & Arias, I. (1990, November). *Application of an investment model of commitment to spouse abuse.* Paper presented at the meeting of the Association for Advancement of Behavior Therapy, San Francisco.

Beck, A. T., Rush, A. J., Shaw, B. F., & Emery, G. (1979). *Cognitive therapy of depression.* New York: Guilford.

Beck, M., Springer, K., & Foote, D. (1992, April). Sex and psychotherapy. *Newsweek,* pp. 53-57.

Belle, D., Longfellow, C., Makosky, V., Saunders, E., & Zelkowitz, P. (1981). *The impact of changing resources on health policy.* Kansas City, KS: American Nurses' Association.

Berger, P. J., & Berger, B. (1979). Becoming a member of society. In P. I. Rose (Ed.), *Socialization and the life cycle* (pp. 4-20). New York: St. Martin's.

Bergman, B., Larsson, G., Brismar, B., & Klang, M. (1988). Aetiological and precipitating factors in wife battering. *Acta Psychiatric Scandinavia, 77,* 338-345.

Berk, R. A., Berk, S. F., Loseke, D. R., & Rauma, D. (1983). Mutual combat and other family violence myths. In D. Finkelhor, R. J. Gelles, G. T. Hotaling, & M. A. Straus (Eds.), *The dark side of families* (pp. 197-212). Beverly Hills, CA: Sage.

Berk, S. F., & Loseke, D. R. (1981). "Handling" family violence: Situational determinants of police arrest in domestic disturbances. *Law and Society Review, 15,* 318-345.

Berkowitz, L., & LePage, A. (1967). Weapons as aggression-eliciting stimuli. *Journal of Personality and Social Psychology, 7,* 202-207.

Bill on violence against women a priority for Biden this year. (1991, February 1). *Criminal Justice Newsletter, 22*(4), 7.

Black, D. (1980). *The manners and customs of the police.* New York: Academic Press.

Blackman, J. (1988, August). *Exploring the impacts of poverty on battered women who kill their abusers.* Paper presented at the annual meeting of the American Psychological Association, Atlanta, GA.

Blau, F. D. (1984). Occupational segregation and labor market discrimination. In B. Reskin (Ed.), *Sex segregation in the workplace: Trends, explanations, remedies* (pp. 117-143). Washington, DC: National Academy Press.

Bograd, M. (1990). Why we need gender to understand human violence. *Journal of Interpersonal Violence, 5,* 132-135.

Bograd, M. (1992). Values in conflict: Challenges to family therapists' thinking. *Journal of Marital and Family Therapy, 18,* 245-256.

Bolles, R. C., Stokes, L. W., & Younger, M. S. (1966). Does CS termination reinforce avoidance behavior? *Journal of Comparative and Physiological Psychology, 62,* 201-207.

Bower, B. (1992). Prior abuse stokes combat reactions. *Science News, 141,* 332.

Bowker, L. H. (1982). Battered women and the clergy: An evaluation. *Journal of Pastoral Care, 36,* 226-234.

Bowker, L. H. (1983). *Beating wife beating.* Lexington, MA: Lexington.

Bowker, L. H. (1984). Battered wives and the police: A national study of usage and effectiveness. *Police Studies, 7,* 84-93.

Bowker, L. H., & Mauer, L. (1986). The effectiveness of counseling services utilized by battered women. *Women and Therapy, 5,* 65-82.

Bradley, E. (1992, May 28). Someone to watch over me. *Street Stories* (CBS).

Bradshaw, J. (1988). *Bradshaw: On the family.* Deerfield Beach, FL: Health Communications, Inc.

Breines, G., & Gordon, L. (1983). The new scholarship on family violence. *Signs: Journal of Women in Culture and Society, 8,* 490-531.

Briere, J. (1987). Predicting self-reported likelihood of battering: Attitudes and childhood experiences. *Journal of Research in Personality, 21,* 61-69.

Broverman, I. K., Vogel, S. R., Broverman, D. M., Clarkson, F. E., & Rosenkrantz, P. S. (1972). Sex-role stereotypes: A current appraisal. *Journal of Social Issues, 28,* 59-78.

Brown, G., Bhrolchain, M., & Harris, T. (1975). Social class and psychiatric disturbance among women in an urban population. *Sociology, 9,* 225-254.

Brown, J. S. (1948). Gradients of approach and avoidance responses and their relation to motivation. *Journal of Comparative and Physiological Psychology, 41,* 450-465.

Brown, J. S., & Jacobs, A. (1949). The role of fear in the motivation and acquisition of responses. *Journal of Experimental Psychology, 39,* 747-759.

Browne, A. (1983). *Self-defensive homicides by battered women: Relationships at risk.* Paper presented at the meeting of the American Psychology-Law Society, Chicago.

Browne, A. (1984, August). *Assault and homicide at home: When battered women kill.* Paper presented at the Second Conference for Family Violence Researchers, Durham, NH.

Browne, A. (1987). *When battered women kill.* New York: Free Press.

Browne, A. (1990, December 11). *Assaults between intimate partners in the United States: Incidence, prevalence, and proportional risk for women and men.* Testimony before the U.S. Senate, Committee on the Judiciary, Washington, DC.

Browning, J., & Dutton, D. (1986). Assessment of wife assault with the Conflict Tactics Scale: Using couple data to quantify the differential reporting effect. *Journal of Marriage and the Family, 48,* 375-379.

Brownmiller, S. (1976). *Against our will: Men, women, and rape.* New York: Bantam.

Brush, L. D. (1990). Violent acts and injurious outcomes in married couples: Methodological issues in the National Survey of Families and Households. *Gender & Society, 4,* 56-67.

Buchanan, D. C., & Perry, P. A. (1985). Attitudes of police recruits towards domestic disturbances: An evaluation of family crisis intervention training. *Journal of Criminal Justice, 13,* 561-572.

Burgess, A. W., & Holstrom, L. L. (1979). Rape: Sexual disruption and recovery. *American Journal of Orthopsychiatry, 49,* 648-657.

Burkhauser, R. V., & Duncan, G. J. (1989). Economic risks of gender roles: Income loss and life events over the life course. *Social Science Quarterly, 70,* 3-23.

Butehorn, L. (1985). Social networks and battered woman's decision to stay or leave. *Dissertation Abstracts International, 46,* 1741B. (UMI No. 8513594)

Buzawa, E. S. (1988). Explaining variations in police response to domestic violence: A case study in Detroit and New England. In G. T. Hotaling, D. Finkelhor, J. T. Kirkpatrick, & M. A. Straus (Eds.), *Coping with family violence* (pp. 169-182). Newbury Park, CA: Sage.

California panel urges reforms to curb gender bias in courts. (1990, May 1). *Criminal Justice Newsletter, 21*(9), 4-5.

Camp, D. S., Raymond, G. A., & Church, R. M. (1967). Temporal relationship between response and punishment. *Journal of Experimental Psychology, 74,* 114-123.

Campbell, J. C. (1986). Nursing assessment for risk of homicide with battered women. *Advances in Nursing Science, 8*(4), 36-51.

Campbell, J. C. (1987, July). *Making sense of the senseless: Women's attributions about battering.* Paper presented at the Third National Conference for Family Violence Researchers, Durham, NH.

Campbell, J. C. (1989a). A test of two explanatory models of women's responses to battering. *Nursing Research, 38*(1), 18-24.

Campbell, J. C. (1989b). Women's responses to sexual abuse in intimate relationships. *Health Care for Women International, 8,* 335-347.

Campbell, J. C. (1990, December). Battered woman syndrome: A critical review. *Violence Update, 1*(4), 1, 4, 10-11.

Campbell, J. C., & Alford, P. (1989). The dark consequences of marital rape. *American Journal of Nursing, 87,* 946-949.

Campbell, J. C., & Humphreys, J. H. (1984). *Nursing care of victims of family violence.* Norwalk, CT: Appleton-Lange.

Campbell, J. C., & Sheridan, D. J. (1989). Emergency nursing interventions with battered women. *Journal of Emergency Nursing, 15,* 12-17.

Caplan, P. J. (1984). The myth of women's masochism. *American Psychologist, 39,* 130-139.

Caringella-MacDonald, S. (1988). Parallels and pitfalls: The aftermath of legal reform for sexual assault, marital rape, and domestic violence victims. *Journal of Interpersonal Violence, 3,* 174-189.

Carlisle-Frank, P. (1991, July). Do battered women's beliefs about control affect their decisions to remain in abusive environments. *Violence Update, 1*(11), 1, 8, 10-11.

Carmody, D. C., & Williams, K. R. (1987). Wife assault and perceptions of sanctions. *Violence and Victims, 2,* 25-38.

Cascardi, M., & O'Leary, K. D. (1992). Depressive symptomology, self-esteem, and self-blame in battered women. *Journal of Family Violence, 7,* 249-259.

Catania, C. (1984). *Learning.* Englewood Cliffs, NJ: Prentice-Hall.

Chang, D. B. K. (1989). An abused spouse's self-saving process: A theory of identity transformation. *Sociological Perspectives, 32,* 535-550.

Chen, H., Bersani, C., Myers, S. C., & Denton, R. (1990). Evaluating the effectiveness of a court sponsored abuser treatment program. *Journal of Family Violence, 4,* 309-322.

Children's Defense Fund. (1979). *American children and their families.* Washington, DC: Author.

Church, R. M. (1969). Response suppression. In B. A. Campbell & R. M. Church (Eds.), *Punishment and aversive behavior* (pp. 111-156). New York: Appleton-Century-Crofts.

Claerhout, S., Elder, J., & Janes, C. (1982). Problem-solving skills of rural battered women. *American Journal of Community Psychology, 10,* 605-612.

Clarke, R. L. (1986). *Pastoral care of battered women.* Philadelphia: Westminster.

Cohen, S., & McKay, G. (1984). Social support, stress, and the buffering hypothesis: A theoretical analysis. In A. Baum, S. E. Taylor, & J. E. Singer (Eds.), *Handbook of psychology and health: Vol 4. Social psychological aspects of health* (pp. 253-268). Hillsdale, NJ: Lawrence Erlbaum.

Cole, T., & Sapp, G. (1988). Stress, locus of control, and achievement of high school seniors. *Psychological Reports, 63,* 355-359.

Coleman, D. H., & Straus, M. A. (1986). Marital power, conflict, and violence in a nationally representative sample of American couples. *Violence and Victims, 1,* 141-157.

Coller, S. A., & Resick, P. A. (1987). Women's attributions of responsibility for date rape: The influence of empathy and sex-role stereotyping. *Violence and Victims, 2,* 115-125.

Corcoran, M., Duncan, G. J., & Hill, M. S. (1984). The economic fortunes of women and children: Lessons from the panel study of income dynamics. *Signs: Journal of Women in the Culture and Society, 10,* 232-248.

Crime Control Institute. (1990). *Predicting domestic homicide: Prior police contact and gun threats.* Washington, DC: Author.

Cummings, N. (1990). Issues of the 1990s. *Response, 13*(1), 4.

Dalto, C. A. (1983). Battered women: Factors influencing whether or not former shelter residents return to the abusive situation. *Dissertation Abstracts International, 44,* 1277B. (UMI No. 8317463)

Davis, L., & Carlson, B. (1981). Attitudes of service providers toward domestic violence. *Social Work Research and Abstracts, 17*(4), 17-39.

DeKeseredy, W. S. (1990). Male peer support and woman abuse: The current state of knowledge. *Sociological Focus, 23,* 129-139.

DePaul, A. (1992, January). New laws in California aid women victimized by violence. *Criminal Justice Newsletter, 23*(2), 5-6.

Deschner, J. P. (1984a). *The hitting habit: Anger control for battering couples.* New York: Free Press.

Deschner, J. P. (1984b). *A review of current theories about battering behavior.* Unpublished manuscript, University of Texas, Arlington.

Dibble, U., & Straus, M. A. (1980). Some social determinants of inconsistency between attitudes and behavior: The case of family violence. *Journal of Marriage and the Family, 42,* 71-80.

Did you know that . . . (1991, August 15). *Bottom Line, 12*(15), 9.

Dinsmoor, J. A. (1952). A discrimination based on punishment. *Quarterly Journal of Experimental Psychology, 4,* 27-45.

Dobash, R. E., & Dobash, R. P. (1979). *Violence against wives: A case against patriarchy.* New York: Free Press.

Dobash, R. P., & Dobash, R. E. (1991). *Gender, methodology, and methods in criminological research: The case of spousal violence.* Paper presented at the British Criminology Conference, York, England.

Domestic Violence Conference Bill to go to Senate for final vote. Right wing target legislation for defeat. (1980, October). *SANENEWS: A National Newsletter on Battered Women, 1*(11), 1.

Domestic violence in the courts. (1989). *Response, 12*(4), 3-6. (Excerpted from *Gender Bias in the Courts,* Report of the Maryland Special Joint Committee on Gender Bias in the Courts, 1989, Annapolis, MD)

Domjan, M., & Burkhard, B. (1989). *The principles of learning and behavior.* Monterey, CA: Brooks/Cole.

Donaldson, M., & Gardner, R. (1985). Diagnosis and treatment of traumatic stress among women after childhood incest. In C. R. Figley (Ed.), *Trauma and its wake* (Vol. 1, pp. 356-377). New York: Brunner/Mazel.

Douglas, H. (1991). Assessing violent couples. *Families in Society: The Journal of Contemporary Human Services, 72,* 525-534.

Douglas, M. A. (1987). The battered woman syndrome. In D. J. Sonkin (Ed.), *Domestic violence on trial: Psychological and legal dimensions of family violence* (pp. 39-54). New York: Springer.

Douglas, M. A., & Colantuono, A. (1987, July). *Cluster analysis of MMPI scores among battered women.* Paper presented at the Third National Conference for Family Violence Researchers, Durham, NH.

Duncan, G. J. (1987). *Economic status of women.* Ann Arbor: University of Michigan, Institute for Social Research.

Dunford, F. W., Huizinga, D., & Elliott, D. S. (1990). The role of arrest in domestic assault: The Omaha police experiment. *Criminology, 28,* 183-206.

Dunkel-Schetter, C., Folkman, S., & Lazarus, R. S. (1987). Correlates of social support receipt. *Journal of Personality and Social Psychology, 53,* 71-80.

Dutton, D. G. (1986). The outcome of court-mandated treatment for wife assault: A quasi-experimental evaluation. *Violence and Victims, 1,* 163-175.

Dutton, D. G. (1987). The criminal justice response to wife assault. *Law and Human Behavior, 11,* 186-206.

Dutton, D. G. (1988). *The domestic assault of women.* Newton, MA: Allyn & Bacon.

Dutton, D. G., & Browning, J. J. (1987). Power struggles and intimacy anxieties as causative factors of violence in intimate relationships. In G. Russell (Ed.), *Violence in intimate relationships* (pp. 163-175). New York: Spectrum.

Dutton, D. G., Fehr, B., & McEwen, H. (1982). Severe wife battering as deindividuation violence. *Victimology: An International Journal, 7*(1-4), 13-23.

Dutton, D. G., & Painter, S. L. (1981). Traumatic bonding: The development of emotional attachments in battered women and other relationships of intermittent abuse. *Victimology: An International Journal, 6*(1-4), 139-155.

Dutton, D. G., & Strachan, C. E. (1987). Motivational needs for power and spouse-specific assertiveness in assaultive and nonassaultive men. *Violence and Victims, 2,* 145-156.

D'Zurilla, T. J. (1986). *Problem-solving therapy: A social competence approach to clinical intervention.* New York: Springer.

Edleson, J. L., & Brygger, M. P. (1986). Gender differences in reporting of battering incidents. *Family Relations, 35,* 377-382.

Edleson, J. L., Eisikovits, Z. C., Guttman, E., & Sela-Amit, M. (1991). Cognitive and interpersonal factors in woman abuse. *Journal of Family Violence, 6,* 167-182.

Eigenberg, H., & Moriarty, L. (1991). Domestic violence and local law enforcement in Texas. *Journal of Interpersonal Violence, 6,* 102-109.

Eisler, R. M., Skidmore, J. R., & Ward, C. H. (1988). Masculine gender-role stress: Predictor of anger, anxiety, and health-risk behavior. *Journal of Personality Assessment, 52,* 133-141.

Ellard, J. H., Herbert, T. B., & Thompson, L. J. (1991). Coping with an abusive relationship: How and why do people stay? *Journal of Marriage and the Family, 53,* 311-325.

Ellis, D. (1989). Male abuse of a married or cohabiting female partner: The application of sociological theory to research findings. *Violence and Victims, 4,* 235-255.

Emery, B. C., Lloyd, S. A., & Castleton, A. (1989, November). *Why women hit: A feminist perspective.* Paper presented at the annual conference of the National Conference on Family Relations, New Orleans.

Epidemiology of domestic violence. (1984, September). *Criminal Justice Newsletter, 16*(17), 4.

Estes, W. K., & Skinner, B. F. (1941). Some quantitative properties of anxiety. *Journal of Experimental Psychology, 29,* 390-400.

Ewing, C. P., & Aubrey, M. (1987). Battered women and public opinion: Some realities about myths. *Journal of Family Violence, 2,* 257-264.

Fagan, J. (1988). Contributions of family violence research to criminal justice policy on wife assault: Paradigms of science and social control. *Violence and Victims, 3,* 159-186.

Fagan, J. (1989). Cessation of family violence: Deterrence and dissuasion. In L. Ohlin & M. Tonry (Eds.), *Family violence* (pp. 377-425). Chicago: University of Chicago Press.

Faludi, S. (1991). *Backlash.* New York: Crown.

Fantuzzo, J. W., & Lindquist, C. U. (1989). The effects of observing conjugal violence on children: A review and analysis of research methodology. *Journal of Family Violence, 4,* 77-94.

Federal Bureau of Investigation (FBI). (1984). *Reporting handbook.* Washington, DC: Government Printing Office.

Federal Bureau of Investigation (FBI). (1989). *Uniform crime reports for the United States.* Washington, DC: Government Printing Office.

Feindler, E. L. (1988, August). *Cognitive-behavioral analysis of anger in abused women.* Paper presented at the annual meeting of the American Psychological Association, Atlanta, GA.

Feld, S. L., & Straus, M. A. (1989). Escalation and desistance of wife assault in marriage. *Criminology, 27,* 141-161.

Felson, R. B. (1992). "Kick 'em when they're down": Explanation of the relationship between stress and interpersonal aggression and violence. *The Sociological Quarterly, 33,* 1-16.

Ferguson, K. E. (1980). *Self, society, and womankind: The dialectic of liberation.* Westport, CT: Greenwood.

Ferraro, K. J. (1979). Hard love: Letting go of an abusive husband. *Frontiers, 4*(2), 16-18.

Ferraro, K. J. (1981). Battered women and the shelter movement. *Dissertation Abstracts International, 42,* 879A. (UMI No. 8115605)

Ferraro, K. J. (1989). Policing woman battering. *Social Problems, 36,* 61-74.

Ferraro, K. J., & Johnson, J. M. (1984, August). *The meanings of courtship violence.* Paper presented at the Second National Conference of Family Violence Researchers, Durham, NH.

Fields, M. (1978). Wife beating: Government intervention policies and practices. In *Commission on Civil Rights: Battered women: Issues of public policy.* Washington, DC: U.S. Commission on Civil Rights.

Finkelhor, D. (1983). Common features of family abuse. In D. Finkelhor, R. J. Gelles, G. T. Hotaling, & M. A. Straus (Eds.), *The dark side of families: Current family violence research* (pp. 17-30). Beverly Hills, CA: Sage.

Finkelhor, D. (1984). *Child sexual abuse: New theory and research.* New York: Free Press.

Finkelhor, D., & Yllo, K. (1982). Forced sex in marriage: A preliminary research report. *Crime & Delinquency, 82,* 459-478.

Finn, J. (1985). The stresses and coping behavior of battered women. *Social Casework: The Journal of Contemporary Social Work, 66,* 341-349.

Fischer, G. (1991). *A community based and dual pronged intervention model to stop domestic violence in the United States Marine Corps.* Position paper from the Family Service Center, Marine Corps Recruit Depot, San Diego, CA.

Flanagan, T. J., & McGarrell, E. F. (1986). *Sourcebook of criminal justice statistics—1985* (NCJ-100899). Washington, DC: U.S. Department of Justice, Bureau of Justice Statistics.

Fleming, J. B. (1979). *Stopping wife abuse.* Garden City, NY: Anchor Doubleday.

Flynn, C. P. (1987). Relationship violence: A model for family professionals. *Family Relations, 36,* 296-299.

Foa, E. B., Olasov, B., & Steketee, G. S. (1987, September). *Treatment of rape victims.* Paper presented at the conference, State of the Art in Sexual Assault, Charleston, SC.

Fojtik, K. M. (1977-1978). The NOW domestic violence project. *Victimology: An International Journal, 2,* 653-657.

Follingstad, D. R., Brennan, A. F., Hause, E. S., Polek, D. S., & Rutledge, L. L. (1991). Factors moderating physical and psychological symptoms of battered women. *Journal of Family Violence, 6,* 81-95.

Follingstad, D. R., Hause, E. S., Rutledge, L. L., & Polek, D. S. (1992). Effects of battered women's early responses on later abuse patterns. *Violence and Victims, 7,* 109-128.

Follingstad, D. R., Polek, D. S., Hause, E. S., Deaton, L. H., Bulger, M. W., & Conway, Z. D. (1989). Factors predicting verdicts in cases where battered women kill their husbands. *Law and Human Behavior, 13,* 253-269.

Follingstad, D. R., Rutledge, L. L., Berg, B. J., Hause, E. S., & Polek, D. S. (1990). The role of emotional abuse in physically abusive relationships. *Journal of Family Violence, 5,* 107-120.

Fortune, M. (1987). *Keeping the faith.* San Francisco: Harper & Row.

Freud, A. (1942). *The ego and the mechanisms of defense.* New York: International Universities Press.

Friedman, L. (1991). Cost-effective compassion. *NOVA Newsletter, 15*(9), 7.

Frieze, I. H. (1979). Perceptions of battered wives. In I. H. Frieze, D. Bar-Tal, & J. S. Carroll (Eds.), *New approaches to social problems* (pp. 79-108). San Francisco: Jossey-Bass.

Frisch, M. B., & MacKenzie, C. J. (1991). A comparison of formerly and chronically battered women on cognitive and situational dimensions. *Psychotherapy, 28,* 339-344.

Gamache, D. J., Edleson, J. L., & Schock, M. D. (1988). Coordinated police, judicial and social service response to woman battering: A multi-baseline evaluation across communities. In G. T. Hotaling, D. Finkelhor, J. T. Kirkpatrick, & M. A. Straus (Eds.), *Coping with family violence: Research and policy perspectives* (pp. 193-209). Newbury Park, CA: Sage.

Ganley, A. L. (1981). *Court mandated counseling for men who batter: A three-day workshop for mental health professional: Participants manual.* Washington, DC: Center for Women's Policy Studies.

Gaquin, D. A. (1977-1978). Spouse abuse: Data from the National Crime Survey. *Victimology: An International Journal, 2,* 632-643.

Garner, J., & Clemmer, E. (1986). *Danger to police in domestic disturbances: A new look.* Washington, DC: U.S. Department of Justice (NIJ).

Geer, J., & Maisel, E. (1972). Evaluating the effects of the prediction-control confound. *Journal of Personality and Social Psychology, 23,* 314-319.

Geffner, R. (1990). Family abuse, the judicial system, and politics. *Family Violence Bulletin, 6*(3), 1.

Gellen, M. I., Hoffman, R. A., Jones, M., & Stone, M. (1984). Abused and non-abused women: MMPI profile differences. *Personnel and Guidance Journal, 62,* 601-604.

Gelles, R. J. (1976). Abused wives: Why do they stay? *Journal of Marriage and the Family, 38,* 659-668.

Gelles, R. J. (1979). *Family violence.* Beverly Hills, CA: Sage.

Gelles, R. J., & Cornell, C. P. (1990). *Intimate violence in families.* Newbury Park, CA: Sage.

Gelles, R. J., & Harrop, J. W. (1989). Violence, battering, and psychological distress among women. *Journal of Interpersonal Violence, 4,* 400-420.

Gelles, R. J., & Straus, M. A. (1979). Determinants of violence in the family: Toward a theoretical integration. In W. R. Burr, R. Hill, F. I. Nye, & I. Reiss (Eds.), *Contemporary theories about the family* (pp. 549-581). New York: Free Press.

Gerow, J. R. (1989). *Psychology: An introduction* (2nd ed.). Glenville, IL: Scott, Foresman.

Gilbert, L., & Webster, P. (1982). *Bound by love: The sweet trap of daughterhood.* Boston: Beacon.

Gilligan, C. (1982). *In a different voice.* Boston: Harvard University Press.

Goetting, A. (1991). Female victims of homicide: A portrait of their killers and the circumstances of their deaths. *Violence and Victims, 6,* 159-168.

Gold, E. R. (1986). Long-term effects of sexual victimization in childhood: An attributional approach. *Journal of Consulting and Clinical Psychology, 54,* 471-475.

Goldenson, R. M. (1984). *Longman dictionary of psychology and psychiatry.* New York: Longman.

Goldstein, J. H., Davis, R. W., Kernis, M., & Cohn, E. (1981). Retarding the escalation of aggression. *Social Behavior and Personality, 9,* 65-70.

Gondolf, E. W. (1988a). *Battered women as survivors: An alternative to treating learned helplessness.* Lexington, KY: Lexington.

Gondolf, E. W. (1988b). The effect of batterer counseling on shelter outcome. *Journal of Interpersonal Violence, 3,* 275-289.

Gondolf, E. W. (1990). The human rights of women survivors. *Response, 13*(2), 6-8.

Gondolf, E. W., Fisher, E., & McFerron, J. R. (1988). Racial differences among shelter residents: A comparison of Anglo, black, and Hispanic battered women. *Journal of Family Violence, 3,* 39-51.

Gondolf, E. W., & Russell, D. (1986). The case against anger control treatment for batterers. *Response, 9*(3), 2-5.

Goodwin, J. (1987). The etiology of combat-related post-traumatic stress disorders. In T. Williams (Ed.), *Post-traumatic stress disorders: A handbook for clinicians* (pp. 1-18). Cincinnati, OH: Disabled American Veterans.

Gotlib, I. H., & Asarnow, R. F. (1979). Interpersonal and impersonal problem solving skills in mildly and clinically depressed university students. *Journal of Consulting and Clinical Psychology, 47,* 86-95.

Graham, D., Rawlings, E., & Rimini, K. (1988). Survivors of terror: Battered women, hostages, and the Stockholm Syndrome. In K. Yllo & M. Bograd (Eds.), *Feminist perspectives on wife abuse* (pp. 217-233). Newbury Park, CA: Sage.

Green, B. L., Lindy, J., Grace, M., & Glese, G. (1989). Multiple diagnoses in post-traumatic stress disorder: The role of war stressors. *Journal of Nervous and Mental Disorders, 177,* 329-335.

Greene, E., Raitz, A., & Lindblad, H. (1989). Jurors' knowledge of battered women. *Journal of Family Violence, 4,* 105-125.

Greenfeld, L. A., & Minor-Harper, S. (Eds.). (1991). *Women in prison* (Special report; NCJ-127991). Washington, DC: Bureau of Justice Statistics.

Guns and dolls. (1990, May 18). *Newsweek,* pp. 58-62.

Gurley, D. (1989, January). *Understanding the mixed roles of social support and social obstruction in recovery from child abuse.* Paper presented at the Responses to Family Violence Research Conference, Purdue University, Lafayette, IN.

Hackler, J. (1991). The reduction of violent crime through economic equality for women. *Journal of Family Violence, 6,* 199-216.

Hall-Apicella, V. (1983, August). *Exploring attitudes of mental health professionals toward battered women.* Paper presented at the annual meeting of American Psychological Association, Anaheim, CA.

Hamberger, L. K. (1991, August). *Research concerning wife abuse: Implications for training physicians and criminal justice personnel.* Paper presented at the annual meeting of the American Psychological Association, San Francisco.

Hamberger, L. K., & Arnold, J. (1991). The impact of mandatory arrest on domestic violence perpetrator counseling services. *Family Violence Bulletin, 6*(1), 11-12.

Hamberger, L. K., & Hastings, J. E. (1986). Characteristics of spouse abusers. *Journal of Interpersonal Violence, 1,* 363-373.

Hansen, M., Harway, M., & Cervantes, N. (1991). Therapists' perceptions of severity in cases of family violence. *Violence and Victims, 6,* 225-235.

Hanson, H., Sawyer, D. D., Hilton, J., & Davis, S. F. (1992, August). *Reported death anxiety in battered and nonbattered women.* Paper presented at the annual meeting of the American Psychological Association, Washington, DC.

Harlow, C. W. (1991). *Female victims of violent crime* (NCJ-126826). Rockville, MD: U.S. Department of Justice.

Harris, M. B. (1991). Effects of sex of aggressor, sex of target, and relationship on evaluations of physical aggression. *Journal of Interpersonal Violence, 6,* 174-186.

Hart, B. (1988). *Safety for women: Monitoring batterers' programs.* Harrisburg: Pennsylvania Coalition Against Domestic Violence.

Hartik, L. M. (1979). Identification of personality characteristics and self-concept factors of battered women (Doctoral dissertation, United States International University, San Diego, CA, 1978). *Dissertation Abstracts International, 40,* 893B. (Order No. 7918190)

Hartmann, H. I. (1981). The family as the locus of gender, class and political struggle: The example of housework. *Signs: Journal of Women in Culture and Society, 6,* 366-393.

Hastings, J. E., & Hamberger, L. K. (1988). Personality characteristics of spouse abusers: A controlled comparison. *Violence and Victims, 3,* 31-48.

Heise, L. (1989). International dimensions of violence against women. *Response, 12*(1), 3-11.

Hendricks-Matthews, M. (1982). The battered woman: Is she ready for help? *The Journal of Contemporary Social Work, 63,* 131-137.

Herman, R. L., & Azrin, N. H. (1964). Punishment by noise in an alternative response situation. *Experimental Analysis of Behavior, 7,* 16-26.

Herrnstein, R. J. (1970). On the law of effect. *Journal of Experimental Analysis of Behavior, 13,* 243-266.

High prevalence for post-traumatic stress. (1991, September 23). *Behavior Today, 22*(39), 7-8.

Hilberman, E., & Munson, K. (1978). Sixty battered women. *Victimology: An International Journal, 2,* 460-470.

Hiroto, D. S. (1974). Locus of control and learned helplessness. *Journal of Experimental Psychology, 102,* 187-193.

Hirschel, J. D., Hutchison, I. W., III, & Dean, C. W. (1992). The failure of arrest to deter spouse abuse. *Journal of Research in Crime and Delinquency, 29,* 7-33.

Hirschel, J. D., Hutchison, I., Dean, C. W., & Mills, A. M. (1992). Review essay on the law enforcement response to spouse abuse: Past, present, and future. *Justice Quarterly, 9,* 247-283.

Hodson, C. A. (1982). Length of stay in a battering relationship: Test of a model (Doctoral dissertation, University of Maryland, 1982). *Dissertation Abstracts International, 43,* 1983B. (Order No. 8226470)

Hofling, C. K., Brotzman, E., Darlymple, S., Graves, N., & Pierce, C. M. (1966). An experimental study in nurse-physician relationships. *Journal of Nervous and Mental Disease, 143,* 171-180.

Holiman, M. J., & Schilit, R. (1991). Aftercare for battered women: How to encourage the maintenance of change. *Psychotherapy, 28,* 345-353.

Holtzworth-Munroe, A. (1988). Causal attribution in marital violence: Theoretical and methodological issues. *Clinical Psychology Review, 8,* 331-344.

Holz, W. C., & Azrin, N. H. (1961). Discriminative properties of punishment. *Journal of Experimental Analysis of Behavior, 4,* 225-232.

Homicides followed by suicide: Kentucky, 1985-1990. (1991, September 27). *Morbidity and Mortality Weekly Report, 40,* 652-653, 659.

Horner, M. S. (1972). Toward and understanding of achievement-related conflicts in women. *Journal of Social Issues, 28,* 157-175.

Hornung, C. A., McCullough, B. C., & Sugimoto, T. (1981). Status relationships in marriage: Risk factors in spouse abuse. *Journal of Marriage and the Family, 43,* 675-692.

Hotaling, G. T., & Straus, M. A. (with Lincoln, A. J.). (1990). Intrafamily violence and crime and violence outside the family. In M. A. Straus & R. J. Gelles (Eds.), *Physical violence in American families: Risk factors and adaptations to violence in 8,145 families* (pp. 431-470). New Brunswick, CT: Transaction.

Hotaling, G. T., & Sugarman, D. B. (1986). An analysis of risk markers in husband to wife violence: The current state of knowledge. *Violence and Victims, 1,* 101-124.

Hotaling, G. T., & Sugarman, D. B. (1990). A risk marker analysis of assaulted wives. *Journal of Family Violence, 5,* 1-13.

Houskamp, B. M., & Foy, D. W. (1991). The assessment of post-traumatic stress disorder in battered women. *Journal of Interpersonal Violence, 6,* 367-375.

Hunt, H. F., & Brady, J. V. (1955). Some effects of punishment and intercurrent anxiety on a simple operant. *Journal of Comparative and Physiological Psychology, 48,* 305-310.

"I'm supposed to be safe . . . Oh my God." (1992, April 23). *Tribune Newspapers of Arizona,* p. A6.

Jaffe, P. G., Hastings, E., & Reitzel, D. (1992). Child witnesses of woman abuse: How can schools respond? *Response, 79*(2), 12-15.

Jaffe, P. G., Suderman, M., Reitzel, D., & Killip, S. M. (1992). An evaluation of a secondary school primary prevention program on violence in intimate relationships. *Violence and Victims, 7,* 129-146.

Jaffe, P. G., Wolfe, D. A., Telford, A., & Austin, G. (1986). The impact of police charges in incidents of wife abuse. *Journal of Family Violence, 1,* 37-49.

Janoff-Bulman, R. (1979). Characterological versus behavioral self-blame: Inquiries into depression and rape. *Journal of Personality and Social Psychology, 37,* 1798-1809.

Jay, J. (1991, November-December). Terrible knowledge. *The Family Therapy Networker,* pp. 18-29.

Jillings, C. R. (1985). Loss and grief: Unravelling two complex phenomena. *Critical Care Nurse, 5*(5), 7-9.

Johnson, I. M. (1988). Wife abuse: Factors predictive of the decision-making process of battered women. *Dissertation Abstracts International, 48,* 3202A. (UMI No. 8803369)

Johnson, J. M., & Bondurant, D. M. (1992). Revisiting the 1982 church response survey. *Studies in Symbolic Interaction, 13,* 287-293.

Jouriles, E. N., & O'Leary, K. D. (1985). Interspousal reliability of reports of marital violence. *Journal of Consulting and Clinical Psychology, 53,* 419-421.

Judiciary committee approves Violence Against Women Act. (1991, August 1). *Criminal Justice Newsletter, 22*(15), 7.

Julian, J., & Kornblum, W. (1983). *Social problems.* Englewood Cliffs, NJ: Prentice-Hall.

Jurik, N. C., & Winn, R. (1990). Gender and homicide: A comparison of men and women who kill. *Violence and Victims, 5,* 227-242.

Justice, A., & Hirt, M. H. (1992, August). *Attachment styles of women with histories of abusive relationships.* Paper presented at the annual meeting of the American Psychological Association, Washington, DC.

Kaci, J. H. (1990). Issues of the 1990s. *Response, 13*(1), 4.

Kahn, M. W. (1980). Wife beating and cultural context: Prevalence in an aboriginal and islander community in Northern Australia. *American Journal of Community Psychology, 8,* 727-731.

Kalmuss, D. S. (1979). The attribution of responsibility in a wife-abuse context. *Victimology: An International Journal, 4,* 284-291.

Kalmuss, D. S. (1984). The intergenerational transmission of marital aggression. *Journal of Marriage and the Family, 46,* 11-19.

Kalmuss, D. S., & Straus, M. A. (1982). Wife's marital dependency and wife abuse. *Journal of Marriage and the Family, 44*(1-4), 277-286.

Kamin, L. J. (1959). The delay-of-punishment gradient. *Journal of Comparative and Physiological Psychology, 52,* 44-51.

Karsh, E. B. (1962). Effects of number of rewarded trials and intensity of punishment on running speed. *Journal of Comparative and Physiological Psychology, 55,* 44-51.

Katz, R., & Wykes, T. (1985). The psychological difference between temporally predictable and unpredictable stressful events: Evidence for information control theories. *Journal of Personality and Social Psychology, 48,* 781-790.

Kemp, A., Rawlings, E. I., & Green, B. L. (1991). Post-traumatic stress disorder (PTSD) in battered women: A shelter sample. *Journal of Traumatic Stress, 4,* 137-148.

Kessler, R. C., McLeod, J. D., & Wethington, E. (1985). The costs of caring: A perspective on the relationship between sex and psychological distress. In I. G. Sarason & B. R. Sarason (Eds.), *Social support: Theory, research, and applications* (pp. 491-506). Dordrecht, the Netherlands: Martinus Nijhoff.

Kilpatrick, D. G., Veronen, L. J., & Resick, P. A. (1979). Assessment of the aftermath of rape: Changing patterns of fear. *Journal of Behavioral Assessment, 1,* 133-148.

King, L. M., & Berrio, M. M. (1992, August). *Gender differences in attitudes about physical aggression within couples.* Paper presented at the annual meeting of the American Psychological Association, Washington, DC.

Kishur, G. R. (1989). The male batterer: A multidimensional exploration of conjugal violence. *Dissertation Abstracts International, 49,* 2409A. (UMI No. 8814496)

Klaus, P. A., & Rand, M. R. (1984). *Family violence* (Special report; NCJ-93449). Rockville, MD: Bureau of Justice Statistics.

Klee, J. B. (1944). The relation of frustration and motivation to the production of abnormal fixations in the rat. *Psychological Monographs, 56*(4).

Koski, P. R., & Mangold, W. D. (1988). Gender effects in attitudes about family violence. *Journal of Family Violence, 3,* 225-237.

Koss, M. P. (1990). The women's mental health research agenda. *American Psychologist, 45,* 374-380.

Koss, M. P., & Burkhart, B. R. (1989). A conceptual analysis of rape. *Psychology of Women Quarterly, 13,* 27-40.

Koss, M. P., Gidyez, C. A., & Wisniewski, N. (1987). The scope of rape: Incidence and prevalence of sexual aggression and in a national sample of higher education students. *Journal of Consulting and Clinical Psychology, 55,* 162-170.

Koss, M. P., Koss, P., & Woodruff, W. J. (1991). Criminal victimization among primary care medical patients: Prevalence, incidence, and physician usage. *Behavioral Science and the Law, 9*, 85-86.

Kramer, T. L., & Green, B. L. (1991). Post-traumatic stress disorder as an early response to sexual assault. *Journal of Interpersonal Violence, 6*, 160-173.

Kristiansen, C. M., & Giuletti, R. (1990). Perceptions of wife abuse. *Psychology of Women Quarterly, 14*, 177-189.

Kuhl, A. F. (1985). Personality traits of abused women: Masochism myth refuted. *Victimology, 9*, 450-463.

Kuleshnyk, I. (1984). The Stockholm Syndrome: Toward an understanding. *Social Action and the Law, 10*(2), 37-42.

Kurz, D. (1990). Interventions with battered women in health care settings. *Violence and Victims, 5*, 243-256.

Kurz, D., & Stark, E. (1988). Not-so-benign neglect: The medical response to battering. In K. Yllo & M. Bograd (Eds.), *Feminist perspectives on wife abuse* (pp. 249-266). Newbury Park, CA: Sage.

LaBell, L. S. (1979). Wife abuse: A sociological study of battered women and their mates. *Victimology: An International Journal, 4*, 257-267.

Lanagan, P. A., & Innes, C. A. (1986). *Preventing domestic violence against women* (BJS Special report; NCJ-102037). Rockville, MD: U.S. Department of Justice.

Landenburger, K. (1989). A process of entrapment in and recovery from an abusive relationship. *Issues in Mental Health Nursing, 10*, 209-227.

Laner, M. R. (1990). Violence or its precipitators: Which is more likely to be identified as a dating problem? *Deviant Behavior, 11*, 319-329.

Laner, M. R., & Thompson, J. (1982). Abuse and aggression in courting couples. *Deviant Behavior, 3*, 229-244.

Lang, D. (1974, November 25). A reporter at large: The bank drama. *New Yorker*, pp. 56-126.

Launius, M. H., & Jensen, B. L. (1987). Interpersonal problem-solving skills in battered, counseling, and control women. *Journal of Family Violence, 2*, 151-162.

LaViolette, A. L. (1991). *Battered women, power, and family systems therapy.* Garden Grove, CA: Newman.

Lehnen, R. G., & Skogan, W. G. (1981). The National Crime Survey. In R. G. Lehnen & W. G. Skogan (Eds.), *Working papers: Vol. 1. Current and historical perspectives.* Washington, DC: U.S. Department of Justice.

Lester, D. (1980). A cross-culture study of wife abuse. *Aggressive Behavior, 6*, 361-364.

Levenson, H. (1973). Activism and powerful others. Distinctions within the concept of internal-external control. *Journal of Personality Assessment, 38*, 377-383.

Levy, B. (1984). *Skills for violence-free relationships* (Curriculum for Young People Ages 13-18). Long Beach: Southern California Coalition for Battered Women.

Lewis, J. E. (1992, August). *Battered woman syndrome: Neglected diagnosis of traumatic brain injuries.* Paper presented at the annual meeting of the American Psychological Association, Washington, DC.

Lloyd, S. A. (1988, November). *Conflict and violence in marriage.* Paper presented at the annual meeting of the National Council on Family Relations, Philadelphia.

Lloyd, S. A. (1989, November). *The stability of physical aggression in marriage.* Paper presented at the National Council on Family Relations Annual Conference, New Orleans.

Logan, F. A., & Wallace, W. C. (1981). *Fundamentals of learning and motivation* (3rd ed.). Dubuque, IA: William C Brown.

Long, G. M., & McNamara, J. R. (1989). Paradoxical punishment as it relates to the battered woman syndrome. *Behavior Modification, 13,* 192-205.

Maccoby, E. E., & Jacklin, C. N. (1974). *The psychology of sex differences.* Stanford, CA: Stanford University Press.

Maertz, K. (1990). *Self-defeating beliefs of battered women.* Unpublished doctoral dissertation, University of Alberta, Canada.

Maguire, M., & Corbett, C. (1987). *The effects of crime and the work of victims support schemes.* Gower, England: Aldershot.

Maier, N. R. F. (1949). *Frustration: The study of behavior without a goal.* New York: McGraw-Hill.

Maier, N. R. F., Glazer, N. M., & Klee, J. B. (1940). Studies of abnormal behavior in the rat: III. The development of behavior fixations through frustration. *Journal of Experimental Psychology, 26,* 521-546.

Maier, S. F., & Seligman, M. E. P. (1976). Learned helplessness: Theory and evidence. *Journal of Experimental Psychology: General, 105,* 3-46.

Maier, S. F., Seligman, M. E. P., & Solomon, R. L. (1969). Pavlovian fear conditioning and learned helplessness. In B. A. Campbell & R. M. Church (Eds.), *Punishment and aversive behavior* (pp. 299-342). New York: Appleton-Century-Crofts.

Main, M., & George, C. (1985). Responses of abused and disadvantaged toddlers to distress in agemates: A study in a day care setting. *Developmental Psychology, 21,* 407-412.

Makepeace, J. M. (1986). Gender differences in courtship violence. *Family Relations, 35,* 383-388.

Malloy, K. A. (1986). Psychological and demographic variables as predictors of women's decisions to leave abusive relationships. *Dissertation Abstracts International, 47,* 6963B. (UMI No. 8629940)

Manley, N. J. (1982). *Battered women: The victim's perceptions.* Unpublished master's thesis, California State University, Sacramento.

Margolin, G. (1987). The multiple forms of aggressiveness between marital partners: How do we identify them? *Journal of Marital and Family Therapy, 13,* 77-84.

Marshall, L. L., & Rose, P. (1990). Premarital violence: The impact of family of origin violence, stress, and reciprocity. *Violence and Victims, 5,* 51-64.

Martin, D. (1978). Battered women: Society's problem. In J. R. Chapman & M. Gates (Eds.), *The victimization of women* (pp. 111-141). Beverly Hills, CA: Sage.

Martin, S. E. (1989). Research note: The response of the clergy to spouse abuse in a suburban county. *Violence and Victims, 4,* 217-225.

Maslow, A. H. (1970). *Motivation and personality* (2nd ed.). New York: Harper & Row.

McCleary, R. M. (1979). Street-corner work with aggressives. *International Journal of Offender Therapy and Comparative Criminology, 10,* 261-267.

McCubbin, H. I., Larsen, A. S., & Olson, D. H. (1982). F-Copes: Family coping strategies. In D. H. Olson (Ed.), *Family inventories* (pp. 101-118). St. Paul: University of Minnesota Press.

McLeer, S. V., & Anwar, R. (1989). A study of battered women presenting in an emergency department. *American Journal of Public Health, 79,* 65-66.

Mercy, J. A., & Saltzman, L. E. (1989). Fatal violence among spouses in the United States, 1976-1985. *American Journal of Public Health, 79,* 595-599.

Milgram, S. (1963). Behavioral studies of obedience. *Journal of Abnormal and Social Psychology, 67,* 371-378.

Miller, D. T., & Porter, C. A. (1983). Self-blame in victims of violence. *Journal of Social Issues, 39,* 139-152.

Miller, I. W., & Norman, W. H. (1979). Learned helplessness in humans: A review and attribution-theory model. *Psychological Bulletin, 86,* 93-118.

Miller, J. B. (1976). *Toward a new psychology of women.* Boston: Beacon.

Miller, K. (1992, April). *Orange County domestic violence cases.* Unpublished statistical data, Santa Ana, Orange County, CA.

Miller, N. E. (1959). Liberalization of basic S-R concepts: Extensions to conflict behavior, motivation, and social learning. In S. Koch (Ed.), *Psychology: A study of science* (Vol. 2, pp. 196-292). New York: McGraw-Hill.

Millon, T., Green, C., & Meagher, R. (Eds.). (1982). *Handbook of clinical health psychology.* New York: Plenum.

Mills, T. (1985). The assault on the self: Stages in coping with battering husbands. *Qualitative Sociology, 8*(2), 103-123.

Mitchell, R. E., & Hodson, C. A. (1983). Coping with domestic violence: Social support and psychological health among battered women. *American Journal of Community Psychology, 11,* 629-654.

Mones, P. A. (1992). Battle cry for battered children. *California Lawyer, 12*(5), 58.

Morgan, R. (1992, April). Sexually explicit lives. *Ms. Magazine,* p. 1.

Morrison, R. L., Van Hasselt, V. B., & Bellack, A. S. (1987). Assessment of assertion and problem-solving skills in wife abusers and their spouses. *Journal of Family Violence, 2,* 227-238.

Mowrer, O. H. (1947). On the dual nature of learning: A reinterpretation of "conditioning" and "problem solving." *Harvard Educational Review, 17,* 102-148.

Muldary, P. S. (1983). Attribution of causality of spouse assault. *Dissertation Abstracts International, 44,* 1249B. (UMI No. 8316576)

Murphy, C. M., & Meyer, S. L. (1991). Gender, power, and violence in marriage. *Behavior Therapist, 14,* 95-100.

Myers, J. E. B., Tikosh, M. A., & Paxson, M. A. (1992). Domestic violence prevention statutes. *Violence Update, 3*(4), 3, 5-9.

National Organization for Victim Assistance (NOVA). (1992). Stress management for caregivers. *NOVA Newsletter, 15*(12), 1-15.

Neidig, P., Friedman, D., & Collins, B. (1986). Attitudinal family violence characteristics of men who have engaged in spouse abuse. *Journal of Family Violence, 1,* 223-233.

Nerney, M. (1987). *Battered women and criminal justice.* (Available from STEPS to End Family Violence, 104 East 107th Street, New York, NY 10029)

Nezu, A. M., & Ronan, G. F. (1986). Social problem solving and depression: Deficits in generating alternatives and decision making. *Southern Psychologist, 2,* 63-71.

Okun, L. E. (1983). A study of woman abuse: 300 battered women taking shelter, 119 woman-batterers in counseling. *Dissertation Abstracts International, 44,* 1972B. (UMI No. 8324256)

O'Leary, K. D., & Arias, I. (1984, August). *Assessing agreement of reports of spouse abuse.* Paper presented at the National Family Violence Research Conference, Durham, NH.

O'Leary, K. D., Barling, J., Arias, I., Rosenbaum, A., Malone, J., & Tyree, A. (1989). Prevalence and stability of physical aggression between spouses: A longitudinal analysis. *Journal of Consulting and Clinical Psychology, 57,* 263-268.

O'Leary, K. D., Curley, A., Rosenbaum, A., & Clarke, C. (1985). Assertion training for abused wives: A potentially hazardous treatment. *Journal of Marital and Family Therapy, 11,* 319-322.

Osthoff, S. (1992). Restoring justice: Clemency for battered women. *Response, 14*(2), 2-3.

Ott, B. J., Graham, D. L., & Rawlings, E. (1990, August). *Stockholm Syndrome in emotionally abused adult women.* Paper presented at the annual meeting of the American Psychological Association, Boston.

Pagelow, M. D. (1980, August). *Does the law help battered wives? Some research notes.* Paper presented at the annual meeting of the Law and Society Association, Madison, WI.

Pagelow, M. D. (1981a). Factors affecting women's decisions to leave violent relationships. *Journal of Family Issues, 2,* 391-414.

Pagelow, M. D. (1981b). *Woman-battering: Victims and their experiences.* Beverly Hills, CA: Sage.

Pagelow, M. D. (1981c). *Women and crime.* New York: Macmillan.

Pagelow, M. D. (1992). Adult victims of domestic violence. *Journal of Interpersonal Violence, 7,* 87-120.

Painter, S. L., & Dutton, D. G. (1985). Patterns of emotional bonding in battered women: Traumatic bonding. *International Journal of Women's Studies, 57,* 101-110.

Panel says battered women may have no choice but retaliation. (1987, August 3). *Criminal Justice Newsletter, 18*(15), 6-7.

Pence, E., & Paymar, M. (1986). *Power and control: Tactics of men who batter.* Duluth: Minnesota Program Development.

Pennebaker, J. W. (1991). Inhibition as the linchpin of health. In H. S. Friedman (Ed.), *Hostility coping and health* (pp. 127-140). Washington, DC: American Psychological Association.

Pennebaker, J. W., & Susman, J. R. (1988). Disclosure of traumas and psychosomatic process. *Social Stress and Medicine, 26,* 327-332.

Peterson, C., & Seligman, M. E. P. (1984). Causal explanations as a risk factor for depression: Theory and evidence. *Psychological Review, 91,* 347-374.

Pfouts, J. S. (1978). Violent families: Coping responses of abused wives. *Child Welfare, 57,* 101-111.

Piet, M. (1989, January). *The need for cooperation between the judicial system and batterer programs.* Paper presented at the Responses to Family Violence Research Conference, Purdue University, West Lafayette, IN.

Pirog-Good, M. A., & Stets, J. (1986). Programs for abusers: Who drops out and what can be done. *Response, 9*(2), 17-19.

Pitts, M. G., Barnett, O. W., Deatherage, J. R., & LaViolette, A. D. (1991, April). *The inadequacy of social support for battered women.* Paper presented at the annual meeting of the Western Psychological Association, Burlingame, CA.

Pizzey, E., & Shapiro, J. (1981). Choosing a violent relationship. *New Society, 23,* 1-15.

Pleck, E. (1987). *Domestic tyranny.* New York: Oxford University Press.

Police Foundation. (1977). *Domestic violence and the police: Studies in Detroit and Kansas City.* Washington, DC: Author.

Poteat, G. M., Grossnickle, W. F., Cope, J. G., & Wynne, D. C. (1990). Psychometric properties of the wife abuse inventory. *Journal of Clinical Psychology, 48,* 828-834.

Prange, R. C. (1985). Battered women and why they return to the abusive situation: A study of attribution-style, multiple-dimensional locus of control and social-psychological factors. *Dissertation Abstracts International, 46,* 4026B. (UMI No. 8522840)

Procci, W. R. (1990). *Medical aspects of human sexuality.* New York: Cahners.

Ptacek, J. (1988). Why do men batter their wives? In M. Bograd & K. Yllo (Eds.), *Feminist perspectives on wife abuse* (pp. 133-157). Newbury Park, CA: Sage.

Quindlen, A. (1992, February 2). Public and private [column]. *The New York Times.*

Report of the Governor's Committee to Study Sentencing and Correctional Alternatives for Women Convicted of Crime, State of Maryland. (1988, June). Annapolis: Governor's Committee.

Rescorla, R. A., & Solomon, R. L. (1967). Two-process learning theory: Relations between Pavlovian conditioning and instrumental learning. *Psychological Review, 74,* 151-182.

Rhodes, N. R. (1992). Comparison of MMPI Psychopathic Deviate scores of battered and nonbattered women. *Journal of Family Violence, 7,* 297-307.

Riggs, D. S., Kilpatrick, D. G., & Resnick, H. S. (1992). Long-term psychological distress associated with marital rape and aggravated assault: A comparison to other crime victims. *Journal of Family Violence, 7,* 283-296.

Riggs, D. S., Murphy, C. M., & O'Leary, K. D. (1989). Intentional falsification in reports of interpartner aggression. *Journal of Interpersonal Violence, 4,* 220-232.

Roiphe, A. (1986, September). Women who make sacrifices for their men. *Cosmopolitan,* pp. 308-313, 319.

Romero, M. (1985). A comparison between strategies used on prisoners of war and battered wives. *Sex Roles, 13,* 537-547.

Rosen, R. (1991, April 8). Women's rights are the same as human rights. *Los Angeles Times,* p. B5.

Rosenbaum, A., & O'Leary, K. D. (1981). Marital violence: Characteristics of abusive couples. *Journal of Consulting and Clinical Psychology, 49,* 63-76.

Rosenblum, L. A., & Harlow, H. F. (1963). Approach-avoidance conflict in the mother surrogate situation. *Psychological Reports, 12,* 83-85.

Rotter, J. B. (1954). *Social learning and clinical psychology.* Englewood Cliffs, NJ: Prentice-Hall.

Rounsaville, B. J. (1978). Theories in marital violence: Evidence from a study of battered women. *Victimology: An International Journal, 3,* 11-31.

Rounsaville, B. J., & Weissman, M. H. (1978). Battered women: A medical problem requiring detection. *International Journal of Psychiatry in Medicine, 8,* 191-201.

Rouse, L. P. (1988). Abuse in dating relationships: A comparisons of blacks, whites, and Hispanics. *Journal of College Student Development, 29,* 312-319.

Rouse, L. P., Breen, R., & Howell, M. (1988). Abuse in intimate relationships. *Journal of Interpersonal Violence, 5,* 414-427.

Roy, M. (1977). *Battered women.* New York: Van Nostrand Reinhold.

Rozee-Koker, P., Wynne, C., & Mizrahi, K. (1989, April). *Workplace safety and fear of rape among professional women.* Paper presented at the annual meeting of the Western Psychological Association, Reno, NV.

Ruch, L. O., Chandler, S. M., & Harter, R. A. (1980). Life change and rape impact. *Journal of Health and Social Behavior, 21,* 248-260.

Rusbult, C. E. (1980). Commitment and satisfaction in romantic associations: A test of the investment model. *Journal of Experimental and Social Psychology, 16,* 172-186.

Russell, M. N., Lipov, E., Phillips, N., & White, B. (1989). Psychological profiles of violent and nonviolent maritally distressed couples. *Psychotherapy, 26,* 81-87.

Saltzman, L. E., Mercy, J. A., Rosenberg, M. L., Elsea, W. R., Napper, G., Sikes, R. K., & Waxweiler, R. J. (1990). Magnitude and patterns of family and intimate assault in Atlanta, Georgia, 1984. *Violence and Victims, 5,* 3-17.

Sandler, J., Davidson, R. S., Greene, W. E., & Holzschuh, R. D. (1966). Effects of punishment intensity on instrumental avoidance behavior. *Journal of Comparative and Physiological Psychology, 61,* 212-216.

Sapiente, A. A. (1988). Locus of control and causal attributions of maritally violent men. *Dissertation Abstracts International, 50,* 758B. (UMI No. 8822697)

Sato, R. A., & Heiby, E. M. (1992). Correlates of depressive symptoms among battered women. *Journal of Family Violence, 7,* 229-245.

Saunders, D. G. (1986). When battered women use violence: Husband-abuse or self-defense. *Violence and Victims, 1,* 47-60.

Saunders, D. G. (1988). Wife abuse, husband abuse, or mutual combat? A feminist perspective on the empirical findings. In K. Yllo & M. Bogard (Eds.), *Feminist perspectives on wife abuse* (pp. 99-113). Newbury Park, CA: Sage.

Saunders, D. G. (1989, November). *Who hits first and who hurts most? Evidence for the greater victimization of women in intimate relationships.* Paper presented at the annual meeting of the American Society of Criminology, Reno, NV.

Saunders, D. G., Lynch, A. B., Grayson, M., & Linz, D. (1987). The inventory of beliefs about wife beating: The construction and initial validation of a measure of beliefs and attitudes. *Violence and Victims, 2,* 39-57.

Saunders, D. G., & Size, P. B. (1986). Attitudes about woman abuse among police officers, victims, and victim advocates. *Journal of Interpersonal Violence, 1,* 25-42.

Schecter, S. (1982). *Women and male violence.* Boston: South End Press.

Schillinger, E. (1988). Dependency, control, and isolation. *Journal of Contemporary Ethnography, 16,* 469-490.

Schneider, E. M. (1986). Describing and changing: Women's self-defense work and the problem of expert testimony on battering. *Women's Rights Law Reporter, 9*(3-4), 195-222.

Schneider, E. M., & Jordan, S. B. (1978). Representation of women who defend themselves in response to physical or sexual assault. *Family Law Review, 1,* 118-132.

Schuller, R. A. (1992). The impact of battered woman syndrome evidence on jury decision processes. *Law and Human Behavior, 16,* 597-620.

Schuller, R. A., & Vidmar, N. (1992). Battered woman syndrome evidence in the courtroom: A review of the literature. *Law and Human Behavior, 16,* 273-291.

Schulman, M. A. (1979). *Survey of spousal abuse against women in Kentucky.* New York: Louis Harris and Associates.

Schwartz, M. D. (1987). Gender and injury in spousal assault. *Sociological Focus, 20,* 61-74.

Schwartz, M. D. (1988). Marital status and woman abuse theory. *Journal of Family Violence, 3,* 239-248.

Scott, R. L., & Stone, D. A. (1986). MMPI measures of psychological disturbance in adolescent and adult victims of father-daughter incest. *Journal of Clinical Psychology, 42,* 251-259.

Sedlak, A. J. (1988a). The effects of personal experiences with couple violence on calling it "battering" and allocating blame. In G. T. Hotaling, D. Finkelhor, J. T. Kirkpatrick, & M. A. Straus (Eds.), *Coping with family violence* (pp. 31-59). Newbury Park, CA: Sage.

Sedlak, A. J. (1988b). The use and psychosocial impact of a battered women's shelter. In G. T. Hotaling, D. Finkelhor, J. T. Kirkpatrick, & M. A. Straus (Eds.), *Coping with family violence* (pp. 122-128). Newbury Park, CA: Sage.

Seligman, M. E. P. (1968). Chronic fear produced by unpredictable electric shock. *Journal of Comparative and Physiological Psychology, 66,* 402-411.

Seligman, M. E. P. (1975). *Helplessness: On depression, development and death.* San Francisco: Freeman.

Seligman, M. E. P., & Meyer, B. (1970). Chronic fear and ulcers in rats as a function of the unpredictability of safety. *Journal of Comparative and Physiological Psychology, 73,* 202-207.

Selye, H. (1946). The general adaptation syndrome. *Journal of Clinical Endocrinology, 6,* 117-230.

Sex abuse: Identifying survivors in adulthood. (1990, December 3). *Behavior Today, 21*(49), 3-4.

Shainess, N. (1977). Psychological aspects of wife battering. In M. Roy (Ed.), *Battered women: A psychosociological study of domestic violence* (pp. 111-119). New York: Van Nostrand Reinhold.

Shepard, M., & Pence, E. (1988). The effect of battering on the employment status of women. *Affilia, 3*(2), 55-61.

Shepherd, J. (1990). Victims of personal violence: The relevance of Symonds' Model of psychological response and loss theory. *British Journal of Social Work, 20,* 309-332.

Sherman, L. W. (1992). *Policing domestic violence: Experiments and dilemmas.* New York: Free Press.

Sherman, L. W., Schmidt, J. D., Rogan, D. P., Gartin, P. R., Cohn, E. G., Collins, D. J., & Bacich, A. R. (1991). From initial deterrence to long-term escalation: Short-custody arrest for poverty ghetto domestic violence. *Criminology, 29,* 821-850.

Shields, N. M., & Hanneke, C. R. (1983a). Attributions processes in violent relationships: Perceptions of violent husband and their wives. *Journal of Applied Social Psychology, 13,* 515-527.

Shields, N. M., & Hanneke, C. R. (1983b). Battered wives' reactions to marital rape. In D. Finkelhor, R. J. Gelles, & G. T. Hotaling (Eds.), *The dark side of families: Current family violence research* (pp. 132-148). Beverly Hills, CA: Sage.

Shotland, R. L., & Straw, M. K. (1976). Bystander response to an assault: When a man attacks a woman. *Journal of Personality and Social Psychology, 34,* 990-999.

Sidman, M. (1953). Two temporal parameters of the maintenance of avoidance behavior by the white rat. *Journal of Comparative and Physiological Psychology, 46,* 253-261.

Skinner, B. F. (1938). *The behavior of organisms.* New York: Appleton-Century-Crofts.

Smith, C. (1988). *Status discrepancies and husband-to-wife violence.* Durham: Family Violence Research Program, University of New Hampshire.

Smith, M. D. (1990). Patriarchal ideology and wife beating: A test of a feminist hypothesis. *Violence and Victims, 5,* 257-273.

Smith, S. (1984). The battered woman: A consequence of female development. *Women & Therapy, 3*(2), 3-9.

Snodgrass, S. E. (1990, August). *Sex role stereotypes are alive and well.* Paper presented at the annual meeting of the American Psychological Association, Boston.

Snyder, D. K., & Scheer, N. S. (1981). Predicting disposition following brief residence at a shelter for battered women. *American Journal of Community Psychology, 9,* 559-566.

Sommer, J. A. (1990). Men who batter: Attitudes toward women. *Dissertation Abstracts International, 51,* 5592B. (UMI No. 9107514)

Sorenson, S. B., & Telles, C. A. (1991). Self-reports of spousal violence in a Mexican-American and non-Hispanic white population. *Violence and Victims, 6,* 3-15.

Spence, J. T., Helmreich, R., & Stapp, J. (1973). A short version of the Attitudes Toward Women Scale (AWS). *Bulletin of Psychonomic Society, 2,* 219-220.

Stacey, W. A., & Shupe, A. (1983). *The family secret.* Boston: Beacon.

Stagg, V., Wills, G. D., & Howell, M. (1989). Psychopathology in early childhood witness of family violence. *Topics in Early Childhood Special Education, 9,* 73-87.

Stahly, G., Ousler, A., & Tanako, J. (1988, April). *Family violence and child custody: A survey of battered women.* Paper presented at the annual meeting of the Western Psychological Association, San Francisco.

Stanton, E. C., Anthony, S. B., & Gage, M. J. (Eds.). (1889). *History of women suffrage: Vol. 1. 1848-1861.* New York: Fowler & Wells. (Reprint of 1881 edition)

Star, B. (1980). Patterns in family violence. *Social Casework: The Journal of Contemporary Social Work, 61,* 339-346.

Stark, E., Flitcraft, A., Zuckerman, D., Gray, A., Robinson, J., & Frazier, W. (1981). *Wife assault in the medical setting: An introduction for health personnel* (Monograph No. 7). Washington, DC: Office of Domestic Violence.

Stark, R., & McEvoy, J. (1970). Middle class violence. *Psychology Today, 4*(6), 30-32.

State v. Wanrow, 88 Wash. 2d 221, 559 P.2d 548 (1977).

Steiner, J. (1966). *Treblinka.* New York: New American Library.

Steinmetz, S. K. (1977). The battered husband syndrome. *Victimology: An International Journal, 2*(3-4), 499-509.

STEPS to End Family Violence. (1987). *Battered women and criminal justice.* New York: Author.

Stets, J. E. (1991). Psychological aggression in dating relationships: The role of interpersonal control. *Journal of Family Violence, 6,* 97-114.

Stets, J. E., & Straus, M. A. (1989). The marriage license as a hitting license: A comparison of assaults in dating, cohabiting, and married couples. *Journal of Family Violence, 4,* 161-180.

Stith, S. M. (1990). Police response to domestic violence: The influence of individual and familial factors. *Violence and Victims, 5,* 37-49.

Stout, K. D. (1988). Intimate femicide: Individual and state factors associated with the killing of women by men. *Dissertation Abstracts International, 48,* 2732A. (UMI No. 8728649)

Straus, M. A. (1976). Sexual inequality, cultural norms, and wife beating. *Victimology: An International Journal, 1,* 54-76.

Straus, M. A. (1979). Measuring intrafamily conflict and aggression: The Conflict Tactics Scale (CT). *Journal of Marriage and the Family, 41,* 75-88.

Straus, M. A. (1980). Victims and aggressors in marital violence. *American Behavioral Scientist, 23,* 681-704.

Straus, M. A. (1983). Ordinary violence, child abuse and wife beating: What do they have in common. In D. Finkelhor, R. J. Gelles, G. T. Hotaling, & M. A. Straus (Eds.), *The dark side of families: Current family violence research* (pp. 213-234). Beverly Hills, CA: Sage.

Straus, M. A. (1986). Medical care costs of intrafamily assault and homicide. *Bulletin of the New York Academy of Medicine, 62,* 556-561.

Straus, M. A. (1991, September). *Children as witness to marital violence: A risk factor for life long problems among a nationally representative sample of American men and women.* Paper presented at the Ross Roundtable on "Children and Violence," Washington, DC.

Straus, M. A., Gelles, R. J., & Steinmetz, S. K. (1981). *Behind closed doors: Violence in the American family.* Garden City, NY: Doubleday.

Straus, M. A., & Hotaling, G. T. (1980). *The social causes of husband-wife violence.* Minneapolis: University of Minnesota Press.

Strentz, T. (1979, April). Law enforcement policy and ego defenses of the hostage. *FBI Law Enforcement Bulletin,* pp. 2-12.

Strube, M. J., & Barbour, L. S. (1983). The decision to leave an abusive relationship: Economic dependence and psychological commitment. *Journal of Marriage and the Family, 45,* 785-793.

Strube, M. J., & Barbour, L. S. (1984). Factors related to the decision to leave an abusive relationship. *Journal of Marriage and the Family, 46,* 837-844.

Stubbing, E. (1990). Police who think family homicide is preventable are pointing the way. *Response, 13*(1), 8.

Sugarman, D. B., & Hotaling, G. T. (1991). Dating violence: A review of contextual and risk factors. In B. Levy (Ed.), *Dating violence: Young women in danger* (pp. 100-118). Seattle, WA: Seal.

Sullivan, C. M. (1991, August). Battered women as active helpseekers. *Violence Update, 1*(12), 1, 8, 10-11.

Swann, W. B., Jr., & Read, S. J. (1981). Acquiring self-knowledge: The search for feedback that fits. *Personality and Social Psychology, 41,* 1119-1128.

Swenson, S. V. (1984). Effects of sex-role stereotypes and androgynous alternatives in mental health judgments of psychotherapists. *Psychological Reports, 54,* 475-481.

Syers, M., & Edleson, J. L. (1992). The combined effects of coordinated criminal justice intervention in woman abuse. *Journal of Interpersonal Violence, 7,* 490-502.

Symonds, A. (1979). Violence against women: The myth of masochism. *American Journal of Psychotherapy, 23,* 161-173.

Szinovacz, M. E. (1983). Using couple data as a methodological tool: The case of marital violence. *Journal of Marriage and the Family, 45,* 633-644.

Tavris, C. (1992, February). *The mismeasure of woman.* Presentation given at the national conference of the Association of Women in Psychology, Long Beach, CA.

Telch, C. F., & Lindquist, C. U. (1984). Violent versus non-violent couples: A comparison of patterns. *Psychotherapy, 2,* 242-248.

Teske, R. H. C., Jr., & Parker, M. L. (1983). *Spouse abuse in Texas: A study of women's attitudes and experiences.* Huntsville, TX: Sam Houston University, Criminal Justice Center, Survey Research Program.

The Oprah Winfrey Show. (1992, May 22). Learning to be assertive.

Thibaut, J. W., & Kelley, H. H. (1958). *The social psychology of groups.* New York: John Wiley.

Thoits, P. A. (1982). Conceptual, methodological, and theoretical problems in studying practical implications. *Journal of Personality and Social Psychology, 52,* 813-832.

Thompson, C. (1989). Breaking through walls of isolation: A model for churches in helping victims of violence. *Pastoral Psychology, 38,* 35-38.

Tierney, K. J. (1982). The battered women movement and the creation of the wife beating problem. *Social Problems, 29,* 207-220.

Tilden, V. P. (1989). Response of the health care delivery system to battered women. *Issues in Mental Health Nursing, 10,* 309-320.

Tinsley, C. A., Critelli, J. W., & Ee, J. S. (1992, August). *The perception of sexual aggression: One act, two realities.* Paper presented at the annual meeting of the American Psychological Association, Washington, DC.

Tolman, R., & Saunders, D. G. (1988). The case for the cautious use of anger control with men who batter. *Response, 11*(2), 15-20.

Toufexis, A. (1987, December 21). Home is where the hurt is: Wife beating among the well-to-do no longer a secret. *Time,* p. 68.

Trimpey, M. L. (1989). Self-esteem and anxiety: Key issues in an abused women's support group. *Issues in Mental Health Nursing, 10,* 297-308.

Truniger, E. (1971). Marital violence: The legal solutions. *Hastings Law Journal, 23,* 259-276.

Turner, S. F., & Shapiro, C. H. (1986, September-October). Battered women: Mourning the death of a relationship. *Social Work,* pp. 372-376.

Ulrich, R. E., Wolff, P. C., & Azrin, N. H. (1964). Shock as an elicitor of intra- and inter-species fighting behavior. *Animal Behavior, 12,* 14-15.

Uris, L. (1976). *Trinity* (1st ed.). Garden City, NJ: Doubleday.

U.S. Bureau of the Census. (1989). *Statistical abstract of the United States* (109th ed.). Washington, DC: Government Printing Office.

U.S. Department of Justice. (1983). *Report to the nation on crime and justice: The data.* Washington, DC: U.S. Department of Justice.

Varvaro, F. F. (1991). Using a grief response assessment questionnaire in a support group to assist battered women in their recovery. *Response, 13*(4), 17-20.

Vaughn, D. (1987, July). The long goodbye. *Psychology Today*, pp. 37-38, 42.

Veronen, L. J., & Resnick, H. (1988, August). *Expert testimony for women who kill: The fear response and perception of threat.* Paper presented at the annual meeting of the American Psychological Association, Atlanta, GA.

Victim agencies struggle with domestic violence and DUI cases. (1992, June 15). *Criminal Justice Newsletter, 23*(19), 5-7.

Violence and women offenders. (1990). *Response, 13*(1), 7.

Waaland, P., & Keeley, S. (1985). Police decision making in wife abuse: The impact of legal and extralegal factors. *Law and Human Behavior, 9,* 355-366.

Waits, K. (1985). The criminal justice system's response to battering: Understanding the problem, forging the solution. *Washington Law Review, 60,* 267-329.

Walker, L. E. (1979). *The battered woman.* New York: Harper & Row.

Walker, L. E. (1981). Battered women: Sex roles and clinical issues. *Professional Psychology, 12,* 81-91.

Walker, L. E. (1983). Victimology and the psychological perspectives of battered women. *Victimology: An International Journal, 8,* 82-104.

Walker, L. E. (1984). *The battered woman syndrome.* New York: Springer.

Walker, L. E. (1985a, June 7). *Psychology of battered women.* Symposium conducted at the Laguna Human Options Conference, Laguna Beach, CA.

Walker, L. E. (1985b). Psychological impact of the criminalization of domestic violence on victims. *Victimology: An International Journal, 10,* 281-300.

Walker, L. E., & Browne, A. (1985). Gender and victimization by intimates. *Journal of Personality, 53,* 179-194.

Warren, J., & Lanning, W. (1992). Sex role beliefs, control, and social isolation of battered women. *Journal of Family Violence, 7,* 1-8.

Watson, J. B., & Raynor, R. (1920). Conditioned emotional reactions. *Journal of Experimental Psychology, 3,* 1-14.

Wauchope, B. A. (1988). *Help-seeking decisions of battered women: A test of learned helplessness and two stress theories.* Durham: Family Violence Research Program, University of New Hampshire.

Weingourt, R. (1985). Never be alone: Existential therapy with battered women. *Journal of Psychiatric Nursing and Mental Health Services, 17,* 24-29.

Weitzman, L. J. (1974). Legal regulation of marriage: Tradition and change. *California Law Review, 62,* 1169-1288.

Weitzman, L. J., & Dreen, K. (1982). Wife beating: A view of the marital dyad. *Social Casework, 63,* 259-265.

West, C., & Zimmerman, D. H. (1987). Doing gender. *Gender & Society, 1,* 125-151.

Wetzel, L., & Ross, M. A. (1983). Psychological and social ramifications of battering: Observations leading to a counseling methodology for victims of domestic violence. *The Personnel and Guidance Journal, 61,* 423-428.

Willet, S. L., & Barnett, O. W. (1987, April). *Relational consequences of wife beating for violent husbands.* Paper presented at the annual meeting of the Western Psychological Association, Long Beach, CA.

Williams, K. R., & Hawkins, R. (1989). The meaning of arrest for wife assault. *Criminology, 1,* 163-181.

Wilson, M. I., & Daly, M. (1992). Who kills whom in spouse killings? On the exceptional sex ratio of spousal homicides in the United States. *Criminology, 30,* 189-215.

Wilson, M. N., Baglioni, A. J., Jr., & Downing, D. (1989). Analyzing factors influencing readmission to a battered women's shelter. *Journal of Family Violence, 4,* 275-284.

Wolfgang, M. E. (1957). Victim-precipitated criminal homicide. *Journal of Criminal Law, Criminology, and Police Science, 48,* 1-11.

Woman sues husband for abuse. (1988, March 14). *Behavior Today,* pp. 3-4.

Yllo, K., & Bogard, M. (Eds.). (1988). *Feminist perspectives on wife abuse.* Newbury Park, CA: Sage.

Youngstrom, N. (1992, February). Laws to aid battered women backfire. *APA Monitor, 23*(2), 45.

• Index

179

• About the Authors

 **Ola W. Barnett** is Professor of Psychology in the Social Science Division, Pepperdine University, Malibu, California. She received her doctorate at the University of California, Los Angeles, specializing in learning. Her major research and publication areas are the characteristics of maritally violent men, the assessment of marital abuse, and battered women. She coordinates a student-volunteer program for a battered women's shelter and has served as a volunteer facilitator for a batterer's group.

 **Alyce D. LaViolette** (M.S.) is a pioneer in the field of spousal abuse. She has worked with battered women since 1978. In conjunction with this, she has developed Alternatives to Violence, one of the first programs in the country (1979) to work with men who batter their wives. She is a featured keynote and conference speaker. She has appeared on local and national television including the National Public Broadcasting System's "Portrait of a Family." She serves as an expert witness for the court on the

battered women's syndrome and is a consultant to other programs. She has done training for the California Probation Department, the Los Angeles Department of Children's Services, and the victims and perpetrators of abuse. She has written a booklet titled "Battered Women, Power and Family Systems Therapy." She has received a proclamation from Los Angeles County and the Lieutenant Governors's office for her work and is the recipient of the Humanitarian Award from the L.A. Commission on Assaults Against Women.